I Seek My Brethren

Ralph Goldman and "The Joint"

I Seek My Brethren

Ralph Goldman and "The Joint"

Rescue, Relief, and Reconstruction—The Work of the
American Jewish Joint Distribution Committee

Tom Shachtman

Forewords by David S. Wyman and Teddy Kollek

Introduction by Mikhail Gorbachev

NEWMARKET PRESS
NEW YORK

This book is published in the United States and in Canada.

First Edition

10 9 8 7 6 5 4 3 2 1

Library of Congress Cataloging-in-Publication Data
Shachtman, Tom
I Seek My Brethren: Ralph Goldman and "The Joint": Rescue, Relief,
and Reconstruction—The Work of the American Jewish Joint
Distribution Committee / by Tom Shachtman ; forewords by Teddy
Kollek and David S. Wyman ; afterword by Mikhail Gorbachev. —1st ed.
    p.   cm.
Includes bibliographical references and index.
ISBN 1-55704-495-3 (hc. : alk. paper)
1. Goldman, Ralph I. 3. American Jewish Joint Distribution
Committee—Biography. 3. Jews—Charities—History—20th century.
I. Title.
HV3190 .S47 2001
362.84'924'0092—dc21
        [B]   2001044933

QUANTITY PURCHASES
Companies, professional groups, clubs, and other organizations may
qualify for special terms when ordering quantities of this title. For information, write Special Sales Department, Newmarket Press, 18 East 48th
Street, New York, NY 10017; call (212) 832-3575; fax (212) 832-3629;
or e-mail mailbox@newmarketpress.com.

www.newmarketpress.com

Manufactured in the United States of America

For more information about the American Jewish Joint Distribution
Committee, visit their website at www.jdc.org.

CONTENTS

A photograph section falls after page 150.

A SPECIAL THANK YOU

This book was initiated by two JDC leaders and their families:

Heinz and Ruthe Eppler, New York and Palm Beach
and
Louis and Mary Zorensky, St. Louis

*As leaders at times of action and of history making, as well
as at times of history telling, they provided the active support and friendship that made it possible for this story to be
put before the public.*

FOREWORD

The Pathfinders

Before the word *Holocaust* was applied to the mass killing of the Jews during World War II, and before the world took clear notice of its monstrous dimensions, the individual rescue and relief personnel who worked for the JDC managed to find invisible paths to Jews in Nazi-occupied Europe and to save lives. While researching my book, *The Abandonment of the Jews: America and the Holocaust, 1941–1945,* I learned that the "Joint" provided more help to the Jews of Europe during World War II than did all the governments of the world combined.

After the war was over, the JDC undertook the huge task of helping to care for some 300,000 surviving Jews who reached the Displaced Persons camps in Europe. Another 400,000 survivors scattered across Europe received crucial assistance from the JDC. And then—silence fell. The Iron Curtain cut off the Jews of Eastern Europe from the Jewish lifeline of the JDC. Travel was limited; information was scarce; infusion of Jewish knowledge was banned.

Or were they really completely cut off?

This book attempts to unveil part of the answer. It tells the previously untold story of the relentless and sophisticated efforts that the JDC made to find new paths to the Jews trapped beyond the Iron Curtain. In overt and covert ways, the former pathfinders of World War II managed to do it again: to overcome obstacles, reach their brethren, and nourish Jewish life under immensely difficult circumstances. And after fifty years of darkness behind that Iron Curtain, when Communism collapsed, the JDC was standing by, ready to rush back in to repair the fabric of Jewish life damaged by years of repression.

"If these communities survived the horrors of the Nazis and the terrors of the Communists, we are not going to let them suffer and die because of our self-indulgence," proclaimed one president of the JDC, Ambassador Milton A. Wolf.

Through a quiltwork of episodes and tales, personal memoirs and archival documents, this book follows the JDC pathfinders into Communist Europe and to the most remote Jewish communities. The reader can appreciate the miracle-like phenomenon of Jewish renewal and admire the devotion of the leaders and professionals who made it possible.

This book is a significant contribution to the narrative of Jewish survival throughout the twentieth century.

Professor David S. Wyman
University of Massachusetts, Amherst
July 2001

FOREWORD

By now my friend Ralph Goldman has retired twice, but you'll still find him at work. When I visit him in his office at the JDC in New York, I'm always struck by a photograph on his wall: There's a young Goldman, wearing his now signature bow tie, helping David Ben-Gurion put on his suit jacket. The photo is classic Ralph Goldman—a man of tenderness and strength, loyalty, without pretension. The year was 1951. I was with Ben-Gurion on his first visit to the United States as prime minister, and Ralph had been asked to make all the arrangements for what was to be a whirlwind ten-city tour. The logistics were really complicated because we didn't have much time—sometimes we'd stop in a city for just a few hours—but Ralph had anticipated every last detail. Our first stop was West Point, where we placed a wreath at the grave of David Daniel "Mickey" Marcus, the United States Army colonel who served as a brigadier general in Israel's army and was killed by accident in 1948. We then set off for Baltimore, stopping en route in Princeton, where Ben-Gurion met with Albert Einstein.

I first met Ralph in 1947, when I came to the United States from Jerusalem, and we were involved together in some underground work in support of the Haganah. Some of our efforts and adventures are described in these pages, although some, still cloaked in secrecy, must remain untold. In those days, Ralph was—as he is today—a natural diplomat, very talented at dealing with people from all walks of life, at making connections between people and between organizations.

One of the best connections I made was to introduce Ralph to Ben-Gurion. I brought Ralph with me to a Tel Aviv party celebrating the first anniversary of Israel's independence; the two of them spoke about books, and Ralph left with an assignment to find the missing volumes of a set of books on world civilization. Of course he found them.

Ralph is a rare combination of idealist and pragmatist, which means that he has vision and good ideas and also knows how to make things happen. And, he's got a big heart. His contributions to the State of Israel, to the Joint Distribution Committee and its operations around the world, are huge. He was very helpful in nurturing the building of the Israel Museum and the growth of community centers around the country, and through his work at the Joint, he's served the physical and spiritual needs of Jews in need, from Morocco to India to the corners of the former Soviet Union. I take some credit for convincing him to take the job of executive vice-president of the Joint in 1976, and I'm pleased to say that.

If you've ever walked down a street with Ralph, attended a Jewish community event in New York, or accompanied him to synagogue in Moscow, you'll realize that Ralph seems to know everyone. He's the ultimate insider, but prefers the background to the foreground. It's said of some people that they don't take no for an answer—Ralph knows how to turn no to yes.

I've had the pleasure of seeing Ralph in his negotiating mode. There's a phrase in Hebrew, *"Echad nehene v'shani lo chaser,"* "One person benefits, no one loses," and that characterizes Ralph's style. He knows to always leave something on the table for his negotiating partner so that everyone leaves the room feeling that they achieved something. He's one of the few people I know with friends and admirers in governments around the world—these are mostly people he's sat across from at a negotiating table.

Trained as a social worker, Ralph is a true leader. I've never heard him speak in jargon, and he doesn't like labels. Over the years, he's developed a corps of people who share his dedication to the Jewish people. For many of his colleagues at the Joint, and for many of our old friends in Israel, Ralph is a mentor. Wherever he is, he creates community, on personal and professional levels.

If I've made Ralph sound too perfect, it's the privilege of being a friend for more than fifty years—a friend who really knows and loves the man.

Teddy Kollek
Jerusalem, June 2001

INTRODUCTION

The well-known, international Jewish organization, the Joint, asked me to write a note to this book, which is devoted to its recent history.

I am gratified to have been asked to do this. This reminded me of an extremely important page in the history book of *perestroika*. The case in point is the abolition of state anti-Semitism in the USSR, which had been hypocritically disguised but existed in fact. Stalin started it by his campaign against "Cosmopolitanism." This infamous campaign for so many years poisoned the minds of our citizens and inflicted (besides open repressions in Stalin's time) a lot of injustice, abuse, and ordeals on the Jews.

The policy of perestroika, aimed at the radical democratization of an entire society's life, could not tolerate this situation. I have to admit it was difficult to achieve a turn—so deep-seated were the prejudices against the Jews inside the ruling *nomenklatura,* including very high officials. But the situation grew healthier quite soon after a "command from the top" came. This is another confirmation of the fact that the Russian people, the Russian intelligentsia—its vast majority—were alienated by anti-Semitism.

It is also noteworthy that the most difficult period of crisis in my country, the last ten years, has failed to subvert the tradition of normal, close, and somewhat familial relations between the Russians and the Jews that were renewed in the perestroika years. Good relations between Russia and Israel continue to develop, and on the whole there is stronger mutual understanding and empathy between our peoples.

Throughout nearly ninety years of its existence, the Joint has been showing to the world the best face and intentions of the

Jewish people. The Joint's material and moral position is strong because the Jews were able to survive through the horrible ordeals that befell them in the twentieth century. They not only preserved their nation but also supplied a new, unprecedented impetus for a powerful upsurge and prosperity to the entire contemporary international community.

I wish the Joint every success in carrying out its noble activity, and I hope many people have the opportunity to read this book.

Mikhail Gorbachev
May 23, 2001

Moscow, August 19, 1991

A T 4:00 A.M. on Monday, August 19, 1991, Israeli engineer Yitzhak Averbuch was jolted awake in his hotel room across from the Kremlin by the sound of tanks rolling into nearby Red Square. Having been born in the Soviet Union and lived there until he was twenty-three, Averbuch knew instantly that some form of putsch or coup was in the making, and could not get back to sleep. Now he wondered whether he would ever get to meet "Mr. Joint," Ralph I. Goldman, the honorary executive vice-president of the American Jewish Joint Distribution Committee —the JDC—the organization that was Averbuch's employer.

As an outgrowth of President Mikhail Gorbachev's *glasnost* and *perestroika*, and largely through the efforts of Goldman, the Joint had finally succeeded in formally re-entering the Soviet Union in 1988, fifty years after it had been kicked out by Stalin. Averbuch was aware that he JDC had been working with the several million Jews who had not been willing or able to emigrate from the Soviet Union—the third-largest Jewish population in the world, exceeded only by that of Israel and the United States.

In the U.S.S.R., the JDC was assisting local organizations in running soup kitchens, health clinics, libraries, book fairs, *yeshiv-*

ot, educational programs, and Jewish universities in dozens of cities—hundreds of projects. Averbuch, a logistics expert, was to create a logistics system for JDC's expanding operation. He wondered what Goldman, a legend in Jewish philanthropy, would think of him.

In his youth in Odessa, during the 1950s and 1960s, Yitzhak Averbuch had been like many other Jewish-born people in the U.S.S.R., ashamed of their Jewish roots and subjected to severe discrimination because they were identified as Jews, even if they did not practice their religion. Despite the difficulties, Averbuch had begun to think of himself as Jewish, and had emigrated to Israel in 1970; he became a citizen and an officer of the defense forces, married a seventh-generation Israeli, had raised three children and had created a small consulting firm.

Two days ago, when he landed at the Moscow airport at age forty-three, and handed the border control officer his documents, the officer looked at him askance and said, "Listen: you are Russian, living in Israel, and now going to represent an American organization in Russia? Tell me, how did this come about?"

"You want me to tell you the whole story, five thousand years of history of the Jewish people—now?"

The officer smiled and asked just what, precisely, Averbuch was going to do here.

"I am going to help Jews," Averbuch had told him, with the sense of completing his own personal circle.

It was an exciting time to be in the Soviet Union. Since the spring, Gorbachev had been attempting to work out a way of ceding power to the nine republics and gradually eliminating the centralized, tyrannical control that had existed since 1917. A treaty ratifying the new arrangement was due to be signed on Tuesday, August 20, after Gorbachev returned from a vacation with his family on the beaches of the Crimea.

At daybreak on Monday, August 19, radio and television began to interrupt regular programming with the bulletin that Gorbachev was ill and in seclusion in the Crimea, and that in his absence Vice-President Gennady Yanayev had taken the reins of government. It was immediately apparent to Averbuch and many others that the tank movements he heard were part of an attempt to prevent the nine-republics accord from being signed on the next day.

Later media bulletins announcing the eight names of an interim governing committee made it clear that a conservative, perhaps even a reactionary coup was in the making. A conservative coup could mean the repeal of the revival of religious activity, especially of Judaism, which had been a target of the reactionaries.

While glued to the television in his hotel room, Averbuch received telephone instructions from the JDC's temporary office in Moscow to prepare to leave the country within hours or days, depending on what developed in the coup. But nobody told him to abort his planned meeting with Ralph Goldman, later in the day.

They were to meet at the venerable Choral Synagogue in Arkhipova Street, only a few hundred yards beyond Red Square. The engineer walked in that direction. Many of the downtown streets were empty because the army or police had closed them to traffic. Others were overcrowded. As the day wore on, more people and more tanks appeared. Pedestrians seemed low-key but worried.

Averbuch turned on Arkhipova Street, which sloped steeply downward, and found the synagogue near the low end. The large, columned building stood out from those nearby. The synagogue had once been magnificent; great infusions of money, time and effort would be required to return it to grandeur. Inside, small groups of men in *yarmulkes* milled about on the edges of the great hall with its tiled ceiling, while others prayed in side rooms used as libraries and for services for groups from Tashkent or Ukraine. Averbuch decided that of all the people in the synagogue, the seventyish man with the white curly hair, glasses and open, smiling face, the man wearing a bow tie, must be the American.

The engineer introduced himself, and they began to converse in Hebrew, which Goldman spoke as naturally as English.

"You saw the tanks?" Averbuch asked.

"Yes, I saw the tanks," Goldman responded calmly.

"So what are we going to do? What's on our schedule?"

"We have to go to see a building that may be suitable for a new synagogue," Goldman explained.

They climbed into a small, official-looking black car whose driver knew the streets well and also knew how to talk to the policemen guiding traffic. Goldman and Averbuch both assumed that the driver worked for the KGB, though he was employed by the Choral Synagogue, and they guarded their conversation. As they rode along, Goldman told the engineer that the building they were looking for had been promised by the Mos Soviet, Moscow City Council, as a possible site for a synagogue; but he recognized that the announcements on the radio that day had said that the "Gang of Eight" had disbanded the Mos Soviet. Goldman also told Averbuch that while an official from the Soviet Embassy in Washington had been trying to schedule an appointment for him this week with Vice-President Yanayev, he now assumed that such a meeting would certainly not take place.

From the directions Goldman gave to the driver, and other hints, Averbuch gleaned that Goldman knew his way around the city; he shortly learned that the American had been there fifteen times in the past several years, and had picked up more than a few words of Russian. Or perhaps, Averbuch thought, Goldman had recalled some Russian words from his early childhood, since Goldman had been born in Ukraine before his family had emigrated to the United States.

Sensitive to Averbuch's nervousness, Goldman told the engineer that before searching for the new building they would first go to the Hammer Center, and buy Averbuch a ticket to leave the country, as requested by headquarters. Averbuch was grateful.

But the streets were blocked, and despite the resourceful driver's ability to convince the police that the men in the car were on a very important mission, travel was difficult. Finally, the driver talked the police into permitting the car into the area where the "White House" was located—the skyscraper headquarters of the Russian Republic and its recently elected chief,

Boris Yeltsin. An empty highway led up to that White House, but at the end there was a blockade composed of streetcars and tens of thousands of people. Moments earlier, in defiance of the massed troops and the coup, Yeltsin had come out to stand with the people in the streets, and had climbed atop a tank to say, "The reactionaries will not triumph."

Goldman and Averbuch turned back, and because it was after 5 P.M., they also gave up looking for the Hammer Center. However, they did continue to search for the possible site of the synagogue, traveling by alternate routes when direct ones were impossible.

"Here we are," Averbuch thought to himself, "going among the tanks, the traffic, people running, and barricades, so that Ralph Goldman can inspect a building that might be used for a new synagogue!" Sensing Averbuch's amazement, Goldman said, "You know, tanks come and tanks go, but believe me, the synagogue will stay."

They found the site, but Goldman decided that it was not quite right for the operation that the local Jewish community had in mind. They continued to discuss the details of a logistics operation as the car took them back to Averbuch's hotel near the Kremlin.

Goldman said his plan for the next few days was to stick to his prearranged schedule; he would not cancel any appointments on his own, although he recognized that government officials might not be able to meet him as arranged.

"If I were here as an individual, I might go home," he explained, "but since I'm here as an official representative of the JDC, it's important to go about my scheduled business." It had taken him and the JDC too many years, and too great an effort, to earn their way into the Soviet Union—he could not permit himself to be frightened away at this critical juncture. Goldman left Averbuch at his hotel, promising to link up with him in the morning and then to buy him a ticket to Israel.

Through the night, Averbuch thought about going home, but also about the actions of Ralph Goldman, this older American Jew in Moscow. Heavy rain fell during the night, producing a mist that befogged the city. Television and radio revealed no real letup in the crisis, although the White House was not stormed by the 15,000 troops massed nearby, even though that storming had seemed inevitable. Yeltsin continued to support Gorbachev as the legitimate head of state, rather than supporting those who wished to overthrow the government, but Gorbachev was still believed to be in the Crimea: the crisis did not resolve, nor did anyone know when it might be over, nor what would happen afterwards.

On the morning of August 20, Averbuch made his way to the Oktoberskaya Dva Hotel, where Goldman was staying; this was a Communist Party hotel on a quiet side street in the shadow of the giant Foreign Ministry building and a stone's throw from the headquarters of the APN, the Soviet news agency. Tanks were stationed in front of both these important buildings, which were also near the headquarters of the army. Goldman had told Averbuch that he never conducted business in this hotel, because he and the Russians who visited him there assumed the rooms were bugged. So they had always talked outside. Such subterfuge, Goldman confided to the young man, was not to his liking. He always preferred to do things in a straightforward way, but he had been willing to endure such indignities in order to assure the prize of the JDC being able to work inside the Soviet Union, to succor and revitalize the large Jewish population there.

When Goldman emerged from the hotel, Averbuch embraced him, kissed him on both cheeks in the Russian manner, and said, "I'm staying. If you can stay and try to go through the barricades to find a place for a synagogue in Moscow, I'm staying, too."

CHAPTER ONE

A Brief History of "The Joint"

RALPH GOLDMAN has been associated with the American Jewish Joint Distribution Committee ("The Joint") for so many years that many who know him are unable to untangle their sense of the organization from that of the man. Actually, both Ralph Irving Goldman and what would become the Joint were born in 1914—Goldman in the Ukraine, and the organization in New York City. This and the next chapter recount their separate histories before they joined forces in 1968.

THE JOINT IS BORN: 1914–1918

On August 31, 1914, Jacob H. Schiff, the prominent New York Jewish businessman and philanthropist, received a cable from Henry Morgenthau, the United States ambassador based in Constantinople, Turkey. It said:

> PALESTINIAN JEWS FACING TERRIBLE CRISIS BELLIGERENT COUNTRIES STOPPING THEIR ASSISTANCE SERIOUS DESTRUCTION THREATENS THRIVING COLONIES FIFTY THOUSAND DOLLARS NEEDED BY RESPONSIBLE COMMITTEE DOCTOR RUPPIN CHAIRMAN TO ESTABLISH LOAN INSTITUTE AND SUPPORT FAMILIES WHOSE BREADWINNERS HAVE ENTERED ARMY CONDITIONS CERTAINLY JUSTIFY AMERICAN HELP WILL YOU UNDERTAKE MATTER

In the first days of August 1914, the Great War had begun, pitting Great Britain and France against imperial Germany. Turkey entered the war as an ally of Germany, and czarist Russia entered as the ally of the British and French. All this proved highly dangerous to the 85,000 Jews living in scattered settlements in Palestine, under Turkish domain. Many elderly Jews there had depended on money sent from relatives and friends in Russia, while younger Palestinian Jews had been selling their agricultural products to Western European markets. Now, neither Russian money nor Palestinian agricultural products could cross international borders. Worse still for Palestinian Jews, the Turkish government cut off food to settlements, causing widespread hunger and starvation.

Ambassador Morgenthau had good reason to believe his cable would spur action. He had sent it to Schiff and Louis Marshall, both officers of the American Jewish Committee, a national organization founded in 1906 to defend the rights of Jews. Along with Morgenthau, Schiff, and Marshall were leaders of an elite group of wealthy German-American Jews. The ambassador knew that they all subscribed to the traditional belief, expressed in the Talmud, that all Jews are responsible for fellow Jews. Charitable actions based on this belief had sustained Jews in the diaspora for many centuries, had enabled whole villages to survive when only a few residents managed to earn wealth, and continued to direct the philanthropy of those who had climbed out of poverty. American Jews were especially responsive to such appeals, conscious of their good fortune in what had become for many immigrants the land of opportunity.

Schiff answered the cable with a check for $12,500. His colleague, Nathan Straus, contributed an equal amount, and the American Jewish Committee added another $25,000; the amassed $50,000 was transferred to Constantinople.

In the ensuing months, the armies of the czar forced a half-million Jews out of their homes in the Pale, an area comprising parts of Poland and Ukraine. One hundred thousand were pushed deeper into Russia, and 400,000 were shoved in the other direction, toward the Austro-Hungarian Empire. These refugees and other Jews of Central and Eastern Europe and the Middle East all required immediate assistance from outside sources.

In response to this crisis, the leaders of forty American Jewish organizations met in New York in October 1914 and established the American Jewish Joint Distribution Committee, which soon came to be referred to as the JDC or simply The Joint. The participants at the October meeting acknowledged the gravity of the problem by pledging $1.5 million for refugee relief—thirty times the amount that Morgenthau had initially sought for Palestine's Jews. In today's terms that would be equal to nearly $50 million.

"All Jews of every shade of thought, irrespective of the land of their birth," the new organization's first communiqué said, "are solemnly admonished to contribute with the utmost generosity." And they did contribute, because of the sharp focus of the JDC's purpose—relief of the refugees—and because of the foresight of leaders Marshall, Schiff, and Schiff's son-in-law Felix Warburg, who managed to thrust into the background serious issues that had earlier separated American Jews into feuding camps divided along ethnic, class, and religious lines.

It was possible to keep this sharp focus and to supercede the old, divisive issues because the JDC came into being in response to an emergency, and it was perceived by its founders as a temporary agency with a narrow mission. The founders further presumed that all the Jews needing help were in Eastern Europe or Palestine, and that once the war ended, they would be able again to take care of themselves and the JDC would cease operations. These were reasonable assumptions at the time—most nations believed the war would be over in a season or a year, after which things would return to normal.

"The lamps are going out all over Europe; we shall not see them lit again in our lifetime," British Foreign Secretary Edmund Grey had said prior to the outbreak of war. Few then believed him, but the Jews of Eastern Europe understood his remark as apt prophecy, because for them the lamps had been steadily going dark for the past thirty years. Since the pogroms in the Pale during the 1880s, and increasingly since the turn of the new century, Jews had become the focus of hatred and persecution that had led to impoverishment and uprooting; the start of the Great War exacerbated their condition.

Thus, while the founders of the JDC had only a dim perception of long-term danger, they realized the need to establish a broadly based organization to call upon the resources of *all* of America's Jews. To raise $1.5 million, files of potential contributors were established, local and state committees empanelled, and mail and press solicitations begun. A year later, as the war continued without an end in sight, Nathan Straus raised the next campaign goal to $5 million, to which he personally pledged $100,000. President Woodrow Wilson declared a Jewish War Sufferers Relief Day, and this governmental recognition, along with the willingness of the Red Cross to collect for the cause and substantial pledges from some of the wealthiest American Jews, achieved the goal.

During 1916, American Rabbi Judah L. Magnes, an educator and community leader, toured the sections of war-torn Poland under German rule and reported to the fledgling JDC that at least $10 million would be required in the next campaign. In the fall of 1916, as pressure mounted for American entry into the war, a kick-off meeting at Carnegie Hall in New York raised $1 million for the JDC's work. An additional $1 million from Julius Rosenwald of Sears Roebuck, contingent on the committee raising the remaining $8 million, stimulated further organizational work. In New York City, for example, where the goal was $5 million, a list of 150,000 prospects, divided by occupations, was given to volunteer teams for solicitation. The United States' entry into the war in the spring of 1917 further spurred donations to the JDC cause.

BEYOND THE FIRST CRISIS: 1918–1932

By November 11, 1918, when the Great War officially ended, it had become obvious that the return of peace would not immediately end the suffering of Jews in war-torn Europe.

During a meeting at Versailles, Western European leaders Vittorio Orlando, Georges Clemenceau, and David Lloyd George, with the reluctant agreement of Wilson, placed draconian conditions on the former Austro-Hungarian Empire. The extent of war reparations to be repaid by the losing belligerents, as well as the fallout from the revolutions that brought the Communists to power in Russia and dissolved the remaining bonds of the Austro-Hungarian empire, increased the work that was desperately needed to be done by the JDC, as did a year-long war between Russia and Poland in 1920–21. Fought mainly in territories predominantly occupied by Jews, the Russo-Polish War killed several hundred thousand people and left 275,000 orphaned Jewish children. Among those who received help from the Joint in the war's aftermath was author Isaac Bashevis Singer, who much later in life would tell Goldman, "I can still feel the warmth of the blanket I received from the Joint."

The establishment of independent states in Eastern Europe stirred up nationalistic fervor and antagonism toward Jews in countries such as Estonia and Poland in the north and Czechoslovakia and Yugoslavia in the south. In *A Continuing Task: The American Jewish Joint Distribution Committee, 1914–1964,* Oscar Handlin writes that within these economically unstable states:

> The desire to encourage national entrepreneurs was often directed at the Jew; the cooperative movement usually supported by the new governments also weakened his position, for he was frequently deliberately excluded from these organizations. Meanwhile he bore a disproportionate share of the heavy taxes, [and] boycotts and quotas undermined the ability of the Jew to compete with his rivals, so that he suffered more than others from the effects of economic dislocation and currency depreciation.

Back in 1917, while the war was still being openly waged, British Foreign Secretary Arthur James Balfour had issued an open letter, the Balfour Declaration, which pledged British support for the permanent establishment of a Jewish homeland in Palestine. This important document was made partly in response to the rising tide of Jewish refugees from the war and partly in response to pressure from Zionist organizations.

In 1920, Great Britain took dominion over Palestine from Turkey, and Jews' hopes were raised that the Balfour Declaration's promise of establishing a permanent homeland for the world's Jews would be fulfilled. The arrangement was indeed ratified in 1922 by the newly formed League of Nations. It was expected that some refugees of the recent and ongoing European wars would resettle in Palestine, but there were so many Jewish refugees that the absorption of any significant fraction seemed improbable. Moreover, Arabs in Palestine continued to oppose large-scale immigration of Jews; Great Britain yielded to their pressure and set quotas on the number of Jews who could resettle there.

The United States' massive relief effort for Europe was led by engineer Herbert Hoover. Among his other responsibilities, Hoover was given authority over all railroads in Eastern Europe, so that he effectively controlled supply lines for the distribution of relief. At a meeting in 1919, Hoover told JDC President Felix Warburg that Jews would be treated no differently than other war victims, a position that refused to take into account that Jews had previously been singled out for ill treatment in the war-torn lands, or that all signs pointed to a continuation of anti-Semitic policies by the new governments. In exchange for Warburg's pledge of a $3.3 million JDC contribution to the general relief effort, Hoover granted the JDC the right to undertake its own, separate relief efforts to Eastern Europe. This generosity was made possible by donations in 1919–20 that totaled $27 million—equal to about $800 million in today's dollar terms.

JDC efforts in the immediate postwar years included operating soup kitchens; rebuilding hospitals; establishing orphanages and schools; and distributing food, medicine, and clothing throughout Eastern Europe, though principally in Poland. The first organized delegation of JDC workers to sail across the Atlantic Ocean in 1920 included 126 doctors and other public-health workers, among them Rabbi Bernard Cantor. (Later that year, Cantor and Dr. Israel Friedlander, a distinguished professor at The Jewish Theological Seminary in New York and also a JDC emissary, were murdered while on a mission to Poland's Marshal Pilsudski to investigate the fate of Ukrainian Jews. It would not be until the year 2000 that the graves of Cantor and Friedlander would finally be discovered in Ukraine.)

For generations, the United States had provided a haven for persecuted European Jews, permitting several million to emigrate and begin new lives. But with the enactment of new immigration laws in 1921, the gates symbolized by the Statue of Liberty began to close, and by 1924, they were firmly locked. The gates would not reopen for a decade.

In reaction to the end of the Russo-Polish War, the murder of two JDC activists, the closing of national frontiers to emigration, and the lessons the JDC had learned from operating in Eastern Europe for a half-dozen years, the JDC's mission and methods evolved. Still perceiving its function as a temporary one, in 1921 the JDC decided to henceforth assist imperiled Jews not by direct relief but through the funding of local, on-site agencies and other Jewish agencies of specific focus, such as ORT (Organization for Rehabilitation through Training), a worldwide vocational training group. Moses A. Leavitt, a JDC executive, expressed the philosophy that underlay the JDC's new direction:

> The JDC is a humanitarian agency [that] makes the basic assumption that Jews have a right to live in countries of their birth or in countries of their adoption; they have a right, as human beings, to reside there with full rights. . . . It is the policy of JDC to help Jews to help themselves. The success of the JDC will lie in the speed with which it can make Jews and Jewish communities self-supporting and, thereby, liquidate its activities.

As part of the new philosophy, the JDC cooperated in the 1920s with the Polish health agency TOZ to enable Polish Jews to assume the management of the organization and to take over a steadily increasing share of its budget. Coordination with the ORT was similarly aimed at the future, since the ORT's mission was to retrain Jews who were no longer able to practice the trades that had once sustained them, and who needed new skills and new occupations. Toward the same goal—self-maintenance— the JDC helped set up over three hundred locally operated Eastern European cooperative credit unions, whose capital assets grew into the millions of dollars, and whose loans established Jewish-owned businesses or enabled them to continue to exist.

The Agro-Joint, the JDC's program in the Soviet Union for the resettlement and retraining of Jews in the western sections of Russia and Ukraine, was a point of pride for the organization for a different reason. During the previous century, relatively few Jews in Eastern Europe or Russia had been farmers, since laws in almost every locale had forbidden Jews to own land. Under the Communist system, land ownership was held by the government, and farming was an occupation open to anyone willing to do the hard labor associated with it. The notion of the JDC working hand-in-glove with Russia's Communist government initially sparked a furor in the governing council of the JDC because some among the leadership did not wish to tacitly condone Communism in any way. But proponents of the idea argued that the JDC's nonpolitical stance permitted it to cooperate with governments whose aims or policies differed from those embraced by the United States. This view eventually won out, and the JDC aided Jews within Russia's borders by teaching 250,000 of them how to farm and by providing the necessary seeds and tools, such as the eighty-six tractors brought over in the program's first year.

The Agro-Joint became a signal success. In 1928, John D. Rockefeller wrote to the American chair of the Agro-Joint that "The studies which my associates have made of the various programs and statistics . . . have impressed us all with the value of this activity as a notable and creative example of social engineering." He enclosed a check for $500,000. Herbert Hoover, soon to become president of the United States, also wrote to praise the JDC endeavor.

Smaller JDC programs in the Soviet Union supplied machinery used to manufacture clothing to disenfranchised Jews, enabling them to earn a living in the big cities. These programs also funded a large Jewish dining hall in Moscow, created cooperatives to teach Jews such trades as furniture-making, and helped Jews sent to Siberia to find homes and sustenance during their exile.

The complement to the JDC's nonpolitical stance in its early years was a non-Zionist policy: the organization neither encouraged nor discouraged activity aimed at transplanting Jews from the diaspora to Palestine. When Zionist leader Chaim Weizmann objected to the JDC's spending of millions of dollars to restore Jewish life in Eastern Europe rather than using the money to resettle those Jews in Palestine, JDC leaders and major contributors argued for Jews to have the right to live anywhere and in any manner they wished.

There was equivalent controversy over another tenet of policy that emerged in this era: the belief that the JDC should support Jews remaining in Eastern Europe rather than encouraging emigration. Many American socialists and some German-born Jews in the JDC were indifferent to the desire to build or rebuild Jewish educational and cultural institutions. However, the consensus of JDC leadership favored helping Jews remain in Eastern European countries by providing major support for such institutions.

Having made these arrangements, in the mid-1920s the JDC almost closed up shop entirely. Donations and disbursements fell to little more than a million dollars a year—the lowest level since operations had begun. There was talk of this being a last period for the JDC, of its work "coming to an end." The ORT and other institutes were reaching the point of being self-sustaining, as was the Agro-Joint.

Pogroms and other anti-Semitic excesses in Eastern Europe during the years of 1925–27 provided new impetus to keep the JDC alive, and for donors to contribute to it. But the 1929 stock market crash and the onset of the Great Depression in the United States decreased the ability of the JDC's patrons to donate. In 1932, only $385,000 was raised. Oscar Handlin wrote that in this period, the JDC's "activities were cut to a minimum and its voice was barely audible."

The JDC and World War II, 1933–1945

Hitler's ascension to political power in Germany in 1933 brought with it his belief that Jews were responsible for Germany's economic and social problems, and the passage of the first laws mandating removal of the Jews from civil service and other positions. The JDC transferred its European headquarters from Berlin to Paris and began operating once again on an emergency basis, though its funds were still severely limited by the Depression. As the 1930s continued, and the Depression's economic toll on the United States lessened, more money was found to assist Jews in escaping from Germany, Poland, and Romania, where Nazism and other nationalistic cults made life for Jews increasingly untenable. The JDC's mission had long been referred to as "the three R's": Relief, Reconstruction, and Rescue. Prior to 1933, the organization had focused on Relief and Reconstruction; now in response to the changing needs of the Jewish community, it shifted to the third "R": Rescue. Assistance from the JDC helped a quarter-million Jews to leave Germany and 125,000 Austrian Jews to leave Austria.

Hitler took over Austria and the Sudetenland of Czechoslovakia by mid-1938 and was threatening to overrun the rest of Czechoslovakia. In November of 1938, a German embassy official in Paris was assassinated, and the deed was traced to a teenaged Polish Jew, Herschel Greenspan, who had wanted to punish the Nazis for what they were doing to Jews. His deed—and its rationale—was used by the Nazis as an excuse to trigger the outbreak of violence thereafter known as *Kristallnacht*. On November 8, 1938, roving gangs of German "civilians" in plain clothes (but wearing storm trooper boots) ransacked synagogues and Jewish-owned storefronts in Berlin, killing nearly a hundred Jews and setting off waves of related

anti-Semitic violence and further crackdowns on Jews throughout the growing Nazi empire.

In response to Kristallnacht and other Nazi pogroms, the
JDC and the other major Jewish fund-raising organization in
the United States, the United Palestine Appeal, joined forces to
raise money for overseas operations. Together they created the
United Jewish Appeal (UJA) and collected tens of millions of
dollars to help Jews suffering in Nazi-occupied Europe.

It is important to recall that the threat to the Jews of
Germany, Austria, and of the other territories annexed by the
Nazi regime was not a cause to which all non-Jewish Americans
were sensitive in 1936. Although the majority of Americans de-
tested Hitler in 1938, there were many whose sentiments
echoed those of right-wing radio priest Father Coughlin, who
took to the airwaves to charge that Jewish money had funded the
Communist revolution in Russia, and that the anti-Semitic
measures being taken by the Third Reich deserved the support
of Americans. That entire countries were willing to turn their
backs on Europe's Jews was underlined by the plight of the *SS
St. Louis* in 1939, when the JDC-chartered ship bearing nine
hundred Jews fleeing Hitler was turned away at every free port
in the world and was eventually forced to disembark its passengers again in Europe, where many of them became victims of
the Holocaust.

Through the 1930s, the JDC's Morris Troper, Moses A.
Leavitt, and Bernard Kahn had taken leading roles in helping
Jews emigrate from Europe. In September of 1940, one year after
war had begun in Europe, and well before the full horrors of Nazi
violence against Jews had become known to the world, Troper
told the JDC's board of directors that "I stand before you this
morning . . . not as Morris Troper alone; I am here as Hirsch of
Berlin, Loewenherz of Vienna, as Giterman, Guzik and
Neustadt of Poland, as Eppler of Budapest and Friedmann of
Prague, Grodzensky of Lithuania, and Ussoskin of Romania. . . .
They have nothing to look forward to except starvation, disease,
and ultimate extinction."

Troper told the board that henceforth the JDC's "sacred task" would be to keep alive as many Jewish brethren as possible, in the teeth of the mounting ferocity and diligence with which Hitler and satellite Nazi regimes were pursuing Jews. The vast preponderance of the Jews in the lands occupied by the Nazis—some six million Jews, half the Jews in the world—perished in the Holocaust. But between 1939 and 1944 the JDC was able to aid 81,000 Jews in emigrating from Europe to other countries, to provide support to Jews who had made their own way to Switzerland, and to send money behind Nazi lines to assist Jews. Funds were secretly parachuted into occupied Poland, where $1 million helped keep the Warsaw ghetto's Jews alive and resisting for several years.

In *Out of the Ashes*, Yehuda Bauer wrote that between 1939 and 1944, the JDC's leadership "did not grasp the full impact of what was occurring to Europe's Jews." But during the war, few people could even imagine that the Nazis were actually gassing, shooting, strangling, or starving to death four thousand people each day, every day, for more than four years. Nonetheless, at the time enough was known about the Nazis' killings to spur JDC funding levels during World War II to reach the equivalent of those attained during World War I, about $15 million annually.

The Postwar JDC and the Establishment of the State of Israel

The full revelation of the existence of the death camps and the various methods of mass killing employed in them shocked and repulsed nearly everyone in the Western world. The horror of the Holocaust and the plight of the flood tide of refugees from the Holocaust spurred JDC contributions and distributions to multiply nearly five-fold, to almost $70 million in the peak year of 1947—in today's terms, more than $2 billion. It was a historical moment that demanded the greatest possible effort, and the Jews of America responded with utmost generosity, contributing through UJA and working through the JDC, which at this time became the most widely effective sectarian agency in the world.

Between 1945 and 1950, the JDC put into effect what Goldman later labeled a "Jewish Marshall Plan," spending $280 million in reconstruction assistance to Europe's Jews. Today there is general agreement among historians that had this massive effort not been mounted, or had it been attempted on a smaller scale, most of the Jews who survived the Holocaust would have perished in the war's aftermath. "It would be no exaggeration," the *Encyclopedia of the Holocaust* suggests, to contend that in the immediate postwar era, the Jews of Eastern Europe "were kept alive, in part at least, by the JDC, directed by Joe Schwartz." Goldman refers to Schwartz, director of overseas operations, who succeeded Morris Troper in 1940, as a model of compassionate caring for Jews, one of the great unsung Jewish heroes. During the war years, he was a master at reaching Jews behind enemy lines. Schwartz thought about questions affecting Jewish communities abroad in terms Goldman characterizes as encompassing a "global Jewish perspective," and during his own tenure, Goldman embraced this tradition.

Although JDC assistance to the Jewish victims of the war started even before the surrender of Germany—with a five-million-franc allocation to France to restore schools and synagogues—it was only in the weeks following the German surrender in May of 1945 that the enormous dimensions of the task facing the Jewish world became clear. One and a half million survivors of Nazi concentration camps, ghettos, and refugee lines were being housed in various places throughout Europe, a quarter-million of them in temporary quarters. Some, like the 150,000 surviving Polish Jews, sought to emigrate to Israel or to return to their wrecked homeland. Most surviving European Jews, however, had no place to return to because buildings and societal infrastructures had been destroyed, and they knew that they were not wanted in places such as Poland. An additional three million Jews were believed to be living, under adverse circumstances, in Russia and other areas controlled by Russian satellite governments—areas closed to outside assistance.

Working hand in hand with the United States Army and the United Nations Relief and Rehabilitation Administration

(UNRRA), the JDC managed to assist 750,000 Jews in Europe in 1946 and 1,000,000 in 1947. The JDC operated hospitals, schools, soup kitchens, and rehabilitation and retraining centers; it also provided funds for Yiddish theater, newspapers, and other cultural activities for the reestablishment of Jewish life. Other organizations also supplied shelter and food, but the JDC saw its main role as providing spiritual sustenance. One project was a joint JDC and U.S. Army reprinting of the Talmud, for distribution to the dispossessed. The JDC employed more than two thousand people to directly administer its programs, as doctors, teachers, and transporters of the displaced.

Despite heroic efforts, the magnitude of the dispossessed was nearly beyond the capacity of relief organizations to properly succor. In many places, the terrible postwar conditions in Europe turned neighbor against neighbor. In 1946, one such instance took place in Kielce, Poland, when forty-two Jewish survivors who returned to their hometown were brutally murdered by Christian neighbors. Kielce was a revelation for the Jewish world that anti-Semitism was still deeply entrenched in much of Europe. Soon, once-repatriated Polish Jews began again to travel westward—with the Joint's help—to resettle in more hospitable countries such as France and Belgium, or to seek transport to Palestine.

The early postwar years also saw the final stages of agitation and maneuvering toward the establishment of the State of Israel in 1948. This event was closely linked to the influx of more than 200,000 refugees from Europe, the vast majority of them transported to Palestine with funds provided by the JDC. In those years there were few destinations for the Jews of Europe other than Palestine. Laws in the United States still limited the total number of immigrants permitted to land on its shores each year, and these laws imposed country quotas that had the effect of further limiting the number of Jews in each country's annual contingent. Canada and Latin American nations could only absorb a small fraction of all those Jews who wished—indeed, needed— to find a country in which to start a new life. Some refugee transport activities in which the Joint found itself engaged were legal;

others were designed to skirt the emigration limitations. Despite the strong opposition of some on the JDC's executive committee, Joe Schwartz persuaded the committee to allocate $1 million for what the British called "illegal immigration to Palestine."

Many groups of Jews needed Palestine as a place to live: the large group of refugee immigrants, the Jews already residing in the still-small settlements of Palestine, additional victims of the Holocaust who were shortly to arrive, and the increasing number of refugees from the Communist-controlled countries. The existence of these groups put additional pressure on the United Nations to accede to the partitioning of Palestine that would allow Jewish control of a portion of the area. The vote in the General Assembly in favor of partition passed by the narrowest of margins in November of 1947. Sensing that the moment was ripe, on May 14, 1948, David Ben-Gurion proclaimed Israel's independence.

THE JDC'S REACH EXPANDS

Some had believed that with the establishment of the state of Israel and the winding down of efforts to resettle European Jews, the JDC's work would lessen. It did not. Rather, it expanded in four distinct directions: assistance to those in Israel, to European Jews, to Jews behind the Iron Curtain, and to Jews in Moslem countries. The categories of relief and the personnel who handled them were interrelated. For instance, Moses Beckelman, JDC's Director-General for Overseas Operations from 1951 until his death in 1955, not only helped move displaced persons from their camps to better destinations, but he also had a hand in obtaining recompense for Holocaust victims and in saving the Jews of Shanghai and Japan. Beckelman was the moving force behind the JDC's assistance to the aged in Israel.

Many refugees who went to Israel were too old or disabled to make new lives for themselves; their dependency was a great burden for the young country to bear. However, the JDC, privately-funded from abroad, *could* meet that need. Early on in Israel's modern history, the JDC developed and supported many initiatives to care for these immigrants. The JDC also assisted other populations who could not care for themselves: the disabled, the mentally retarded, the aged and infirm. Support for programs within the state of Israel included the operation of hospitals for tuberculosis and other communicable diseases, and of schools and yeshivot.

As Jews returned from the refugee camps to their European homelands, they made up substantial (and largely impoverished) populations in France, Belgium, and other countries released from Nazi domination. The JDC supported local organizations that assisted these populations and rebuilt parts of Jewish communities that had been laid waste, such as synagogues in Venice, Amsterdam, Stockholm, and Madrid. After 1951, money from the Claims Conference—reparations paid by Germany for crimes against Jews during the war—was also used for these purposes. Following the principle of helping local people help themselves, the JDC steadily transferred both financial and practical responsibility for support of Jewish life in Europe to local organizations, so that JDC funds and energy could be redirected to assist Jews elsewhere to care for themselves.

The largest faction of Jews needing help was shut off from the world when the Soviet Union closed itself and its satellites in 1946, creating what Churchill labeled the Iron Curtain. Over the next several years, it became increasingly difficult for the JDC to directly reach the three million Jews living behind that Curtain. While immediately after World War II the JDC had been invited into Hungary, Poland, Czechoslovakia, Yugoslavia, Romania, and Bulgaria, by 1953 the organization was no longer welcome in Hungary, Poland, and Czechoslovakia. In some places, the JDC was openly accused of espionage and anti-Communist activities.

Stalin fanned the flames of the anti-Semitism that had surfaced throughout Eastern Europe. Already hard-pressed economically, these countries became involved as "satellites" of the USSR, and were involved in a Cold War with the United States and its democratic allies. When Soviet Jews in Moscow gave a warm reception to Golda Meir, Israel's first ambassador to the

USSR, Stalin ordered the arrest, imprisonment, and torture of many Soviet Jewish intellectuals, army leaders, and political rivals. This anti-Semitic trend spread with the arrest in 1951 of fourteen officials of the Communist Party—eleven of whom were Jewish, including Rudolf Slansky, the Party's secretary-general. This anti-Semitic culminated in the so-called "Doctors' Plot" against Stalin in 1952–53, which the dictator charged had been instituted by Jewish medical doctors in the Kremlin.

Unable to function directly in the satellite countries, the JDC established and quietly funded entities like the *Societé de Secours et d'Entr'Aide* (SSE), a social service organization in Geneva, to fill the breach. In other third-party arrangements, trusted individuals and companies in Great Britain, France, and the Scandinavian countries sent packages and even managed to transfer some funds to Jews behind the Iron Curtain. The uprising in Hungary in 1956, which resulted in 20,000 Jews fleeing into Austria, where the JDC could assist them, and the expulsion of 20,000 Jews from Russia to Poland in 1957–58, where the JDC continued to be active, provided isolated opportunities for the JDC to directly assist Soviet-satellite Jews.

The JDC had long insisted that Jews from Muslim countries, whose physical appearance was different from European Jews, should be considered by American Jews as equal-status brothers, just as they considered Eastern European Jews to be. This even-handed challenge was put to the test during the establishment of the Jewish State and the subsequent attempts of nearby Arab countries to tear it apart. The Arab-Israeli wars of 1948 and 1956 produced great pressure on the dwindling Jewish enclaves in Muslim lands, where some Jewish communities had existed side by side with Muslims for two thousand years. During this period of conflict, the JDC helped the Jews of Muslim lands emigrate to more hospitable shores. It assisted the Jewish Agency and other organizations in transporting whole communities from Muslim countries to Israel—50,000 from Yemen in "Operation Magic Carpet," many thousands more from Iraq and Kurdish areas in "Operation Ezra and Nehemiah," 32,000 from Libya, and others from Egypt and Syria. Even after the conclusion of these operations, the JDC continued to assist Jews who remained in place throughout the Middle East and North Africa.

THE JDC'S MISSION CONTINUES

In 1964, Oscar Handlin observed in his fiftieth anniversary history of the JDC that "Much of the excitement of fund raising in earlier years was gone, along with much of the uncertainty [of Jewish existence]" but that the sort of tasks that the JDC had undertaken in Poland and Russia in 1914 "still occupied it in Morocco and Iran" in the 1950s and 1960s. The Joint's main mission, Handlin continued, remained clear: To bring to Jews in all corners of the world "not only bread but also the promise of future reconstruction [of their communities] on a basis sounder than in the past."

In an era of cold war, this became increasingly difficult to accomplish, especially in the aftermath of the 1967 Six-Day War between Israel and several of its neighboring Arab states. Israeli troops reclaimed East Jerusalem and captured the Golan Heights, Sinai, and other strategically important objectives, despite the Arab countries having been armed and advised by Communist bloc countries. A cease-fire, however, did not end the tensions. Shortly after the conclusion of the fighting phase of the war, Charles Jordan, the JDC's chief executive, was abducted and murdered in Prague, Czechoslovakia. Rabbi Moses Rosen of Romania, with whom Jordan had spent several days in Bucharest just prior to the abduction, was later told by Romania's intelligence service that Jordan had been killed by Egyptians, who had mounted three unsuccessful attempts against the JDC executive in Bucharest before Jordan traveled to Prague. Others believed that the murder had been a mistake and that the assassins had thought Jordan was Shaike Dan, an Israeli operative. The Czechoslovakian government refused to press the Egyptian government on the issue and mounted only a cursory investigation that identified no suspects. Years later, a Czechoslovak defector who had worked for the country's intelligence service asserted to those who debriefed him in the United States that Jordan had been murdered by Egyptians, but no acknowledgement was made of this by that Czechoslovak government or subsequent ones. In the year 2001, the murder of Executive Vice President Charles Jordan remains officially unsolved—a reminder of the many difficulties and hazards faced by the JDC in aiding Jews around the world during the depths of the Cold War.

It was after the murder of Charles Jordan that Sam Haber took over the professional leadership of the JDC. Haber had been an integral part of the organization since the Holocaust, and was ideally suited to help the JDC carry out its missions of Relief, Reconstruction, and Rescue. Among the first people who Haber sought to hire for the JDC was a man who had already become one of the best-known Jewish social workers, the professional leader of the Israel Education Fund, Ralph I. Goldman.

CHAPTER TWO

Preparations

Becoming "Mr. Joint"

R ALPH IRVING GOLDMAN, the man who would eventually
replace Sam Haber as the professional leader of the JDC
and would come to be known among the peoples the JDC served
as "Mr. Joint," was born in Lechovitz, Ukraine, in 1914, and emigrated with his family to the United States at a very early age.

GOLDMAN'S EARLY EDUCATION AND
INTRODUCTION TO PUBLIC SERVICE

Goldman spent most of his childhood and youth in Dorchester,
Massachusetts, a lower-middle-class suburb of Boston that was
then predominantly Jewish. While his mother raised the small
family, his father, who in Ukraine had been the proprietor of a
fabric store, worked as a "peddler who sold things from his car,"
Goldman remembers. "He bought jewelry, home furniture, and
furnishings, and sold them to individuals on the installment
plan, which meant having to collect weekly payments from
them." Goldman also recalls that his father frequently had to obtain loans of a few hundred dollars from the Hebrew Free Loan
Society—no-interest loans he would pay back within weeks.
The Goldman home was a religiously observant and hospitable

one; Goldman's mother was never certain how many would be at her dinner table. By the time Goldman was in junior high school, he was also attending the Beth-El Hebrew School five afternoons a week, along with many other children in the community. A classmate and close friend there was Theodore H. White, who wrote his first short story before his fourteenth birthday and who would later become one of the country's leading journalists. White's memoir, *In Search of History: A Personal Adventure,* recalls that Hebrew school:

> Most of our teachers were then newly arrived young immigrant scholars, who had come from post–World War I Europe to seek a secular education in Boston's universities. . . . They were rigorous in their teaching of the young, and violent of temper when the tired children failed to respond. They despised Yiddish . . . and as a matter of principle they would speak no English in class, for their cardinal principle was Zionism. They were about to revive the Hebrew language and make it a living tongue. . . . The Bible was explained to us in Hebrew, pounded into us in Hebrew, and we were forced to explain it to one another in Hebrew. It was a nightmare education, but I came to love it.

Goldman has fond memories of himself and White buying bologna sandwiches, large enough to sustain them through a whole day's studying, for five cents apiece. The main subject of the friends' recurring debate was: Should we save the Jews, or save Judaism?

"Teddy would take one side or the other," Goldman recalls, "but I always argued that we should save both." Goldman's firm conviction was that it was possible to save individual Jews as well as to make sure Jewish culture survives; both goals were essential and complementary. This belief, formed early in life, became a touchstone and a guide for him throughout his career.

Goldman and White's deep belief in Judaism sometimes took them into the streets. One Saturday night in 1936, they put up signs outside of a Woolworth's store in Dorchester to protest the sale of goods from Germany and Japan. For their efforts, the two were dragged into the local police precinct, but were soon released.

Graduating from the five-day-a-week Hebrew school, Goldman and White continued their studies at Boston's Hebrew College, which they attended daily throughout the remainder of high school and beyond. They took Hebrew College classes through the years when they were also students at secular colleges such as Boston University and Harvard, in effect shouldering a double academic load throughout their teens and early twenties. "Teddy White and I also taught Hebrew to make some money," Goldman recalls.

The faculty of the Hebrew College was as eclectic as it was intellectually advanced, made up principally of European émigrés, who taught, in Hebrew, such subjects as economics and psychology—not normally the fare for high-school age children in the United States. Many students who stayed the course through to diplomas went on to distinguished careers as academics, surgeons, and businessmen. The bonds formed in the school continued long afterward, and many of Goldman's classmates, including the late Theodore H. White, remained his close friends throughout life.

Goldman received diplomas from Boston's Hebrew College and Boston University in 1937. In those years, Goldman remained committed to Judaism, but his observance took on a more personal sensibility. His father wouldn't drive on Shabbat, but would lend his car to his son. For Goldman, this was an early lesson in how different people could live together with respect, according to their own standards.

In 1937, he also received his first fellowship, from Avuka, a student Zionist organization (for which he had served as New England area chairman). This enabled him to visit Palestine, an all-consuming experience that had a profound impact on the rest of his life. Goldman found it "exhilarating" to work on a kibbutz, help establish a settlement, and pave a road, because all these activities qualified as building the country. Every aspect of the fellowship year abroad fed into his education and burgeoning love for Palestine. These were the years of riots in Palestine and of guerrilla actions by Arabs against new settlements. Goldman recalls being shot at by Arabs while in a communal shower building in a northern outpost. By chance, he roomed with friends at Golda Meir's home when she was out of the country. He audited courses at the Hebrew University in Jerusalem, and—demonstrating the sort of leadership that would become his hallmark—successfully petitioned the Jewish Agency to hold a series of high-level seminars for himself and other fellowship students; among the speakers were men who would later sign Israel's declaration of independence when Israel became a state.

A British royal commission had recently recommended that Palestine be partitioned, and while Goldman was in Palestine the students participated in the Jewish community's great debates about the recommendation. Goldman favored partition, and he was particularly struck by the refusal of the famous Zionist leader Abraham Menahem Mendel Ussishkin, then the Chairman of the Jewish National Fund (and the leading opponent of partition), to shake his hand because of Goldman's position on the issue.

From this trip, Goldman became more than ever convinced of the necessity of someday establishing a sovereign state that would be a Jewish homeland.

Coming home, Goldman entered the world of the founder of the Hebrew College, Louis Hurwich. Hurwich had only a shoestring budget on which to educate his students, but nonetheless was able to invite distinguished scholars and community activists to address Goldman and the other young men in weekend supplementary seminars. Among the visiting lecturers were Salo Baron of Columbia University, the dean of Jewish historical studies in the United States; Harry R. Lurie, director of the Bureau of Jewish Social Research; and Graenum Berger, then the director of a community center in the Bronx and later in life the founder of the American Association for Ethiopian Jews.

In 1938, Hurwich devised an experiment: he would help a

few of the graduates enter community service work, principally in order to raise the Jewish content of such work. "In those days," Goldman recalls, "the Jewish Federations around the country were run by social workers, but not necessarily by people who had a deep background in Jewish matters. Hurwich's idea was to produce social workers with more extensive Jewish knowledge." Goldman was awarded a fellowship of $750 a year and lived at home while working daily at Hecht House, a settlement house in the Boston area. Goldman aspired to enter a Jewish school for social work in New York, but when that facility closed, Hurwich stepped in and helped Goldman to attend Harvard Graduate School of Arts and Science and the School of Social Work at Boston University. For three years, Goldman took classes at Harvard and obtained a master's degree in social work to go along with his bachelor's degree in education. Meanwhile, Goldman continued at Hecht House, doing case work and individual therapy in conjunction with the Jewish Family Service Agency. In his book, *Memoirs of a Jewish Educator,* Hurwich recalled the young Goldman and his classmate Charles Zibbell in their work at Hecht House and at the Y.M.H.A. in Roxbury:

> They introduced a new tone into the clubs, which caught the warm attention both of the professionals as well as the laymen on the board. Generally, there was no organized training for directors of the clubs [but] these two . . . had introduced a Jewish tone in their administration of the club. This spark had gotten hold of the youngsters who were part of their club, and from all corners rumors came flying about the enthusiasm for the work and the holidays arranged [by the pair] that had content as well as an attractive Jewish form.

Dean Hurwich considered the "experiment" in training Goldman and Zibbell highly successful, and continued it with other promising students. Goldman recalls with pride that they were indeed able to engage the young club members as well as their leadership with Jewish content. In those days, he and his fellow social work students would gather to discuss their work, over pastrami sandwiches and green pickles, and debate the pressing issues of the day.

Goldman has always resisted the label of "social worker," feeling it does not adequately describe what he does or his ways of approaching the world, but he says he always "liked community work and wanted to go on with it. I probably would have ended up as the director of a community center in some large city," but the war intervened.

INTO THE STORM: WORLD WAR II

In June of 1942, Goldman entered the United States Army and was sent to boot camp at Fort Meade, near Baltimore. During his basic training, Goldman worked in intelligence, and later, as an assistant to a psychiatrist and to a chaplain.

In boot camp, his personal life took a new direction as well. Back during the second year of his social work studies, Goldman had supervised a first-year graduate student; this connection led to Goldman's receiving at Fort Meade a letter from Helen Goldberg, a young woman friend of that grad student's wife. The correspondence between Goldman and Helen soon developed into a romance. He and Helen were married in June of 1943, and a daughter, Judy, was born in 1944. In November of that year, he was sent to a base in England in a town named Dorchester; a month later, his unit, the 66th Infantry Division, was sent to France, and in early 1945 moved into Germany.

After the end of the war in Europe, Goldman was sent back to France, to an army unit near Arles. While he and his mates waited to be shipped to the Far East to continue the war against Japan, Rabbi Abraham Haselkorn, the Jewish chaplain, recruited Goldman to help with the flood of displaced persons, many thousands of whom were housed in temporary quarters in the area.

Work in the displaced person (DP) camps became his second most important formative experience, for the plight of the tens of thousands of refugees, many of them Jewish, moved Goldman, especially in light of what were then recent revelations about the extent of the Holocaust. No Jew could fail to be deeply shaken by the fact of the Holocaust; but those like Goldman, who came in contact with Holocaust survivors immediately after the end of the war, developed a perhaps more intense sense of the effects of the Nazis' killings and an equally intense determination to aid Holocaust survivors in every way possible.

Goldman applied his ingenuity to helping supply the displaced persons camps, commandeering a truck to take surplus from Army warehouses to camps near Marseilles. That the supply camps were manned by German prisoners of war also struck Goldman: "Seeing them distributing U.S. supplies made me feel that my mission to help the DPs was even more sacred and of critical importance." One memorable supply prize was 40,000 boxes of Milky Way candy bars; the Army rejected them because they were not properly double-wrapped, but Goldman helped the bars find their way to the camps.

Goldman's commitment to help those who had suffered because they were Jews helped form his belief that the refugees should be aided in reaching Palestine, every Jew's rightful homeland. Toward that end, he taught Hebrew to young people in the camps, who were more likely to travel, legally or illegally, to Palestine to begin a new life, rather than return to Poland or other countries to the east. But some could not imagine a life other than the one they had known; Goldman is still troubled by the memory of a bright twelve-year-old boy in one of his classes who ran away, back to Poland, to search for his family. "I still wonder about his fate," Goldman says.

It is difficult to pinpoint just when any individual's special sensitivity becomes well-enough developed to determine the path of his or her life's work, but those who know Goldman believe, as he does, that his experiences assisting Jews in need in the DP camps affected him profoundly, to the point that from that moment on he devoted himself to helping fellow Jews in need (and often in distress). In short, the direction of Goldman's future was set in these months at the close of World War II, working around the DPs.

Performing his tasks, Goldman came in contact with people

engaged in *Aliya Bet*, or illegal immigration operations for the transfer of displaced persons to Israel. Jewish leaders in Palestine distinguished between immigration (*aliya*) permitted by the British, which they called type A or *Aleph*, and immigration not permitted by the British, which they called type B, or *Bet*. Those colleagues suggested that when he was demobilized from the army, he see Ya'acov Dori, the secret head of the Haganah (the pre-state defense force that eventually became the backbone of the Israeli army), and join the New York part of their operations. But Goldman had already promised an army friend whom he had befriended that he would become his second in command at a Jewish community center in Canton, Ohio. Goldman worked diligently enough in Canton for nine months, but, as he later recalled, "That was not the job for me, certainly not in '46. Fortunately, I took sick and was hospitalized, and I had to leave Canton. When I got out of the hospital, Eddie Parsons—a former schoolmate of mine and a fellowship partner when we were in Palestine before the war—arranged for me to take a job in New York as director of the Palestine Vocational Service, a one-man front organization for the clandestine recruitment of personnel for what the British called 'illegal ships' taking immigrants to Palestine."

ISRAEL: BIRTH OF A JEWISH STATE

While Goldman had been in France, David Ben-Gurion had met in New York City with eighteen American Jewish leaders from various parts of the United States and Canada, and had given to them his evaluation of the prospects for a Jewish homeland in Palestine. In this secret meeting, Ben-Gurion predicted that the end of the war would precipitate a change in government in Great Britain, and that this, along with other international problems, such as the burden of the Displaced Persons camps and Jewish resistance to British governance in Palestine, would produce, within two or three years, the surrender of the British Mandate and the establishment of a Jewish state. After the new state was formed, Ben-Gurion also predicted it would have to fight the surrounding Arab states in order to survive. The new Jewish state would need arms and personnel for that fight, and these could only be obtained in America. "On that memorable day," participant Rudolf G. Sonnenborn later recalled, "we were asked to form ourselves into an . . . American arm of the underground Haganah," and to agree to perform activities that were, in the eyes of American law, illegal—but that Sonnenborn and the other men assembled believed were legitimate. The group pledged several million dollars, which would be used to buy or lease airplanes and ships to transport immigrants by roundabout routes to Palestine, as well as to provide for the armed forces of the not-yet-formed Jewish state.

It was this buying and staffing effort that Goldman joined when he returned to New York City. From an office on East 71st Street in Manhattan, Goldman functioned as a recruiter of personnel for the ships and planes, and as a buyer and leaser of transports. He recalls his work at this time as being an "aide-de-camp and a confidante" of the high officials of the Haganah and of others who would later take important positions in the state of Israel. He functioned "well enough to be trusted" by Ya'akov Dori, who became first chief of staff when the State of Israel was established. It was at this time that he first met Teddy Kollek, who would become the long-term mayor of Jerusalem. The two young men started a lifelong friendship during a half-block walk from one meeting to another. "Ralph was our intelligence and security officer," Kollek recalls, and he depicts Goldman as more integral to the effort of funneling people and material to Palestine than Goldman gives himself credit for.

Testament to Goldman's role was his part in his group's chartering of ships like the *Exodus,* which became famous for its voyage to Palestine, filled to capacity with 4,500 "visa-less" Jews from DP camps. Though unarmed, the *Exodus* was fired upon and was seized by the British seventeen miles offshore, in international waters, and became a symbol of British intransigence and Jewish determination and courage. The spectacle of the British military preventing Holocaust survivors from reaching a

Jewish homeland evoked worldwide sympathy for the victims and helped to prevail on the British to relinquish their mandate. Members of a United Nations committee sent to Palestine to research partition of the country watched the events surrounding the *Exodus* unfold from their balconies in Haifa, and returned to UN headquarters convinced of the necessity of establishing a Jewish state.

Between 1946 and 1948, the ships chartered by the New York group and manned by volunteers, many of whom the 71st Street office had recruited, transported some 32,000 immigrants to Palestine. Goldman recalls that "the FBI was after us," because the group's recruiting and purchasing activities skirted the borders of legality; as a result, Goldman recalls, "I would never meet a prospective recruit at the office, only at a café or other neutral location." One Saturday morning, a barrel broke on a loading dock in Jersey City, and all present could see that it contained not the agricultural tools listed in the cargo manifest, but guns. Goldman's job became helping the men handling that cargo to "disappear" before they could be arrested and the story was made public. To accomplish this, Goldman sent the cargo handlers to Canada, and Eddie Silver, Assistant United States District Attorney, enlisted the help of New York Mayor Robert F. Wagner in covering their tracks.

Goldman also recalls having a minor role in rounding up the votes in the United Nations for the partition of Palestine on November 29, 1947—the event that led to the establishment of the state of Israel in May 1948. At the exact moment of Israel's birth, Goldman was unable to celebrate—he was working behind-the-scenes, helping to set up of a secret radio station from which Ben-Gurion could announce the deed to the world. In New York, several hours before the State of Israel was declared, Goldman received confirmation from a UN source of the Arab nations' impending attack and had some frustrating moments when he was unable to find anyone in New York to directly communicate this critical news to Ben-Gurion in Tel Aviv.

GOLDMAN AND BEN-GURION

Although Goldman was not present in Israel at the birth of the country, he continued to work for the infant state in New York; he did, however, travel to Israel in 1949 and was present for its first anniversary celebrations. He worked there for six weeks with the small group of insiders in the nascent government. At a joyous Foreign Office party, Goldman remembers that he and Abe Harman, who would later become Israel's ambassador to the United States and President of Hebrew University, toasted Ben-Gurion with a bottle of brandy, celebrating long into the night. The next evening, after a reception at the Ministry of Defense, Kollek summoned him to at last "meet the old man," Ben-Gurion himself.

"Come with me," Ben-Gurion said to Goldman as they were introduced and brought him into an inner courtyard of the ministry building. "He made sure that I had pen and paper," said Goldman, "and proceeded to recite the titles and publication dates of two books, part of a series of fifty volumes on the civilizations of the East, published over several decades in the 19th century." Goldman had learned earlier of Ben-Gurion's continuing efforts to obtain these volumes and had in fact already helped other emissaries buy some of them. When Goldman returned to New York, he searched for months to find and buy the missing volumes, but to no avail. The two existed only in the New York Public Library; he rebuffed the importuning of friends who told him to steal the volumes and instead prevailed upon his brother-in-law for an emergency grant of $500 to photostat them and to bind the copies. Years later, Goldman would discover that Ben-Gurion kept these bound copies at his home, along with the others in the set.

Goldman became a representative of Prime Minister Ben-Gurion, working in the Israel consulate in New York, to recruit personnel—now openly—for scientific and technical positions with the new state. He also became publisher of *Israel Speaks,* a biweekly of twelve to sixteen pages. Written in English, it was distributed to paying customers and to the journalistic community, which used it as an authoritative source of news about Israel.

In 1951, Goldman received what he calls one of his most thrilling assignments, to do logistics and appointments work for Ben-Gurion on a month-long tour of the United States as Ben-Gurion established the Israel Bonds organization. It was to be the first time that a prime minister of Israel had made a visit to the United States. Moved by the honor of the assignment but bound by secrecy, Goldman was unable to inform his parents of it until an entire month had passed. Preparations were so extensive that Goldman once had to make three plane trips between Washington and New York in a single day to nail down the details, among them, an "unofficial" visit to President Harry S. Truman.

Ben-Gurion was "not a person with whom you could chitchat," Goldman says, but Goldman remembers that he learned much from the older man, such as the value of taking every spare moment to read and the importance of placing great emphasis on education. He noted how delighted Ben-Gurion was when Goldman arranged for him to talk, in Hebrew, to a group of students at Goldman's old school in Boston, the Hebrew College. On a refueling stop for Ben-Gurion's airplane in Tulsa, Oklahoma, four hundred people showed up at two in the morning, just to catch a glimpse of the prime minister; that, too, impressed Goldman. In Los Angeles, Mrs. Sam Goldwyn phoned and asked Goldman to tell Ben-Gurion that he reminded her of the Gilbert Stuart painting of George Washington. When Goldman conveyed the message, Ben-Gurion responded, "I wish I looked like Abraham Lincoln."

In the middle of the month of the tour, Ben-Gurion asked Goldman to bring together a few people to whom he could present a special idea. Goldman organized the gathering, and Ben-Gurion told them of his dream to have the world's classics translated into Hebrew. "He did not want Israel to be a Levantine state," Goldman says. "He wanted Israelis to be an '*Am Segulah, Or Lagoyim,*' a people of destiny, a light unto the nations."

On September 3, 1951, Ben-Gurion wrote to Goldman that

Jews always "believed in the supremacy of the *spirit*," and that the "historical test of Israel" would not be of its military might, its economy, or its ability to increase its population, "but of its *spirit*, vision, and prophetic and messianic mission." Therefore—and in order to bring together the Jews in Israel and those in the diaspora—the spirit must be renewed and refreshed, by means of Hebrew culture and the translation into Hebrew "of all the works worthy to be passed to future generations."

The enterprise never quite came together in the form that Ben-Gurion had envisioned, but the sentiments about *Am Segula*, the importance of Hebrew culture, and of the written word in it became part of the core beliefs underlying Goldman's life's work.

Of equal importance to him was Ben-Gurion's steady adherence to principle, even when political exigencies might have suggested otherwise. Goldman finds one particular incident memorable in this regard. In 1955, when Pinchas Lavon resigned as Minister of Defense after a disastrous intelligence operation in Egypt, Prime Minister Moshe Sharrett's government appointed a commission that investigated the matter and cleared Lavon. But when Ben-Gurion returned as prime minister, he rejected the commission's findings, insisting that in a democratic state only a judicial tribunal could resolve such an issue. Goldman remembers Ben-Gurion saying that a committee appointed by the government to clear one of its own ministers would always be suspect. For years, Ben-Gurion was maligned for insisting on such a judicial tribunal. "He was called stubborn, vindictive, a recalcitrant old man," Goldman recalls, "but he clung to his principles because he felt that having a judicial tribunal and then acting on its recommendation, whether or not it was favorable to the government, was the only way Israel could be true to itself as a democracy, as the land of the Jewish people."

After the 1951 trip, Ben-Gurion crossed back to Europe by ship, and Goldman went with him; daily, on board, along with his other duties, Goldman would play poker with Ben-Gurion, Ben-Gurion's wife Paula, and his military attaché, Nechemia Argov—Goldman and the attaché managed to lose artfully to Paula.

POINT FOUR AND OTHER AID PLANS IN JERUSALEM

After Goldman's work on the prime minister's American tour, Kollek asked him to accept an assignment in Israel—the leadership of the Technical Assistance Department of the prime minister's office, with which he had been working at the consulate in New York. In that position, Goldman would direct the Israeli part of the Point Four program, wherein Israel received money and technical aid from the United States government and a parallel United Nations program. Earlier, Deputy Defense Minister Shimon Peres, with the approval of Ben-Gurion, had asked Goldman to become Secretary General of the Israeli Ministry of Defense, the second position in that critical department. But Goldman decided that he could do more good for Israel in technical assistance, and he accepted Kollek's job instead. It was "an opportunity to be involved in how the country evolved," Goldman recalls. He was eager to have a multimillion dollar budget with which to help shape that evolution and to work at the side of his hero, Ben-Gurion. As for Kollek and Ben-Gurion, they were happy to have on their team a man who had already proved his worth to the prime minister, to Jewish causes, and to Israel.

Goldman moved to Jerusalem with Helen and their two children, Judy, aged nine, and David, then five. A third child, Naomi, was born in Jerusalem.

The Point Four technical assistance program was an outgrowth of the Marshall Plan's provision for helping war-torn countries, providing aid not only with funds but also with expert technical assistance in rebuilding and fellowships for promising people from countries being helped. Its later version was proposed by President Truman, who declared in his 1949 inaugural that, "We should make available to peace-loving people the benefits of our store of technical knowledge in order to help them realize their aspirations for a better life." One of the recipients of this assistance was Israel, partly because of American desire to have the State of Israel grow, and partly because Israel was also the target of much attention and some technical help from the USSR. Under the United States program, American experts of all sorts streamed into Israel to train the people in everything from vocational education to transportation, the use of water resources, and tourism. The money and resources from the Point Four program in Israel were coordinated by Goldman's Technical Assistance Office, providing Goldman the opportunity to oversee the growth of the new nation.

Goldman recalls with distaste that the British had frequently spoken and written of limitations on the "absorptive capacity" of Palestine, by which they meant its ability to absorb immigrants. The area was thought to be constrained by geography and by the extent of arable land. The problem, Goldman realized, was economic, not geographic. In the early 1950s, with immigrants still streaming into Israel, Goldman saw "a need for the economy to change from agricultural towards industrialization," partly to modernize, and partly to increase the country's ability to absorb the continuing influx of immigrants. Point Four provided the technical expertise to assist this change. "We also worked with various United Nations programs for technical assistance, the ILO (International Labor Organization), UNICEF, and so on," he said. Experts came from all over. Goldman remembers that one expert, the government's advisor on aeronautics, was a British subject, and that he made a radical recommendation: that Israel not buy the most advanced and expensive machinery then available—full jet planes—but put its limited resources into turboprop planes for its commercial fleet. These, he said, were adequate for Israel's purposes, available immediately, and so low-priced that they would allow Israel to offer lower fares than those of competing airlines.

The Point Four program's philosophy resonated with Goldman, who believed in its generous spirit and in the importance of providing technical assistance to help local people perform their own tasks better. He would one day continue this philosophy at the JDC.

It was a time of austerity in Israel; Helen Goldman recalls that meat and eggs were rationed, and she was proud that her husband's work resulted in projects that developed meatier chickens, better roads, and improved irrigation for crops—things that made life better for Israel's inhabitants.

Point Four and associated programs brought Goldman into interaction with the senior ministers of the government of Israel and increased the circle of those who had confidence in his abilities. He and Helen would occasionally be asked to private dinners of between a half-dozen and a dozen people held at Ben-Gurion's home. Goldman recalls that once, on a private visit, Paula Ben-Gurion wanted her husband's assistance in fixing one of their American-built kitchen appliances. On another visit Goldman was amused to see Ben-Gurion come down the stairs with a plate on which there was a peach pit, throw the pit into the garbage, and wash the plate in the sink. "My wife has not forgotten that," Goldman recalls; "to this day she reminds me that if B.G. could wash the plate, so can I."

Frequently, the outside experts brought in under plans administered by Goldman could recommend courses of action to Israel that would have been politically difficult for the state to accomplish on its own. For instance, the UN adviser on social administration, at Goldman's urging, recommended that Israel change its way of awarding public assistance "so as to provide for a basic subsistence level for all persons and families," even though to do so would mean "higher budgets for the municipalities" and a reorganization of the state ministries responsible for welfare, children, and families. The old welfare plan, a leftover from British mandate years, was too much like the dole, a now-discredited form of assistance, but until then, no one inside the government had been able to change it because of resistance from entrenched bureaucrats.

These funds could also occasionally be used by Goldman for seed funding for projects not high on the state's priority list, but ones that he saw as ultimately worthwhile, such as a $5,000 grant to help sustain a group of Atlas Mountain Moroccan immigrants engaged in a special sort of wool-weaving; later, this developed into a self-sustaining handicrafts operation.

Another aid plan administered by Goldman sprang from

some $5 million in United States funds that had been accumulated in Israel by American publishers, who had sold their books in the country and received local currency as payment. The American government appropriated $10 million worldwide to pay back the publishers in dollars and decreed that the money held in such countries as Israel would be spent, in those countries, in support of scientific, educational, and cultural projects approved by the United States Congress and the government of the country where the books were sold, with all the money going to the government of that country. Among the projects proposed and funded in Israel, Goldman recalls, was a version of Ben-Gurion's dream of having the world's classic literature translated into Hebrew. Others that were funded included Fulbright scholarships, artists' colonies, a home for the deaf, a science wing for the Bar-Ilan University, vocational training for underprivileged boys, community centers, teacher-training schools, the restoration of archaeological sites, and the building of cultural centers. Perhaps the most important grant was an initial $822,000 for what would become Israel's national museum in 1965. This grant represented about 20 percent of the cost of the museum's construction; Goldman later came to believe that "if it hadn't been for this very significant initial contribution of the United States government, I doubt that the voluntary funds raised subsequently would have followed."

An additional plan sent Israelis abroad to study technical subjects, from metal finishing to telephone installation and the administration of post offices in the United States, Latin America, Great Britain, Belgium, Holland, Switzerland, and other European countries.

A summation of the impact of the various aid programs underwritten by the United States itself and as the principal funder of United Nations' programs was penned by Goldman for the prime minister's office in 1955. It provides insight into the effects of these programs on the still-young State of Israel:

> The assistance extended by the United States Government . . .
> has been a vital element in the expansion of the Israel economy,

in the creation of the productive facilities required to permit Israel's suddenly enlarging population to begin to earn its own way. . . . Without it, living standards in Israel today would be below their present levels, the number who could be employed in any sort of useful and productive work would be far smaller today, and the goal of self-support would be much farther in the distant future. . . . Economic assistance by one government to another . . . is not a new phenomenon in world history. What is new and what is the special contribution of the United States to world history is the extension of such assistance without interference in the political life and affairs of the country assisted and without an abridgement of the political independence of these countries.

New Challenges: Promoting Culture and Education

In 1958, Goldman was chosen to return to New York to coordinate the tenth anniversary celebration of the birth of Israel, as a representative of the prime minister's office. Friends at a farewell dinner were amused by parodies of telegrams from various governments around the world purportedly alarmed by Goldman's change of post, and the likelihood that wherever he landed, he would increase tourism there at the expense of other locales.

After completing his assignment in New York, Goldman was recruited to become the executive director of the America-Israel Cultural Foundation (AICF), headquartered in New York City. It was a job for which he was ideally suited, since it involved coordinating the efforts—and egos—of senior Israeli government officials, American-Jewish philanthropists, many competing cultural institutions, aspiring artists, and established artists such as conductor Leonard Bernstein, impresario Sol Hurok, and violinist Isaac Stern.

Goldman's first action at the America-Israel Cultural Foundation was to broaden its backing of the arts. "To me," Goldman reports, "culture has always been more than just music.

The Foundation was a heavy supporter of music, but only supported art in Tel Aviv, and our worst offense was lack of interest in literature. We, the Jews, are 'the people of the book'—and yet the Foundation wasn't doing much to fund literature."

Among the activities that the AICF supported were tours of the United States, Canada, and Mexico by the Israel Philharmonic Orchestra; the publication of archaeological studies; support of three leading Israeli theater groups, including the National Theater, Habimah; exhibits by Israeli artists in galleries and museums outside the country; the acquisition of important works of art by Renoir, Pissarro, and Lipschitz to be exhibited in Israel's museums; the Israel Composers League; a Pablo Casals competition for young musicians in Jerusalem; and fellowships for two hundred promising young Israeli artists and musicians, some of which allowed them to study abroad.

Competition for the fellowships, especially for those to enable young people to study abroad, was intense, and the winners were chosen by committees of educators in the particular fields. In one instance, the process created a dilemma for Goldman. Itzhak Perlman, the violinist crippled by polio in his early years, had received fellowships from the AICF, in Israel, from age seven until he reached thirteen, as did other young artists who went on to become classical music stars, such as Pinchas Zukerman and Daniel Barenboim. But then Perlman was invited to New York to appear on *The Ed Sullivan Show* and wanted afterwards to continue his studies at the Juilliard School of Music. "I had met Itzhak and thought he was terrific," Goldman recalls. "But I agreed with the rule that no one at the Foundation in New York should make a decision on who received a fellowship, and the music committee in Israel had turned him down because they weren't involved in his decision to come to New York. I could have overruled that decision, but felt I shouldn't, because of the problems that would create within the organization."

Instead, Goldman and members of his staff worked to find ways for Perlman and his mother to exist in New York while the teenager attended Juilliard. "Every few weeks, I would receive a telephone call from Mrs. Perlman, who took in laundry in order to make ends meet, pleading for a grant of a few dollars." Goldman would somehow manage to find the money. When Itzhak had reached the age of seventeen, Goldman finally managed to convince Isaac Stern to come and listen to the boy at a concert held at a patron's home. It was a hot summer day, and the setting was magnificent—a house on a hill, with the concert in the open air. Perlman was sitting on a chair on the hillside, with the audience sitting below him. Goldman brought Stern and was soon delighted to find the older virtuoso drawing with a pen and pad while he listened to Perlman. "Isaac was so excited that he was sketching a chair for Perlman to use so that it would appear he was standing—all other violin soloists stood when performing—when he was actually sitting." Shortly, Stern took Perlman to meet impresario Sol Hurok, who arranged a concert tour that launched Perlman's career.

In a second and much larger instance, Goldman found himself at odds with the AICF board over building and funding the Israel Museum. As recounted earlier, during Goldman's Point Four days he had helped seek the initial grant from the United States government for the establishment of an Israeli national art museum. When he became executive director of the America-Israel Cultural Foundation in 1958, Goldman asked its board to allocate major support to the construction of the museum, as it had done when it had contributed one-third of the funding for the building facilities for the Israel Philharmonic Orchestra. Since this would be the first national Jewish museum, Goldman told the AICF board it was "inconceivable" that a foundation dedicated to promoting culture in Israel "should not be involved." Nonetheless, the board refused to participate at that time.

Never one to take a defeat lying down, Goldman then proceeded to help raise monies for the museum, with some success. The plans for the museum, to be situated on a Jerusalem hillside, continued apace, and eventually the AICF began to contribute to it, though in a modest way.

A breakthrough occurred when Goldman helped broker an unusual gift to the Israel Museum from Broadway producer

Billy Rose. Earlier in life a columnist for the *Jerusalem Post,* Rose maintained an affectionate regard for the State of Israel. Rose also had one of the largest and most significant sculpture collections in private hands: works by Rodin, Maillol, Archipenko, Picasso, and Henry Moore, in addition to Jacques Lipschitz, Sir Jacob Epstein, and other artists.

When Gershon Agron, founding publisher of the *Jerusalem Post* and later mayor of Jerusalem, learned that renowned Jewish leader Dr. Nahum Goldmann had suggested Rose donate his sculpture collection to Israel, Agron sent his former columnist a note lauding the idea. For a museum to have such a collection would instantly place it in the forefront of art institutions. The potential donation was mired in difficulties, but they were eventually unraveled by the combined efforts of Goldman and Karl Katz, Director of the Bezalel National Museum of Jerusalem. Katz came to New York with the blessings of Kollek, then Director General of the prime minister's office. Katz would help with the planning of fund-raising to obtain $1 million for the Bezalel National Museum at an event for which Rose had agreed to donate one Epstein sculpture. Mulling over strategy, Goldman and Katz decided that Katz would invite Rose to the kick-off committee meeting for an art auction.

"There were many problems associated with making the announcement of the Rose donation then and there," Goldman recalls. Among them was that the Epstein sculpture was entitled *The Annunciation*. Since this would obviously be inappropriate for a Jewish-themed museum in Israel, Katz and Goldman renamed the sculpture *Hannah*. Rose unveiled it at the AICF Festive Dinner, announced the gift of his entire sculpture collection, and also raised the ante by further announcing that he would fund the construction of a special, sprawling five-acre garden adjoining the museum to display the sculptures.

Goldman was so excited by this potential gift that he dropped other duties to concentrate on facilitating it. Rose liked to work quickly. "I'll try to run as fast as you can run," Goldman said to him. Within days, Goldman met at Rose's home with Katz and famed architect and sculptor Isamu Noguchi, whom Rose wanted to design the garden, and arranged for them to visit Israel. But there were objections from Israel, on secular and religious points. The secular point was the difficulty of obtaining the extra land. The greater stumbling block was the deeply-held Jewish belief, based on the book of Leviticus (26:1), that Jews should not "make unto yourselves idols and graven images . . . and do not bow unto them." This could be construed as a prohibition on openly exhibited sculptures, although a commentary on Leviticus suggests that Jews were permitted images, statues, and monuments so long as they did not bow to them. The question did not resolve easily or quickly, and when the delays on the Israeli side lengthened, Goldman and Katz cabled Kollek and others, who prodded the project from their end. In New York, Rose appointed Goldman as secretary of a separate fund established for the purpose of building the sculpture garden and installing the sculptures in it.

The several difficulties eventually crystallized into a polite, but critical, debate that took place between Billy Rose and General Yigael Yadin in Kollek's home in Jerusalem. Yadin had been Chief of Staff of the Israeli Armed Forces, a renowned scholar, and the man whose father had received the Dead Sea Scrolls from a bedouin. An official of the new museum, Yadin was adamant about the need to integrate Rose's sculptures into the rest of the museum and believed they should be spread throughout the museum's entire acreage rather than concentrated in an adjoining garden. Rose was equally adamant about keeping the sculptures together as a group, with the implied threat of not making good on his donation if his demands were not met. Since Goldman and Katz felt that the two principals must settle the matter themselves, they left Yadin and Rose alone in the room. Goldman recalls that he "came in from time to time, and was also called in several times in order to ease the situation a bit," but he knew both men to be "good fighters" and was content to watch from the sidelines this "battle of words between a great modern general and a civilian Napoleon."

Rose won. The sculpture garden was constructed on the plan of a Japanese rock garden, a *ryoanji*, providing magnificent sites in which each monumental piece can be viewed in all its splendor. In what amounted to a coup d'etat within the museum structure, Rose was appointed head of the museum's fine arts committee and the AICF's art committee for the Jerusalem museum. An opportunity to further augment the sculpture collection presented itself while the garden was under construction: Jacques Lipschitz decided to fulfill an earlier pledge and donate three hundred original clay plaster casts of his sculptures—some fifty years of work—to the museum.

QUALITY OF LIFE: EDUCATION AND COMMUNITY CENTERS

At about the same time, Ben-Gurion was preparing to retire from the government for the last time, a departure that created an opportunity and a challenge for Goldman. Ben-Gurion let it be known publicly that he had two dreams for Israel. The first was to change the electoral system to foster greater democracy, and the second was to revolutionize the country's secondary education so that every child could receive a free high school education.

"I agreed wholeheartedly with both objectives," Goldman recalls, "but I couldn't do much to help the first." In pursuit of the second, however, he accepted an invitation from Kollek to leave AICF and become Director-General of an "education fund" that would be linked to the United Jewish Appeal (UJA), yet would operate as an independent fund-raising body. "Actually, the invitation had come from Ben-Gurion, and Teddy [Kollek] had already said 'yes' on my behalf, knowing that I would accept. Had I needed personal appeals for my services, Teddy was prepared to obtain them from Prime Minister Levi Eshkol and Finance Minister Pinhas Sapir." On the day the Israel Education Fund was established, Goldman wrote to tell Ben-Gurion that the enterprise would be in the service of the former prime minister's dream.

The educational need was acute. Grade school in Israel was available to all children, but not high school, and as a result only 12.5 percent of the country's high-school-aged children attended high school. Furthermore, most of those who did attend high school were of European background. The drop-off rate for Jewish Children of Asian or North African origin was substantial—only about 40 percent of those children who had attended grade school went on to high school. It was an indication that the lack of free high schools was widening the cultural divide between Jews of European parentage and those of Asian-African parentage. The plan of the Israel Education Fund was to raise money from American Jews to pay for the construction of new schools, believing that in time, local communities and the central government would become able to pick up the schools' operating expenses. Other ancillary facilities, such as community centers, public libraries, and prekindergarten schools were also part of the program.

Establishing these institutions was not without political repercussions in Israel, and this was a time of upheaval, with a new breakaway party being formed by the "Young Turks," Kollek, Moshe Dayan, and Shimon Peres, in the teeth of the express disapproval of Prime Minister Eshkol and Minister of Finance Sapir. There was also American Jewish politics to be wary of: for instance, Goldman had not known that the UJA was hesitant to have the Israel Education Fund appeal undercut its regular one. Without Goldman's knowledge, the UJA and those backing the Israel Education Fund idea had jointly decided that the new fund would only accept donations of a minimum of $100,000, and that whoever donated to the fund would first have to continue to donate to the annual campaign the same amount to the regular UJA campaign as before. Lacking experience in fund-raising, Goldman found it "no easy task" and decided that "the only way to accomplish it was to 'exploit' my friends." So whenever a high official from Israel, such as Sapir or Kollek, came to the United States, Goldman would prevail upon them to make appearances in behalf of the fund.

Goldman considers his years with the Israel Education Fund to have been among the most productive and satisfying of his life, even though he did not fulfill the ultimate goal of making high school education free and available to all. "We raised $28 million in four years. We were able to assist the State of Israel in establishing seventy high schools, plus thirty community centers, public libraries, and prekindergarten schools."

While the notion of universal free high school education was Ben-Gurion's, the libraries and particular type of community centers were largely Goldman's idea. These ideas emerged from his American background; his deep belief in informal as well as formal education, along with his enthusiasm for American-style free public libraries and community centers, would carry over from his years at the Israel Education Fund into his later work with the JDC. He had been impressed with the Carnegie libraries dotting the American landscape that had become the focal points for literary and cultural activities in so many communities, and he sought to reproduce that paradigm in Israel.

While the libraries were straightforward enterprises that Israelis could understand, the building of American-style community centers in Israel was more controversial. Goldman's fondness for them reflected his early training, his work at Hecht House, and his years of graduate study in social work. During his four years at the Israel Education Fund, Goldman spent much time and energy trying to persuade the authorities of Israel to develop community centers rather than youth clubs, which were then the prevailing facilities run by the government and voluntary agencies. Youth clubs generally offered meeting facilities for athletic young people in the community, but didn't cater to other groups, such as children, seniors, and women, who were already underrepresented.

According to Dr. Shaul Lilach, later the leader of the Israel Association of Community Centers (IACC), some four hundred of these youth clubs existed throughout the country in the late 1960s. A coordination committee was appointed under the direction of Chaim Zippori, who would become the first director of the Israel Corporation of Community Centers—the state-funded entity that eventually evolved into the IACC.

"When Ralph proposed the idea of real, multipurpose community centers on the American model, all the departments in the Ministry of Education were against it," Lilach recalls. In 1966, there was very little cooperation among departments in the education ministry, and they competed with each other for funds. "Ralph countered this with a brilliant organizational idea: he suggested to Zalman Aranne [then Minister of Education] that the money for the new centers come from several divisions, and that each division get, in effect, a share of the new enterprise. The result was a strange arrangement: people who were initially against the idea, all sitting on the board that governed the community centers."

"Ralph was the main architect and main influence on the community centers," recalls Margot Pins, an expert in early childhood education who was also associated with the centers for two decades. "Without Ralph, the community centers would have remained just an idea." Today, because the centers are successful, many people claim to have originated and carried forward the idea. But those with long memories, such as Kollek, credit Goldman as the father of Israel's community centers.

At the time of their inception, American-model community centers were seen as a way of integrating the European (Ashkenazi) and Asian-North African (Sephardi) sectors of Israeli society. Today there are 180 centers, in all the larger towns and many communities; among them are nearly twenty in predominantly Arab areas. They operate mostly independently of the government and of the JDC, though some money for them still comes from those sources. Of the previous 400 youth athletic clubs, Lilach points out, "not a one remains."

Dr. David Macarov, now an emeritus professor at the Paul Baerwald School of Social Work at the University of Jerusalem, attributes the success of the Goldman version of the community centers to three improvements, obvious in the new centers, but that had been lacking in the old ones: "The new ones were capable of being used for a variety of functions; they were free of political affiliation; and they had completely open membership."

Since 1948, Goldman and high officials of the JDC had been talking with one another and occasionally interacting as representatives of their respective organizations; during the ensuing twenty years, several overtures had been made to Goldman to join the organization, but for various reasons having to do with timing, responsibilities, and location of the work, Goldman had been unable to accept a position with the JDC.

Finally, having established the Israel Education Fund, Goldman felt he could move on. In 1968, he received an invitation from the Joint to serve as Associate Director of its programs in Israel under Director-General Harold Trobe, with a particular assignment for the reorganization of the Joint's work in Israel. But before starting work with the JDC in 1968, Goldman had to deal with what would be Ben-Gurion's last tour of the United States, in 1967, on behalf of the UJA. Perhaps because his fund-raising work for the Israel Education Fund had been done so independently (and so successfully) within the UJA, the leaders of the UJA initially did not want Goldman involved in Ben-Gurion's tour, though they knew he was close to Ben-Gurion. A personal letter from the former prime minister to the UJA, especially requesting Goldman to accompany him, mooted that objection. The trip was conducted successfully, raising many millions of dollars—among which, Goldman recalls, were $2 million that Ben-Gurion managed to extract from the sponsors for support of a regional high school at his kibbutz, Sde Boker, as the price of his agreeing to make the trip.

CHAPTER THREE

Transitions

Ralph Goldman's Early Years With the JDC

GOLDMAN FORMALLY JOINED THE JDC in late 1968, at a moment when both he and the organization were at points of transition. He was fifty-four years old, eager to join the organization—even willing to accept a lower title and starting salary than he had been making—because he agreed with the JDC's sense of mission and had definite ideas as to what future directions the JDC ought to take in Israel.

The JDC was recovering from a year of what an official report labeled "unanticipated crises and emergencies." These emergencies included an exodus of Jews from Czechoslovakia following a Soviet invasion, the increased emigration of Jews from Poland and North Africa that occurred in the wake of the 1967 Mideast War, and a funding crisis in France as a result of the political unrest that shook France in the spring of 1968. Other pressures resulted from the government of Israel's inability to adequately fund social programs because it needed to spend large amounts of money on national defense.

Twenty years after the establishment of the State of Israel, the JDC was entering a new phase in its relationship with Israel. The activities that had been appropriate—even essential—to assuring the health of the new nation in its formative years were no longer as urgently needed. The JDC in Israel required substantial change—the phasing out of some programs, the handing-off of other programs to the care of local agencies or governments, and the radical alteration of the JDC's mode of operation.

ESHEL: A New Concept of Service

One of Goldman's first tasks at the JDC was to oversee MALBEN. MALBEN had initially begun in 1949 as an offshoot of the JDC that provided services to the disadvantaged—the aged, the chronically ill, the handicapped. But by 1968, rising costs had reduced the organization's ability to provide beds, and Israel's growth had made it more possible for the government to take over direct provision of these services itself.

"When I joined JDC-MALBEN in 1968, it was already becoming obsolete," Goldman recalls. Because of budget limitations, JDC had been forced to make cutbacks in services. One of these cutbacks involved limiting its MALBEN operations to only take care of people who had been in the country less than five years. This resulted in problems, perhaps best illustrated by the plight of an old man who had served as a pioneer in drying up the swamps and had been in the country with his wife for forty-nine years. He wanted to have his wife admitted to a MALBEN home, but the family was ineligible for JDC support because they weren't newcomers.

One of the reasons that Goldman agreed to work for the JDC was the understanding that MALBEN would shortly go out of business in its current configuration, and that the JDC itself would cease being a provider of direct services; instead, the organization would take on other functions, becoming a forum for ideas, a planner and designer of innovative projects like the Point Four program or Israel Education Fund, and a donor of seed money for them.

Ralph Goldman became the executive chairman of a new offshoot of the JDC, the organization that became ESHEL (a Hebrew acronym for the Association for Planning and Developing Services for the Aged). As he often did, in order to give focus to an idea, Goldman developed a catchy name for the entity that was being planned: in addition to being an acronym, *eshel* was the name of a type of oak tree associated with Abraham.

The ESHEL program was a serious effort that reflected the philosophy of Goldman and the evolving stance of the JDC. As executive chairman of ESHEL, Goldman galvanized a national effort to deal with a national problem: an aging population that had risen from 3.5 percent of the total Israeli population in 1948 to 7 percent of the total population in 1968, a moment when Israel's population had itself quadrupled in size. Virtually no other countries in the developed world were planning for an ever-increasing elderly population when Israel, through ESHEL, began to do so. ESHEL helped develop comprehensive services for the aged population: the delivery of community services to the aged in their own communities and homes, the construction and staffing of old-age homes, and the establishment and upgrading of geriatric sections in general hospitals. Gradually, ultimate responsibility was to be shifted from ESHEL to central and local governments, allowing the JDC to slowly withdraw from the picture.

"ESHEL changed the nature of being elderly in Israel," says Dr. Yitzhak Brick, who in the 1970s was Deputy Director of the Ministry of Labor and Social Affairs. "It changed how the care was delivered, the quality of the care, the percentage of people who have to be cared for in nursing homes, and the cost of the care. It virtually halted the excess construction of institutions for the elderly by helping to maintain people, in good health, in their own communities and through day-care centers." Israel's continued low rate of institutionalization of the elderly, Brick avows, is the direct result of the existence of ESHEL.

ESHEL's most important structural innovation may have been Goldman's insistence that the board of ESHEL include high-ranking representatives of three governmental ministries concerned with the elderly. The board included members from the finance ministry, together with an equal number of members from the JDC, and it was under the permanent chairmanship of a JDC appointee. This was not done just to assure equal representation or to give the JDC a veto, since another important principle embedded in the structure was that when any program came up for review, even one "nay" vote on the board could reject it. All votes had to be unanimous, which assured that whatever ESHEL did was done by consensus. The board and voting structure that Goldman helped establish made ESHEL strong enough to survive the appointment and removal of individual ministers, and even changes in governments.

Dr. Jacob Menczel, a leading gerontologist and a former director general of the Ministry of Health, recalls that one reason ESHEL was so effective and influential was that its structure included the government's minister of finance as a full partner. Another key to its effectiveness, Menczel maintains, was that the JDC retained the ability to act by itself when there was a need that the government could not move rapidly enough to address or for which it did not have enough funds. Menczel discovered that his own hospital was sending elderly patients home too quickly after they had strokes or coronaries; Goldman and JDC medical director Dr. Itzhak Margulec convinced the JDC board to fund the country's first geriatric facility inside a hospital and made certain that it was also connected to a research laboratory and an academic institution. This sort of thoroughness, Menczel contends, characterized the approach of Goldman and the JDC to many matters: "When it came time to turn over the MAL-BEN nursing homes to the government, JDC first renovated them. JDC also established groups of organizations interested in the elderly in every community, as support for the work of ES-HEL. That was Ralph's personal initiative—he thrives on bringing people together."

Economist Arnon Gafni recalls those early days from another perspective. In the late 1970s and 1980s, Gafni served as governor of the Bank of Israel (similar to the Federal Reserve Bank in the United States) and earlier worked in the Finance Ministry under Pinhas Sapir. The Sapir-Goldman friendship and working relationship, he contends, were central to the establishment of many important social engineering programs. "Sapir had a good sense of economic priorities," Gafni points out. "One time he asked us to keep in mind, 'How many schools could you build for the price of a wheel of a Phantom jet?' It was an indication of his understanding of the real priorities of the country. This, and his interest in the absorption of immigrants made him a natural ally of Ralph Goldman and the Joint."

For a sovereign government to willingly share power with a private entity, as Israel does with the JDC in ESHEL, was extraordinary at the time that the JDC proposed it in the early 1970s, and remains so today. Goldman now believes that this unusual cooperation was made feasible by two aspects of the partnership: "One, that the JDC was known to be *nonpolitical*, and two, that the JDC and its services were *nonpermanent*—that we had no intention of building a bureaucracy that would stay around and run programs forever."

COMMUNITY CENTERS, DAY CARE, AND THE "TWIN SCHOOLS" INITIATIVE

A second focus for Goldman in his position at the JDC was a continuation of the work he had done with community centers at the Israel Education Fund. Studies had discovered that the gap between the functional levels of children from "more privileged" families and those from "disadvantaged" families was so large that it was preventing equal accomplishment as early as first grade; therefore, intervention was needed before that age, when the children were infants and toddlers.

Goldman and ESHEL decided to tackle these problems head-on. In some communities, he and his colleagues noticed that young women weren't attending the centers. They realized that many women, particularly those whose families came from Moslem countries, were told by their husbands and fathers that they belonged at home, rather than at a center taking courses. Goldman came up with the idea to place washing machines and dryers in the community centers, and then women were permitted to frequent the centers to do their laundry. While waiting for the machines, they attended courses arranged for them in home sanitation, nutrition, and toddler care. And while the

mothers were busy, the children participated in activities organized by the Early Childhood Education department.

"This was a time when Israel was vulnerable," recalls early
childhood specialist Margot Pins. There had been uneasy
changes in Israeli society from the 1967 and 1973 wars, changes
that did not permit recent waves of immigrants to be well absorbed. For instance, at the close of the Yom Kippur war, many
fathers remained on active duty with the armed forces rather
than being permitted to return home, resulting in a situation
that left mothers in need of child care. Lacking such care, mothers could not do errands outside of their homes or even take jobs
to help support their families. Insularity and slower absorption
into the wider society resulted. Part of the answer to such problems, Goldman believed, could be provided by childcare and education offered at local community centers, and by programs
aimed as much at parents as at children.

Pins recalls that Goldman had a unique way of approaching
the problems and potential solutions. "He was never the kind of
official who said 'We know and you don't,' and went on to impose an idea from outside. He was always respectful of the people in charge, at the ministries and at the local level. By carefully
including people from the government in the decision-making
process, he ensured that they would bring their financial commitment to the project."

Goldman hired Pins to help establish a network within the
community centers. Together, they enrolled various women's
voluntary organizations in the task. "We set a standard for early
childhood education in the country," Pins recalls, "and at the
same time moved early childhood education out of the hands of
low-paid mother's helpers and into those of professionally
trained staff." Educational enrichment programs, after-school
care programs, and home care for babies all followed in short
order.

Shlomit Shimron, formerly the director of the Haim Zippori
Center, an educational facility for training community workers,
was the assistant director of a small community center in the
Negev desert when Goldman and Pins came calling in the early

1970s, seeking to establish an early childhood facility in her center. There had been no facilities in the area for children aged one to three years, and there was no money to build a separate facility for such a purpose. "Ralph had an idea about using equipment that could be set up for the children in the morning but easily taken down and rolled away for storage in the evening, when we had to use the same space for adult cultural programs," Shimron remembers. She loved the idea and recalls Goldman positively responding to her enthusiasm. "Ralph believes in people," she explains. "You sense his love and care in every detail. He's thinking about improvements all the time, looking for new ideas that will help."

The JDC's pilot day-care programs concentrated on working with the parents as well as with the children. After two pilot projects wholly funded by the Central British Fund for World Jewish Relief proved successful, the JDC provided seed money that enabled the Israel Association of Community Centers to obtain funds for a nationwide program from the Ministry of Welfare, Ministry of Education, and other agencies.

Another of Goldman's passions was for finding ways to combine religious and secular facilities. "You would have a town of, say, five thousand people," Goldman recalls, "and they would want a religious high school and a secular one, even though they didn't have enough pupils to warrant building separate facilities for each." From his core belief in the oneness of the Jewish people, and the importance of both religious and secular aspects of Jewish culture, Goldman evolved a simple scheme to bring together the two sides.

To address the needs of such towns, Goldman worked out a "twin schools" plan, later adopted throughout Israel. On one end of a single building were classrooms for a secular school, and on the other end, classrooms for a religious school, while in the middle were facilities that could be used by either group, such as a gymnasium, a cafeteria, and a science laboratory. Considerably less expense was involved in building such a school than for constructing and maintaining two separate schools; the dual-purpose nature of the twin-schools buildings also made them much easier for communities to use for ancillary activities.

OTHER INITIATIVES IN SOCIAL WORK

One of the early programs of the JDC had been to establish the Paul Baerwald School of Social Work at the Hebrew University in Jerusalem. "This was an independent school, not well accepted at first by the university because its mission was practical—to train social workers," recalls Dr. David Macarov, an emeritus professor. Its very independence made for some difficulties, among them, the inability of professors there to gain tenure because they did not have doctorates. Using the Baerwald School model, and with JDC seed money, other schools were later established to train professionals to serve in programs for the aged, the mentally ill, and the handicapped.

After the Baerwald School became successful, the school began a new program—at Goldman's insistence, and over the initial opposition of the Baerwald School itself—named for former JDC leader Dr. Joseph J. Schwartz, to train people who would become directors for the country's burgeoning community centers.

Another early focus for the JDC in Israel, the care of the elderly, was taken to another level in the early 1970s as the JDC created the Brookdale Institute of Gerontology and Adult Human Development in Jerusalem. The governance structure was similar to that of ESHEL. Among the moving forces behind the institute were Herbert Singer, a lawyer and philanthropist associated with Beth Israel Hospital in New York; Dr. Martin Cherkasky, president of Montefiore Hospital in New York and chairman of the JDC's professional advisory committee on health and welfare; and Brookdale's first director, Dr. Israel Katz, previously director of the Baerwald School. Dr. Katz, who would later become Minister of Labor and Social Affairs for the government, had the foresight to insist that Brookdale's official name include the phrase "and Adult Human Development," which positioned Brookdale to become a policy organization dealing with a wide range of central issues not limited to the aged.

As Katz's nomenclature suggested, the basic purpose of the institute was "an attempt to influence all of Israeli society through the disbursement of knowledge," says Jack Habib, who is today the Brookdale Institute's director. He points out that Brookdale emerged in the same time period, and in the same spirit, as the transition of the JDC's work in Israel from a service provider to a program developer; Brookdale provides the research that must underlie any good program development. In establishing Brookdale as a research institute, the JDC was recognizing another unmet need of the State of Israel—the need for the sort of basic statistical and social research that in other countries is often done by government departments or by universities, but that was not being done in a still-young country. Today, says Habib, the institute has gone beyond research on the elderly to become the nation's premier institution dealing with health policy from infancy to old age. "We provide independent research on problems, and evaluations of programs, to the government, private funders, and institutions in the field—social intelligence that can be used in developing policies and finding out how well they are working."

TAKING STOCK: THE JDC IN TRANSITION

After the 1973 war, and twenty-five years after the establishment of the State of Israel, there was a desire in the JDC to reevaluate the organization's mission and structure.

Having raised and spent hundreds of millions to aid the Jews of the world during its more than sixty years, the Joint had outgrown the concerns of its 1914 founders and was challenged by some fundamental dichotomies. The JDC had been set up as a temporary organization whose goal was to go out of business after the needs of its "clients" had been met, but it was continuously busy and seemed likely to never stop being so. It was an American organization, but its functional activities took place in Israel and other countries where Jews were having difficulty existing as Jews. It was formally known as a "committee," but it was actually a broad agency whose governance and organizational structures were a mismatch. And although a determinedly "nonpolitical" agency, it dealt with governments whose activities were profoundly political, which meant that the JDC's own activities often had a decidedly political impact.

In March 1975, at the instigation of JDC president Jack D. Weiler, a self-audit committee of the JDC was convened. The committee was under the direction of Henry L. Zucker, executive vice-president of the Jewish Community Federation of Cleveland, and other leading Jewish communal professionals, including Professor Herman Stein of Case Western Reserve. Goldman was an active participant in the group, termed "the Zucker Committee."

The Zucker Committee's study concluded its work at a seminal time in the history of the twentieth century. The war in Vietnam was coming rapidly to a close, and détente between the United States and the USSR was blossoming. The development of the Organization of Petroleum Exporting Countries (OPEC), dominated by Arab states, was altering the power balance of the world by drastically raising its price for oil, on which the economies of the Western countries deeply depended. The combination of these trends produced a shift in American attitudes on many matters. Among them was the American stance vis-à-vis Israel and toward Jewish refugees in general; more attention was being directed to current refugees from East Asia—the boat people of Vietnam—than to potential Jewish refugees from Eastern Europe. At the same time, there was also recognition of the possibilities of further breakthroughs in American relations with the vassal states of the Soviet bloc.

The study's first recommendation was that the JDC not continue to emphasize the idea that it was devoted to putting itself out of business. The JDC, according to the study, needed to develop long-term planning capabilities, anticipate future trouble spots, and work with local authorities on contingency plans for prospective emergencies. The study recommended reinforcing the organization's historic mandate to transfer programs and responsibilities to local community auspices as quickly as possible, rather than to have them continually run or supervised by JDC personnel. Toward this end, the JDC must also commit itself to developing Jewish professional and lay leadership throughout the world, which would assist local communities and organizations to properly manage their own programs, and to keep the Jewish content of them sufficiently high. Both of these objectives—emphasizing local control and developing professionals to run local programs—were personal goals of Goldman.

In general, the study recommended that the JDC should model its future transitions on the way that MALBEN yielded to ESHEL, and on the evolution of the Association of Community Centers. To help Israel develop an "effective infrastructure of community services," since the JDC would no longer operate facilities, fewer JDC staff members would be required in Israel in the future, allowing the remaining ones to concentrate on completing and supervising programs already begun.

As for programs already in place to deal with the needs of Jews in communities throughout the world, the study recommended a continuation of the work in Romania and an appraisal of the good and bad aspects of what had happened in Romania as a guide for determining how to assist the other Jews in Eastern Europe. The study also recommended major changes in the governance of the JDC, eliminating an unwieldy structure in which a "national council" of ten thousand people served as a governing body, but retaining these people, in the report's words, "as a body of informed JDC *supporters*," and convening instead a smaller board of 150 directors. An executive committee of 40, divided into working committees, would review units of JDC work in geographic areas such as Eastern Europe, or functional areas such as Budget and Finance. "Previously," Goldman recalls, "every year a committee of five to seven people would go to Geneva to hear reports from the field directors and would have little way of truly evaluating what the staff said it was doing; policy would be made, *de facto,* by people in the field." Thereafter, closer board involvement would be exercised by a committee in continual touch with the work to be done; as a side benefit, this arrangement would involve more lay people with each specific policy and its implementation.

In concert, the staff and the headquarters would be reorganized and augmented. Administration would continue to be located in New York, and would operate there and through two regional offices, in Jerusalem and Geneva. New York would cover Latin America, Jerusalem would cover Israel but also a major program in Iran and in the Middle East when peace would come, and Geneva would cover Europe and Eastern Europe. The effect of the entire package of reorganizations was to democratize the governance and decision-making process.

Henceforth, the JDC would look in three main directions for its work: toward the captive Jewish peoples in Eastern Europe and the Soviet Union; toward Israel, the center of Jewish life in the world; and toward other Jews of the diaspora.

Unspoken in the thoughtful and detailed study, but uppermost in the mind of Goldman, was the belief that the time had come for the JDC to take more charge of its own programs and the spending of its funds, to give proper emphasis and direction to the JDC's objectives, to bolster those programs in which it had an intense interest, and to concentrate on aiding Jews in place, principally in Eastern Europe and inside the Soviet Union, before all traces of Jewish culture in those areas permanently died out.

TAKING CHARGE

Goldman's close work with the Zucker Committee went hand in hand with his being chosen in 1975 to replace the retiring Samuel Haber as executive vice-president of the JDC—the organization's professional leader—an appointment that would become effective on January 1, 1976. Almost sixty-two years old, Goldman had little expectation of remaining in his new position for more than a few years. But he was ready and eager for the task.

In December 1975, Goldman faced a set of transition problems. He was scheduled to finally close down JDC-MALBEN, in Tel Aviv, on December 31. Control of MALBEN's one-hundred-bed hospital and three nursing homes, as well as its eight hundred employees, were to become the responsibility of the government of the State of Israel. After that date, the JDC in Israel would no longer operate facilities or provide services directly; it would enter a new phase in its relationship with the state, beginning with the opening on January 1, 1976, of the JDC-Israel's new headquarters in Jerusalem. "The closing and reopening were in the spirit of *Simchat Torah*, the completing of the reading of the Five Books of Moses and starting afresh to read them," Goldman recalls. Also on January 1, Goldman was to become the JDC's executive vice-president for world operations, and a few days later, he was scheduled to move back to New York, the world headquarters of the JDC.

But on December 29, 1975, though Goldman had removed himself from the negotiations, other JDC-MALBEN officers were still negotiating with the union representing the bulk of the eight hundred employees. To transfer them from private to government employ was a delicate task; there were severance and retirement pay issues still to be resolved, and a late demand by the union brought the bargaining to an impasse. When Goldman learned of the demand, he thought it extravagant, but he also calculated the cost of the new demand and weighed the need to bring the negotiations to a close. "We needed $100,000 to $125,000 more to close the gap," he recalls. "So I telephoned Jack Weiler, the president of the JDC, in New York, and recommended that the money be paid, even though I thought the demand unjustified. Weiler agreed, and the JDC pledged the extra money. That broke the logjam."

It was a typical Goldman maneuver: finding a path around a bureaucratic roadblock in order to attain a desired goal. Another such stratagem was demonstrated when finding a home for JDC-Israel in Jerusalem. Some time earlier, the president of the Hebrew University in Jerusalem—a city only under full Israeli sovereignty since the 1967 war—had asked Goldman when he would be moving there from Tel Aviv. "Give me a building, and

I'll move," Goldman had said, only partially kidding. One of his main tenets was that Jerusalem was central in the hearts of Jewish people, as well as being the seat of government for the state of Israel, and he believed the JDC ought to be sited in Jerusalem.

The university actually had a building it wanted to sell, on an isolated hill equidistant from part of the university and from a phalanx of government ministerial offices, including that of the prime minister. After a slew of technical and legal details were ironed out, plans were made for the JDC to locate its Israel headquarters in the building, along with those of its Brookdale research center.

"The transfer of the Joint from Tel Aviv to Jerusalem was a symbolically important act for Jerusalem," recalls Teddy Kollek, the long-term mayor of that city. "If the Joint could come to Jerusalem, why couldn't others?" He notes that others followed, including important nongovernmental organizations which earlier had been hesitant to move there.

On December 31, 1975, as Goldman was preparing to travel, he learned that because of bureaucratic mix-ups, the driver who had long been assigned to him, a JDC-MALBEN employee, had not received his severance pay. "There's a statement in the Bible to the effect that you shouldn't keep the salary of an employee overnight," Goldman points out and recalls that he was furious that the man was being deprived both of the sum that was due him and of the interest it could earn. Goldman reached for the telephone and would not stop his calls until the money was in the driver's bank. Only then could Goldman head for Jerusalem, to open the JDC–Israel and to begin his work as the chief executive of one of the most venerable and resourceful philanthropic organizations in the world.

CHAPTER FOUR

Cracking the Wall

The JDC Peers Behind the Iron Curtain

WHILE RIDING HIS BICYCLE along the streets of Herzliya at 6:00 a.m., Ralph Goldman tried to collect his thoughts on the main challenges facing the JDC as he became its new steward. One was the JDC's attempt to restore a direct connection to the Jewish communities inside the Communist bloc. Another was to oversee the transformation of the JDC's work in Israel from being a direct service provider to being a strategic force in the development of the country's social programs and policies. The final challenge was the need to conceive and develop what Goldman would eventually label as a "global Jewish strategy" to better enable the JDC, other Jewish philanthropic organizations, and the state of Israel to jointly address the problems and crises facing world Jewry.

A later visit to Argentina's thriving Jewish community helped Goldman further clarify the interrelationship of these problems. The health of an outlying Jewish community, he came to understand, relied on what he called the "trilateral relationship." It rested on three legs: its own vitality; its connection with a healthy diaspora community (in Argentina's case, that of American Jews); and, as essential, its continuing connection with Israel. Henceforth, Goldman would work to ensure that any external assistance program for Jews living beyond Israel and the Western European democracies aim to firm up the bonds of their trilateral relationship. That would mean developing programs to strengthen the local community, to finely tune the response of the JDC to that community, and to determine ways to enhance that community's continuing connection with other diaspora communities and with Israel.

"What permeated my thinking throughout my years at JDC," Goldman recalls, "was a phrase from the story of Joseph in the book of Genesis. It was the theme of a speech that I heard an eight-year-old in Morocco deliver in Arabic, Hebrew, and English, and it stuck with me: '*et achai anochi m'vakesh,*'— I seek my brethren. That says it all—encompasses all the varied things we tried to do."

Behind the Iron Curtain: The JDC in Communist Eastern Europe

During the first sixty years of the JDC's existence, the organization's bywords had been *rescue, relief,* and *reconstruction.* Now, in the mid 1970s, the several million Jews behind the Iron Curtain—the largest population of Jews in the world beyond the borders of Israel and of the United States—were in need of just those services. After the Holocaust, and since the onset of Communist rule, members of that community had been subjected to having their Jewish identities steadily eroded to the point of virtual annihilation of Jewish religious and cultural life, even though Jewish life had previously been vibrantly alive in that area of the world for more than a thousand years.

"The JDC prided itself that there was not a Jew in an outlying country around the world that we could not somehow reach and help in some way," Goldman recalls. "And we were already helping some of those Eastern bloc Jews, though in a roundabout way and not as effectively as we knew it was possible to do when we worked directly in a country." Because of the opposition of Communist-bloc governments to direct assistance from JDC, the organization's help to Eastern European Jews had to be provided through third party and surrogate organizations like SSE. Help was thus constrained by the inherent difficulties of working through middlemen and by the inability of these intermediary organizations to adequately assess the real requirements of the Eastern European Jews. "While 80 percent of what we give is material assistance," Goldman maintains, "the last 20 percent is cultural, educational, and spiritual assistance, and that part is essential to helping Jews live as a minority inside a dominant majority culture."

The Jews of Eastern Europe were both injured and vulnerable. Having lost millions of their family members in the Holocaust, they consisted mainly of many survivors who were old and sick, and who moreover had been discriminated against by their governments—denied old-age payments, or given substandard ones when compared to others in their countries. Many of these older Jews had no family support, since many of their children had emigrated. And the younger Jews who still remained had to contend with the liability of being a Jew in a society deeply tainted by continuing anti-Semitism.

Goldman familiarized himself with the most critical of the JDC's Eastern European programs: those being carried on in several Eastern European countries through the Société de Secours et d'Entr'Aide (SSE), headquartered in Geneva. The SSE had been established by the JDC in 1953 to distribute JDC monies and assistance in countries from which the JDC was officially barred, including Hungary, Poland, Czechoslovakia, and other Soviet satellites. According to its statutes, the SSE functioned "to lighten the burden of [local and national] social service organizations" by distributing funds which originated from "contributions to Jewish philanthropic organizations."

The significant difficulties for outside organizations in working in Communist-bloc countries were caused by the natures of the economic system and the totalitarian governmental system, the long-term mistreatment of people within such Communist states, and the peoples' attitudes toward themselves and toward outside assistance. Encapsulating these difficulties were a set of principles evolved by the JDC for the behavior of JDC personnel in Communist-bloc countries, as elucidated by Goldman, his associate Dr. Akiva Kohane, and his protégé Michael Schneider, who is today the executive vice-president of the JDC. Earlier in his career with the JDC, Schneider served as country director for several Eastern European countries.

"First," Schneider recalls, "we always had to assume that every conversation we had in an indoor space, or even in a car, was being recorded by the government. The rule was never to say anything privately that you wouldn't want to say in front of a microphone." Goldman adds, "The reason for this was not only to protect against spying but also because we wanted what we said and did to be always correct and unassailable."

"That means you never discuss politics," Schneider points out, "or let yourself be drawn into a conversation in which you appear to be taking sides on a controversial issue."

"We would always try to deal directly with the government and with the local Jewish organizations that were authorized by the government," Goldman says. According to Schneider, the "rules" mandated that they not do a number of things, including visiting people in their homes, befriending youngsters and meeting them alone, and even mentioning Israel. In their efforts to help the community, Schneider would make special efforts to show the government that he was not a threat politically, not an activist, "that I was not trying to whip up the Jewish community against Communism." In order to win the trust of people listening in on his conversations, Schneider would say things that he knew they liked to hear—lines like "It's possible to be a good Hungarian and a good Jew."

BEGINNINGS IN HUNGARY

In terms of number of Jews served in the 1970s in Eastern Europe, the most significant JDC/SSE program was in Hungary. Back in 1941, the Nazis had classified an estimated 850,000 people in Hungary as Jews. More than a half-million of them died in the camps during World War II, and approximately a quarter-million survived. Although anti-Semitism was officially banned in Hungary after the war, strong anti-Jewish sentiment still existed, and many blamed Jews for the country's postwar economic problems. Moreover, Communist nationalization of many industries deprived Jews of the means for making a living.

Between 1946 and 1952, when the JDC was permitted to work directly in Hungary, the JDC spent over $50 million to succor and rehabilitate its Jewish communities. Then, in consequence of the anti-Semitic actions of 1952–53 in all Soviet-bloc countries, the JDC was accused of espionage against Hungary, and many of the local Jewish leaders with whom the JDC had worked were imprisoned. There were threats that the JDC would itself be indicted and placed on trial in Hungary, though such a trial did not take place.

After 1953, forced to aid Jews in Hungary indirectly, the JDC established the SSE for that purpose and set up its headquarters in Geneva under the leadership of Maître Erwin Haymann, a Swiss lawyer who had saved many Jews during the war and aided emigration of refugees to the Jewish homeland. He was variously described by those who worked with him as "courageous," "steely," "selfless," and as "quiet and secretive as a Swiss banker." Haymann took many personal risks to negotiate SSE entry into Communist countries, and he bristled at the notion that his agency was merely a pass-through funder for the JDC. He conceived of his work as importantly assisting the Jews in countries from which the agencies of the West had been ousted, and as providing reports to those agencies about the conditions of the Jews behind the Iron Curtain and the ways in which donations were being spent. While insisting on his independence, he accepted direction and insight on how to deal with the various Eastern European governments and indigenous Jewish communities from Shaike Dan and Motke Yanai, old friends and secret operatives of the government of Israel who traveled frequently on the fringes of the region (and sometimes inside it).

Secret operatives in spy fiction are often men that stand out in a crowd; in reality, spies are those most able to lose themselves in crowds. Motke Yanai and Shaike Dan had those attributes:

graying men with few memorable features, able to move easily from place to place without drawing attention. "Things prohibited to others were permitted to the Swiss," Motke Yanai recalls, "and Maître Haymann could go in to see what we couldn't get to see ourselves."

The initial SSE budgets for Hungary were small—in the tens of thousands of dollars per year. Following the 1956 uprising in Hungary, in which the Soviet Union ruthlessly put down an incipient liberalizing revolt and installed a harsher puppet government, there was a new and substantial emigration from Hungary to Israel of rabbis and lay leaders, which deprived the local communities of leadership. Jewish life in Hungary was further eroded by renewed emphasis on socialism and an insistence that Hungarians identify only with the state, and not with religious or ethnic groups. The Jewish population in Hungary declined to less than 100,000. Things continued to deteriorate after that, particularly in the aftermath of the 1967 and 1973 Middle East wars, when articles in the Soviet press warned that Hungary was falling under the influence of Zionist and imperialist propaganda.

During the winter of 1974–75, according to Dr. Alexander Scheiber, leader of the Jewish Theological Seminary in Budapest, Hungarian Jews in high posts in the government, in the Communist Party, and in communications media lost their jobs; moreover, a recently-signed agreement between the Hungarian and West German governments for war reparations was twisted by the Hungarian government to preclude most Hungarian Jews from collecting benefits from the suffering endured during World War II. In the same time period, the Hungarian economy turned sour, and the government sought foreign trade with the West to sustain it. Hungary reinstated relations with the United States, receiving an official visit from Secretary of State William P. Rogers, and concluding an arrangement to settle claims from American citizens for property confiscated in Hungary in exchange for Hungary receiving Most Favored Nation Status (MFN) from the United States.

The rapprochement between the United States and Hungary reached a symbolic peak on January 6, 1978; Secretary of State Cyrus Vance returned to the Hungarians Saint Stephen's crown and "coronation regalia" that had been in storage at Fort Knox since 1945, when they had been given to the United States Army by a member of the Hungarian Royal Guard to keep them out of Soviet hands.

By 1977–78, some $750,000 was being spent annually by the SSE to aid certain sectors of a Hungarian Jewish population concentrated largely in and around the capital city of Budapest, and consisting of Holocaust survivors and of those Jews who had not emigrated in the wake of the 1956 uprising. Most of those being aided were elderly, female, and lived alone. Compared to the postwar Jewish populations of other satellite countries, such as those of Romania and Yugoslavia, which had lost more of their Jews to war and emigration, Hungary still retained quite a large number of Jews, between 80,000 and 100,000 people. Hungarian Jews ostensibly enjoyed the privilege of living and worshipping openly as Jews, but to do so exposed them to sanctions from the government and from their fellow Hungarians.

Hungary, however, did have some resources. There were more than twenty synagogues in Budapest. The country was unique in the entire Eastern bloc for having the only rabbinical seminary that was supported by the government. It also had a Jewish Museum built on the birthplace of Theodore Herzl, the father of political Zionism; behind the museum was a courtyard cemetery where two thousand Jews had been shot and buried in a mass grave; the cemetery also contained Jewish tombstones that dated from the third century. There were seventy-two functioning congregations in Hungary, but only twenty-eight rabbis shuttling between the congregations; many of the country's 150 synagogues were no longer suitable for holding services. Communist rulers did not permit the teaching of religion to anyone in Hungary under the age of eighteen, yet the Jewish community was able to provide Sunday school classes for hundreds of children in the entire country. An American Jewish

Committee report summed up this and the many other contradictions in Hungary:

> According to [Hungarian Jewish] community leaders, the relationship between them and government officials is one of friendly cooperation ... so that the . . . congregations in Hungary practice religious traditions with a great deal of freedom and acceptance. The other side of the coin is that the community also is careful never to ask for anything beyond the scope and limitations imposed upon it.

In the mid-1970s, before Goldman took office as executive vice-president, some JDC board members had begun to visit Hungary as private citizens and to return with reports citing the urgent and unmet needs of Hungarian Jews. There had also been inklings since 1972 that the Hungarian government might look favorably on a JDC return, but hints passed to JDC representatives by Hungarian Jews had not been followed by any official overtures from the government in the ensuing half-dozen years. Without a governmental invitation, Goldman felt, there was no hope for a direct return. A July 1974 memo written by Goldman's predecessor, Samuel Haber, cited meetings Haber and Haymann held with Minister of State Imre Miklos in Geneva. "Nothing of real importance took place," Haber noted, "but Miklos wanted the record to show that the request to visit Hungary emanates from us and not from him." Six months later, a glum Haber memo concluded, "I doubt very much whether we have any chance now to start a 'direct' operation in Hungary."

The week after Goldman assumed the leadership of the JDC, Ted Feder, the JDC's European regional director, who was based in Geneva, sent a memo concerning a possible official JDC return to Hungary. Conditions seemed riper than ever for the JDC to receive an official invitation.

Goldman discussed strategy for exploiting a possible opening with his closest confidantes, including Shaike Dan. Dan was a legend in Israel for his exploits of parachuting behind German lines in World War II to reach beleaguered Jews, and for his postwar efforts that resulted in extra thousands of Jews being able to immigrate to Palestine. Dan and Goldman had actually worked for the same cause, long before they met: Goldman in New York purchasing the ships onto which Dan in Europe secretly boarded thousands of Jews from refugee camps. Another Goldman confidant was Kohane, a longtime JDC field director born in Poland and educated as a lawyer, who had a wide acquaintance with Eastern European affairs. Goldman also consulted with Feder and with Dr. Lavoslav Kadelburg, a distinguished jurist and the leader of Yugoslavia's Jewish community. Goldman sums up their advice at that meeting as "Every opening leads to another door," which he interpreted to mean that he should take whatever first opportunity turned up to reenter the Eastern bloc, because upon going through it, he would have a better chance of opening all the other doors.

TWO INTRIGUING EXAMPLES: ROMANIA AND YUGOSLAVIA

In addition to the advice received from associates, Goldman recalls, "I had the examples of Yugoslavia and Romania before me." There were crucial and instructive differences in the thrust of the JDC programs in each country.

Before World War II, Romania had been a thriving center of culture, its capital city of Bucharest known as "little Paris." Romania had a strong Jewish life practiced by 800,000 Jews, half of them in Bucharest and the other half spread in dozens of communities throughout the country. Some streets near the center of Bucharest had numerous synagogues, cheek by jowl, built by associations of Jewish tailors, carpenters, or artisans. The huge Choral Synagogue, built in the 1860s to resemble a Roman basilica, with great vaults and arches and decorated with Byzantine tile and ceiling mosaics, was full to the rafters for every holiday service and on many Sabbath celebrations.

During the Holocaust, 150,000 Romanian Jews perished in the extermination camps, and an equivalent number died from starvation and illnesses in concentration camps in Moldavia. Many who returned alive were in an area of the country that was later claimed by Hungary, and they became part of that country's Jewish population rather than Romania's. Many thousand more Romanian Jews immigrated to Israel immediately after the war, further reducing Romania's Jewish communities.

The JDC had been expelled from Romania in 1948 but had been invited back in 1967, principally due to the efforts of the country's chief rabbi, Moses Rosen, who was also the leader of the Romanian Jewish community and a member of the country's parliament.

According to Rabbi Rosen's lifelong friend, Dr. Nicola Cajal of Bucharest, Rabbi Rosen towered above other Jewish religious leaders in Romania as "a writer and orator of great force," as a man who could attract and lead people, and as "a great diplomat." Being able to work with Romania's president, Nicolae Ceausescu, Dr. Cajal points out, was "no easy task." Perhaps Rosen had the strength to deal with Ceausescu because Rosen had been a principal in continuing Jewish resistance during the war and had survived. After the war, Rosen had been appointed as chief rabbi.

Romania had not permitted the SSE to operate in the country in the 1950s and early 1960s. But in the mid-1960s, Rabbi Rosen began to meet the JDC's Charles Jordan abroad, in Warsaw and other venues, during meetings of European Jews, and to tell Jordan that he was in the process of persuading Ceausescu to allow the JDC to return to Romania. Tens of thousands of Romania's Jews had registered with the government to be permitted to immigrate to Israel, and perhaps this potential mass exodus worried the government. According to Rabbi Rosen, a condition placed on the JDC's reentry was that the JDC would have to bring in at least $200,000 per year that would be spent inside Romania, bolstering the local economy. Rosen traveled to the United States to make appeals for this funding, and according to his memoir, "managed to raise $600,000." He also prevailed upon the Romanian government to give the JDC a favorable exchange rate, so that its dollars would buy more goods within Romania. Still, the process of gaining full access took several years; in the interim Jordan arranged for Rosen to import huge quantities of wine and brandy, which he then resold and used the proceeds to aid the Jewish population. By 1967, the success of Israel in the Six-Day War encouraged tens of thousands more Romanian Jews to consider emigrating. Eventually, some 300,000 did emigrate.

Beginning in 1967, the JDC started to send in money that enabled what was known as FedRom, the central federated council of Romanian Jews, to give food packages to the country's Jews nine times a year, to establish eleven kosher kitchens, to forward monthly stipends to individuals, to purchase good clothing and resell it to Jews at a discount in its shops, to have a meals-on-wheels program for the aged, and to staff and maintain several old-age homes. "No Jew in Romania now suffers from hunger; no Jew is inadequately dressed or shod," Rosen boasted in an autobiography. Just as important to Rabbi Rosen, a trend toward assimilation and rejection of religious rituals had been reversed largely through his own zealous efforts and also through assistance rendered by the JDC in the form of religious books, prayer shawls, and other ceremonial necessities.

The true origin and character of that early assistance has remained secret until this day. In a recent interview, Motke Yanai revealed one aspect of it. At the behest of Israeli agencies, and with the cognizance of the JDC, Yanai and Shaike Dan arranged a meeting with a representative of Romanian Jewry at a conference outside the country. "We used the code phrase, 'Believe in God, and you'll do good,'" Yanai recalls. The former Mossad agents emerged from the meeting with a plan to ship into Romania a train-car load of prayer books in Hebrew, which also included Jewish calendars, alphabet lessons, and other educational materials. The books were to be printed in Switzerland at JDC expense and shipped into Romania. When the shipment was finally made, Romanian guards at the border crossing seemed more interested in the ornate boxes in which the books were shipped than in the books themselves. Later, Yanai and Dan entered the country surreptitiously, the latter disguised as a rabbi, and helped to distribute the boxcar load of books. The manuals made it possible for more Jews to observe holidays and take part in prayer services.

A sense of what the welfare programs meant to the recipients was gained on trips to Romania by various board members and JDC delegations. JDC executive board member Marshall Weinberg described such a group's 1974 Romanian trip as being so momentous an experience that he could be neither "objective" nor "very intelligent" about it. "We spent five solid days from early morning until night seeing food distribution, going to medical cabinets, talking to doctors, going through old-age homes, the clothing distribution." They were amazed to find numerous young people speaking English, and those in old age homes weeping with gratitude at the very mention of "the Joint" or of "America." They met a seventy-year-old man who traveled with his horse and cart thirty-one miles just to pick up a semiannual food package of "two bottles of oil, a little pasta, some soap, a chocolate bar, and a little sugar." They listened to a rabbi tell how 17,000 people went to Auschwitz from one city and only 1,500 returned, how a city of seventy-two synagogues now had just two. "He said, 'We're just trying to hang on,' and I'll never forget the expression, he started to cry before us. He said 'It's the last struggle [and] we're on the ramparts. Don't let us down.'" Another who cried in Weinberg's arms was a twenty-year-old man who said that he had to spend his entire life lying in order to survive in the Communist state because he had been blocked in emigrating to Israel. When Weinberg asked a Romanian doctor what would happen to his patients if the JDC money and supplies ceased, he was told that they would die.

After many such experiences, Weinberg and his fellow board members were almost ashamed at their own wealth and good fortune. At a synagogue in Iassi, Weinberg was asked to speak to children of a Romanian congregation.

> I told them ... that they had given us this greeting as if we were gods and lords, [but] that we were not important people. And I wanted them to believe that when we meet in New

York that we do not look at them as the poor Jews. That we are privileged to be able to help them and that we care and are concerned for them. And that it was a privilege for us who haven't suffered [to come] here to understand what suffering was for the first time in our lives. And to see people holding on to their heritage. . . . And I told them that after looking at all the young people like that after seeing all the old people, it made me feel there was a chance for Jewish survival, and . . . I started to cry [and] for the first time in my life I couldn't even talk any more. . . . I felt even sadder when I came back and listened to these JDC budget meetings and I knew that I lied to these kids when I said that I felt confidence in Jewish survival [because] I don't feel confidence if we're going to have to cut budgets. . . . The whole community in Romania really depends on us. . . . We've got to fight for every penny that we can because it really means life and hope and help to these people.

The JDC-supported programs in Romania, though considered successful, were continually on the edge of failure and extinction from causes beyond the JDC's control. For instance, in late 1974, the Ceausescu government sharply devalued the Romanian currency, the lei, and on the same day unilaterally decided to breach its agreement with the JDC and stop contributing to Rabbi Rosen's programs two lei for every dollar that the JDC sent into Romania.

In early 1975, Moses Levine, then JDC's country director for Romania, explained in a letter to a board member that Rabbi Rosen was quite shaken by the devaluation. Eventually, though, the rabbi received a call from the Romanian vice president, Bodnares, who said that because of Rosen's past services and what they expected in the way of future services—even though it was completely against Romanian law—the government would continue to contribute two lei for every dollar transmitted by the JDC for social assistance.

There is no question today but that Jewish life would have completely disappeared from Romania had it not been for Rabbi Rosen. Michael Schneider states that "If we had had a half-dozen Rabbi Rosens, there would have been less need for the JDC to have its own personnel in Eastern Europe." Shaike Dan, who had fundamental and long-standing disagreements with Rosen over Rosen's exclusion of some people from the rolls of FedRom and over plans for wholesale emigration of Romanian Jews to Israel, nevertheless told Rosen's successor, former Knesset member Rabbi Menachem HaCohen, that "If we had three more like Rosen in that part of the world, the Jewish people would be better off."

But it was problematic for the JDC to have the survival of Jewish life in any country depend on the actions and control of one individual, no matter how intelligent, committed, and charismatic. Goldman recalls Rabbi Rosen as "very persuasive, a good politician; he could walk into a room and convince people who didn't want to allocate that extra $100,000 to give it to him. He was passionate in what he believed in, and we knew that he didn't live well at JDC's expense." Nonetheless, Goldman points out, Rosen could sometimes act in ways that in the JDC's view were counter to the long-term best interests of the Romanian Jewish community. By the 1970s, the Jewish community in Romania had acquired assets that it might have used to fund its own programs. Over the years, it had taken title to a large number of apartments, either when members of the community died or immigrated to Israel; older Jews on the welfare rolls, in exchange for years of assistance, had been required to write wills that bequeathed their property to the community. The worth of these apartments was estimated at several million dollars. Rabbi Rosen, who effectively controlled these properties, wanted to retain them for whatever emergency might arise in the future—and this stance brought him into conflict with Goldman. "I wanted him to sell or exchange those apartments for money that could shore up the programs the JDC was funding in Romania, and he wouldn't do it." To try to persuade Rosen, Goldman assured him that the JDC would guarantee that if the day ever came when Romanian Jews were threatened, the JDC would give the community the $2 million per year needed to sustain the programs. He also pointed out that the Romanian Jewish community had no way to assure that the value of those apartments would be maintained, for instance if President Ceaucescu died or if some other great change occurred.

A second point of conflict was Rabbi Rosen's wish to have the JDC build a new old-age home. The general JDC policy was to prefer the provision of services to the buying of bricks and mortar; Goldman's own long experience in working with the aged echoed this idea, and so he initially opposed the project. However, JDC staff argued that a new facility would upgrade services in Bucharest, and that the home had to be built to maintain good relations with Rabbi Rosen and the Romanian Jewish community. The construction proceeded to a point at which nearly a half-million dollars was spent before the Romanian government suddenly withdrew the building permit, saying it needed that land for another purpose, but offering to build another home on a different site. Eventually the government did just that. After the old-age home was erected, Rosen then asked the JDC for funds to pay for maintenance. To Donald M. Robinson, president of the JDC, this chain of events was evidence that Rabbi Rosen would have been a "very successful businessman" in a capitalist society.

The JDC's relations with Rabbi Rosen were frequently exasperating, and one of the problems raised by his personality and style highlights another of the organization's policies: the need to activate groups of local people to ensure that the community is properly served. "Rabbi Rosen would travel out of the country at least three months a year," Goldman observes. "Since he was president of the Jewish Federation of Romania, and nothing could be done without his express approval, when he wasn't there, things were not getting done." Pending Rosen's return from some journey or other, clothing sent in by the JDC for distribution to needy families was languishing in warehouses, and packages were not being delivered. Goldman argued that the JDC ought to have a staff person in residence in Romania or visiting there every month to help avoid such roadblocks and to train local staff to keep the pipeline flowing. "But the Jewish population there was too small to really justify a resident staff member, and we had a hard time finding professionals who were prepared to live and work in Romania at that time, so one was never appointed."

The "Underlying Sadness" of Yugoslavia

The situation in Yugoslavia was largely different from that of Romania. Marshal Josip Broz Tito prided himself on his distance from Moscow and expressed that distance in such actions as not becoming part of the Warsaw Pact and in seeming tolerance of religion within the country's borders. Back in 1936, Tito had written that Communists ought to ignore the philosophic differences separating them from religious adherents and concentrate on reforming the economic system, bettering "the hell on this earth, whose flames engulf believers and nonbelievers alike." But in the 1970s, while Yugoslav authorities officially tolerated religion, on a local level religion was discouraged; official actions combined with the devastation wrought by decades of war, emigration, and suffering forced a decline in Jewish religious practice to the point where the Belgrade synagogue could not regularly put together the *minyan* of ten men needed to hold weekly Sabbath services. In 1970, a JDC consultant visited Yugoslavia and applauded the JDC aid that was being given but could not help being affected by a tone of "underlying sadness" in the Yugoslavian Jewish community and a "preoccupation with Jewish cemeteries, museums, and other things connected with the tragic past." The implication was clear: the Yugoslavian community could be aided, but did not have sufficient mass for full renewal.

By the mid-1970s, about six to seven thousand Jews remained in Yugoslavia. The administrative structure of the country was one in which various "ethnic groups" were recognized and legitimized by the government, and every citizen was required to be part of one group or another. Jews were considered just another ethnic group in a country of many minorities—Slovenes, Croats, Serbs, Montenegrins, Macedonians, Bosnians, and Albanians, to name just a few.

There were three major Jewish communities in Yugoslavia and more than a dozen small ones permitted by the government to conduct their traditional affairs with a reasonable degree of freedom. Most of the top leaders of the Jewish communities held high government positions, were members of the League of Communists, and strongly supported Marshal Tito. Within the Jewish communities, traditional Jewish laws covering marriage, divorce, and even dietary practices were hardly observed because of a dearth of qualified religious personnel combined with a strongly secular attitude of the Jewish leadership. It was more practical for the community's leaders to promote Jewish cultural activities, such as an annual summer camp for hundreds of young people, than to promote religious practices in the absence of rabbis, cantors, or kosher butchers. Similarly, the communities readily accepted into their midst people who were the children of mixed marriages between Jews and non-Jews; this acceptance permitted the communities to remain stable in terms of numbers of members from the 1950s through the 1970s. The two Jewish kindergartens in Belgrade and Zagreb were the only facilities for formal Jewish education in the country; considered among the best kindergartens in Yugoslavia, they had only a small percentage of Jewish students in their classes. Similarly, the well-received Jewish choir had many non-Jewish voices in it.

Goldman recalls that the president of the Jewish community in Yugoslavia, Dr. Lavoslav Kadelburg, was a "terrific guy, trusted by the government and the Jewish community alike." Reserved and cultured, a former World War II partisan fighter, Kadelburg spoke or read a dozen languages, including Latin and ancient Greek, as well as Russian, Hebrew, English, and various Serbo-Croat tongues. In his youth he had been a member of a left-wing kibbutz movement, many of whose other members had immigrated to Israel after the war. A lawyer since 1939, he served Yugoslavia in several government posts and as a supreme court judge. After his retirement in 1966 from the post of assistant chief of the country's social security administration, he continued to function as an arbitrator for the Yugoslavian government, traveling all through the country to settle disputes.

He was also the undisputed leader of the country's Jewish communities. Kadelburg was a major force in establishing the country's Jewish museum and helped edit its many Jewish publications. Goldman recalls that Kadelburg "was able to visit Israel more easily than people in other Eastern European countries. He went to Israel frequently—he was devoted to Israel, but he was principally a Yugoslavian patriot, so he had never emigrated to Israel." Kadelburg was not religious but had a deep interest in Jewish cultural life, was known throughout the various Eastern European Jewish communities, and traveled among them with the express knowledge and consent of the Yugoslavian government.

"We do our best to keep the community alive," Kadelburg told a reporter in 1976, but he also stated, "We are not interested in the [Jewish] religion as a religion. We are not religious." Echoing this comment was a contemporary report by an outsider on Yugoslavian Jewry, which stated, "Virtually all the content of Jewish life is confined to the organized [cultural] activities of the community. There is little Jewish life in the home and even less in the synagogue." The report concluded that as a result of the high rate of intermarriage, the lack of Jewish education, and the lack of religious leadership, "it would seem difficult for the next generation to acquire sufficient incentive to remain Jewish."

To remedy that situation, and at the community's request, the JDC had taken some small steps—for instance, continuing and expanding its support for the summer camp, which helped inculcate traditional as well as cultural aspects of Jewish life to many hundreds of Eastern European children every year; underwriting trips by young rabbinical students in Israel to Yugoslavia to conduct holiday services; and sending in kosher food for Passover seders. The JDC's annual support amounted to $170,000, about half of which went for the upkeep of a one-hundred-bed home for the aged in Zagreb, and an additional $50,000 of relief assistance to 160 people scattered throughout the country.

When Goldman looked at a community such as that in

Yugoslavia, he accepted the need to approach it on its own terms—that is, through funding the programs that the community itself desired. "I wanted to do for a community what the community wanted done, not what outsiders thought should be done." This stance brought him to oppose programs that tried to impose anything on a country's communities from outside, such as more overtly religious assistance to replace the current traditional or cultural assistance. Moreover, "I assumed that no matter how many people from an Eastern European country emigrated to Israel, there would always be a remnant who would not emigrate, and that we had a positive obligation to help them, too, live Jewish lives in the countries of their birth."

Henry Taub, president of the JDC during that era, recalls that in this critical period, the JDC was steadfastly oriented toward "the human side of Jewish life, and we never got bogged down in the politics as to whether somebody [in a country being helped] was a Communist or an ex-Communist or an atheist or a Bolshevik. It did not make any difference. We had an organization that [was] concerned with the plight of individuals who needed help."

The professional leadership of that organization was entrusted to a man whose working methods reflected that same concern. Taub recalls Goldman's methodology in those heady days of the first attempts of the JDC to reenter Eastern Europe. The two of them, Taub and Goldman, would be sitting in a room with a government official whom they hadn't met before, and whose language they did not speak, but,

> Ralph had the gift of being sociable even in the most awkward of circumstances. . . . I was always sure that Ralph did not know the language, but he had a way of humoring people along. He'd laugh at the right time, and grunt at the right time, and wave his hand at the right time, and he knew a couple of words. . . . You pick up a few words, and take a few more sips of vodka, and move on. You probably get the gist of what they were trying to say; but they weren't too concerned, either, whether you understood them or not.

When Goldman assessed the assistance being rendered to the Jews of Yugoslavia and Romania, he saw an important difference. "The emphasis in Yugoslavia was cultural, while in Romania it was more religious," Goldman points out. He hoped to incorporate both emphases in Hungary, where waiting for direct assistance was a Jewish population larger than that of Yugoslavia and Romania combined.

HUNGARY: WAITING FOR AN INVITATION

"There was pressure inside the JDC for us to attempt to return to Hungary, and also from Philip Klutznick (then president of the World Jewish Congress and a former United States representative to UNESCO with the rank of ambassador). Klutznick had visited Hungary recently and was a personal friend of United States Ambassador Philip Kaiser," Goldman recalls. "But the Cold War was still actively being prosecuted, and there were also people inside the American Jewish community who didn't want any Jewish organization 'wasting money' going into the Communist bloc countries, who believed that if we sent money there directly, all we would be doing was feeding our dollars to the Communists."

Goldman disagreed with the naysayers. He saw an opportunity not merely to enter Hungary and assist its Jewish population, but also to use the programs in Hungary as a bridge to other existing Eastern European programs and to meld from the best parts of all of them approaches that might one day make it possible for the JDC to reenter the Soviet Union. Therefore, Goldman concluded that it was imperative that the JDC go into Hungary, and do so "through the front door," that is, with full knowledge of both the governments of Hungary and of the United States, and only after an official invitation to the JDC was extended by the Hungarian government through its officially sanctioned Jewish community. The position was not unanimously applauded by the JDC board, but the majority did approve it, and the undertaking was begun.

It took several years to come to fruition. Hints and feints had to be followed and avoided. In a speech in December of 1977, for instance, the Hungarian minister of religion, Imre Miklos, the key figure in Hungary for the JDC, made remarks that seemed at once an invitation and a warning:

> Some of the western circles, groups, and persons are trying, without any authorization, to interfere with the life of Jewry in other countries, including Hungary. They don't take into consideration that only those who live in the given Socialist countries, who know the basic interests, relations and the situation of Jews living in those countries are the responsible leaders of those communities and entitled to involve themselves in the development of the destiny of Jewry and of the Jewish religious community. Consequently, it is self-understood that Hungarian Jewry will establish contacts only with such groups of Jewry and with international organizations of such countries who would respect the principles of equality, sovereignty, and autonomy of others.

The JDC and Hungary each seemed to be waiting for the other to make the first definitive move. In 1978, the United States granted Hungary Most Favored Nation status, and that provided a break in the logjam. In November of that year, after flurries of cables and letters between Washington, New York, Geneva, and Budapest, Ambassador Kaiser was enthusiastic about the notion of the JDC returning to Hungary. A formal invitation from the Hungarian Jewish community finally arrived, and meetings were arranged to take place in Hungary in mid-February of 1979. "We assumed that the invitation had the approval of the leaders of Hungary," Goldman states, "and likely also the approval of the Kremlin—we knew that Miklos, the minister of religion, visited Moscow on official business several times a year."

Imre Miklos's official title was Minister of State and Chairman of the Ministry of Religious Affairs. Miklos had been born Catholic but had had Jewish friends while growing up, and in the days right after World War II, when he and his wife were first married and had nowhere to live, they moved into a Budapest apartment shared with an older Jewish couple. Miklos had entered the government from a position in a labor union as a very junior *apparatchik*, and worked his way steadily up the ladder, demonstrating both his fealty to the leadership and his talent at organization. In the 1990s, in an interview with the JDC, Miklos would characterize the 1950s in Hungary as a period of confrontation between church and state, and of "extremism" on both sides. He recalled that in the 1970s he had to "fight" internal opposition to be permitted to invite the JDC to return to Hungary, just as he also had to fight to permit the Vatican's emissaries to minister directly to their Catholic charges in the country and to make overtures to Protestant sects to do the same.

Michael Schneider was busy in 1979 as country director for Iran; after the fall of the Shah, Goldman would ask him to become the JDC country director for Hungary, and he would develop a long association with Miklos. Schneider recalled in a recent interview that in the late 1970s and early 1980s, Miklos was the "spearhead of religious tolerance," not only within Hungary, but because of the regard in which he was held throughout the entire Soviet bloc. "Miklos always stressed bridges of tolerance even while the two countries—the United States and Hungary—were at loggerheads because of the Communist business."

In mid-February of 1979, Goldman flew to Budapest with Donald M. Robinson, then president of the JDC, and his wife Sylvia Robinson. They were met at the airport and taken to rooms in a hotel that they assumed were bugged, and in which they held only guarded conversations. But Goldman found the night they spent on the town revelatory for the city's openness and level of culture. Budapest had suffered in the bombing during World War II but retained its sophisticated air, along with ten centuries of architectural styles. In company of officers of the Jewish community who also had connections with the government, the JDC visitors dined at a restaurant that served fine food and were treated not only to gypsy music but also to some Israeli music—a startling thing, Goldman felt, because Hungary and Israel did not have diplomatic relations. When a gypsy fiddler played *A Yiddishe Mama*, Goldman noticed that the Hungarian Jews had tears in their eyes, which made him feel close to his hosts.

During the day, the group was taken to visit the various facilities that served the Jewish population. "The people were attractive and likable," Goldman recalls. "They had a certain dignity, even in poverty, and the culture seemed very European and sophisticated." It was clear that the SSE was in direct contact with Holocaust victims and was able to aid them. It was also clear that Hungary was a closed system; those who watched over such facilities as the rabbinical seminary, the Jewish hospital, and the dilapidated central kitchen where eight hundred kosher meals a day were prepared for elderly Jews could well be agents of the government who reported on everything that happened in the Jewish population.

The dilapidated condition of the central kitchen appalled Goldman and Robinson. "In all my JDC travels," Robinson later told the executive committee of the board, "I have never seen something that I felt [more strongly] should be corrected immediately." As a gesture of good faith, and a belief in the future, Robinson and Goldman announced on the spot that the JDC would grant an additional $300,000, over and above the SSE annual budget level of $750,000, to build new kitchen facilities. They were overjoyed at visiting the rabbinical school, which was led by the charismatic professor Alexander Scheiber; the Friday night services and communal meal were attended by a startling three hundred to four hundred people, many of them young, and featured a dynamic choir and a congregation that responded to the services and music "with great spirit." Since only grape juice and *challah* bread were served, it was clear to Goldman that "the hunger and thirst of the people there was not for food, but for being together as Jews." Goldman was delighted to converse with some of the rabbinical students from the Soviet Union—in Hebrew, the only language they all shared in common—about their backgrounds and plans; one was training to go back to Moscow to replace the ailing chief rabbi there.

At a first formal meeting, Miklos referred to the suffering of Jews during the Holocaust, to prior anti-Semitism in Hungary, and the absence of the JDC from the country for many years. He repudiated all such matters as "not our fault" and welcomed the JDC to the country. Both sides acknowledged openly what had previously been unspoken, that the SSE assistance to Hungarian Jews had always been funded by the JDC. Robinson and Goldman responded that the JDC wanted to work directly in Hungary, and was prepared to do so and to increase the size and scope of the programs. They also responded that the JDC would proceed step-by-step, and only after JDC staff had been permitted to come in and assess the needs of the community.

"I recognized that what the Hungarian government really wanted was the dollars, the foreign exchange, which was in short supply," Goldman notes. "They also wanted the JDC to argue their case to the United States government, to act as a nonofficial channel for communications between Budapest and Washington."

The rest of the visit was taken up with emotionally intense activities: attending the ordination of a young Czech rabbi at the seminary, and visiting the cemetery, the Holocaust memorial, and several synagogues, among them the Dohany Synagogue, the largest in Europe, which was closed for the winter because of lack of heat.

Once back in New York, Goldman and Robinson sent Miklos a letter reiterating the JDC's commitment and expectations, and then waited for the invitation to send in staff members to go to work. But for six months there was no response, even after Robinson and Goldman sent a second letter. The silence was deafening.

Goldman realized something had gone wrong and determined to meet Miklos and whatever members of the Hungarian Jewish community the minister might bring along at a site outside the country. He suggested he could meet them at the twenty-fifth anniversary of the SSE in Geneva in early

September of that year. Hearing from the SSE's Maître Haymann that the Hungarians had promised to show up as they had for celebrations at the fifteenth and twentieth anniversaries, Goldman flew to Geneva.

Even though the forthcoming negotiations would obviate the need for the SSE in Hungary, Haymann did everything possible to facilitate the direct relationship between the JDC and Hungary. When Haymann met the Hungarian group at the airport, he was easily able to convince the minister to agree to an early meeting with Goldman at six that evening, in a conference room of a hotel. Goldman visited the room ahead of time and found it set up as though for a formal negotiation. Goldman was in the process of substituting easy chairs when Miklos and Haymann arrived, accompanied by an interpreter and by Dr. Mihaly Borsa.

Then in his seventies, Borsa had survived Auschwitz and Dachau, had been a minister of state in previous governments, and had later directly handled the SSE welfare program in Hungary for many years. In February, the other representatives of the Hungarian Jewish community had consciously tried to keep Goldman from Borsa; but now it was Borsa who accompanied Miklos to Geneva. A curious character, Borsa was later affectionately described by Michael Schneider as "irascible . . . an absolute rogue, in a nice way."

Minister Miklos set an aggressive tone, suggesting that the JDC's mid-May letter had asked for concessions from the government but had not indicated what the agency would do, or why he should cooperate with the JDC. "He referred to the JDC's role in Romania by innuendo—i.e., that we were spending a lot of money on a Jewish population that was one-fifth the size of Hungary's," Goldman would shortly recall in a memo to the files. (There was historic mutual enmity between Hungary and Romania, stemming in part from disputes over the Transylvanian area of western Romania that was for a time successfully claimed by Hungary.) In the conference room, Goldman tried to recover from Miklos's oblique attack, saying the JDC's letter had been misunderstood. The proceedings seemed to Haymann a "wrestling match" destined to end in a stalemate.

Out of the presence of everyone but the interpreter, however, Miklos made a private remark to Goldman that if they could arrange a bilateral arrangement, it would "radiate" and have other effects. This was a very startling comment, which could be interpreted as implying that if the JDC could make inroads in Hungary, this could have a positive ripple or domino effect upon all the Jews in Eastern Europe, perhaps even including those in the Soviet Union. Goldman might have liked to jump for joy, but, ever the diplomat, "let him feel, without being at all specific, that the American Jewish community could be helpful to Hungary," as he put it in a note to the files. Miklos countered with the observation that while they were not dealing in political matters, political implications could not be escaped. "It was all a game of generalizations," Goldman noted, "but we felt that each knew what the other was saying without the specifics."

The "radiate" comment would be chewed over for months, as JDC staff and board members tried to zero in on the exact meaning and all the possible implications.

During the Geneva meetings, Borsa let Goldman know that he, rather than the other Jews in Budapest, had the ear of the minister and implied that unless the JDC was willing to come into Hungary with considerably more money than it had funneled through the SSE, there might be no deal. It became clear to the JDC men that Borsa was the central player in the JDC's potential reentry to Hungary.

There were few discussions at dinner, but the evening was laced with what Goldman noted as "enough wine to facilitate friendships." The next morning, Goldman met with Shaike Dan, whom he had asked to come to Geneva and advise him behind the scenes. As Dan often did when asked for advice, he rendered it in a roundabout way, by reference to a Talmudic saying or a Yiddish joke. In this instance, the lesson was contained in a well-known Yiddish phrase that referred to the punch line of a joke: a mother tells her son, who is about to join the army, "Don't try to shoot them all at once—shoot one and take a rest, shoot another and take a rest." This punch line was Dan's counsel to Goldman in regard to Miklos and Borsa: work on them separately and one at a time. After the JDC men and their several advisors dispersed, Dan, while crossing a street, caught sight of Borsa in the middle, and the two seemed to share a moment of recognizing each other as secret agents now on the verge of coming in from a long war. To Goldman, watching this scene from a vantage point in the hotel, it seemed a positive omen.

At a formal meeting with Goldman and Feder, Borsa lost his temper over an alleged slight that had occurred during an earlier visit to Hungary by Feder, but when Feder calmly denied that he had been there, Borsa seemed embarrassed at his own outburst and thereafter became more cooperative. Shortly, he reversed direction and agreed that the JDC could take over the Hungarian operation from the SSE, effective almost immediately. This changed tone carried over into a luncheon meeting in which Miklos became expansive, repeating his lines about the potential "radiating" effects that might follow from a JDC-Hungary agreement. In an unplanned but heartfelt remark, Goldman called Miklos both a "dreamer" and a "realist," a champion of a small country in a world dominated by large ones.

Miklos later said that he was touched by Goldman's understanding of what was truly important to him, and the basics of the agreement between the JDC and Hungary were quickly set in place. Schneider would make an assessment visit to Budapest with Feder later that month, and JDC money would start flowing in directly by the following month. "Who could have known," Goldman wondered in his memo to the files, "the change of mood that would take place in twenty-nine hours, from Tuesday evening at 6:00 to Wednesday night at 11:00?" It was an early indication, as well, of the importance of individual personalities and chemistries in the relationships between the JDC and the regimes of the Communist satellite countries.

Next day, Miklos gave Goldman a gift of wine, pâté, and Bartok piano concertos, and the two made plans to meet again, outside of Hungary if possible and in the near future, to discuss the JDC's continuing role in Hungary. "I always offered to meet

Communist bureaucrats in Geneva, Paris, Vienna or some oth-er nice place," Goldman recalls, "because they liked to make trips, and it was possible for them to speak a little less formally when they were away from home—though of course they al-ways had someone along who was watching and noting every word they said."

When Michael Schneider began his work as JDC country di-rector for Hungary, he tried to apply the lessons he had learned previously as country director for Iran. He found, he recalls, that the "cultural divide wasn't so big" in Hungary as it had been in the midst of an Islamic society. Although he had entered Hungary with some trepidation, carefully watching his every step, he soon developed a father-son relationship with Borsa. Schneider learned to navigate his way through the labyrinthine paths that intertwined the Jews of Hungary, shuttling between the official Jewish community—to which many Jews did not belong out of fear that membership would compromise their rise in official circles—and the competing groups around Miklos.

The JDC budget for Hungary was set at $1 million a year. While construction was begun on the new kosher kitchen building, JDC direct support for the Hungarian Jewish Community was demonstrated in other ways, too. A 104-year-old woman approached Schneider and Feder during an early vis-it and asked for help in trying to locate a grandson whom she believed had survived the war. The JDC learned that he had been in a Jewish orphanage until 1950, then he had disappeared from view. JDC inquiries prompted the French Jewish commu-nity to place an ad in a magazine. The ad drew a response, and shortly a Paris businessman was reunited with his only living rel-ative. Donors also stepped forward. Goldman learned about the willingness of Dr. Peter Varadi, a Hungarian Jew in Washington, D.C., to restore the magnificent synagogue in Szeged, the sec-ond largest city in Hungary. Because of these and other projects, Goldman was able to convince Miklos that the return of the JDC would bring more to Hungary than the direct aid.

On a larger level, the JDC's patience and attention to detail in Hungary also began to pay off. In mid-June of 1980, a message came to Schneider from a leader of the Hungarian Jewish community who had recently been in Moscow for the inauguration of the new chief rabbi there. The leader had taken the opportunity to pay a visit to the USSR's vice-minister for cultural affairs, a man named Vissov. The vice-minister asked the Hungarian if he could arrange for some religious supplies—including many pounds of matzot—to be sent to Moscow through the Hungarian Jewish community. The Hungarian leader told this to Schneider, who quickly put the request in a "strictly private and confidential" letter to Goldman. Schneider and Goldman believed that this was a breakthrough, the first time a senior Soviet government official had ever asked for something that he knew would be provided by the JDC. The supplies were quickly sent and transshipped. Later on, the hopes raised by Vissov's request were dashed, and the request seen in retrospect as not the harbinger of good things to come that Goldman had hoped for.

Relations between Hungary and the JDC remained exquisitely sensitive to actions in the outside world. At the end of February 1981, Goldman flew to Budapest to meet a very agitated Miklos. The minister had been called on the carpet by his own government to answer for matters which were nowhere under his control: President Reagan's recent charge that Hungary was supplying arms to the El Salvador rebels; and an action by Israel's prime minister, Menachem Begin, convincing the Knesset to declare Jerusalem to be the capital of Israel, an action with which the Hungarian government disagreed. The behavior of the Western leaders, Miklos told Goldman, "caused us big problems." What the minister wanted, Goldman recalled, was for President Reagan to differentiate in his foreign policy between the Soviet Union and Hungary, which was increasingly pursuing a separate path. Goldman recognized that he was expected to convey the Hungarian's thoughts to the American authorities, and said he would do so, to Miklos's evident relief.

On another visit to Hungary, on what was a very cold day, Goldman and Schneider took an unaccompanied walk along the concrete path that abuts the Danube. With the sound of the rushing river as cover, the electronic devices that the pair assumed were tracking them and recording their conversations might be left behind for a few moments. "Ralph had a huge view of the world," Schneider recalls, and on that day "he mapped out his whole vision." The vision was part of a global strategy for the Jewish future, which had as one pillar the JDC helping Jewish communities beyond Israel's borders toward renewal and shoring up the means for them to remain in place, while simultaneously supporting Israel as the center of Jewish life. To achieve that goal, the JDC had to be able to aid all Jews behind the Iron Curtain, as well as those in Europe and more accessible places. The entry into Hungary, Schneider remembers Goldman saying, "was the beginning, it was the foot in the door, it was a wedge into the Communist bloc, it had greater implications than simply the Jewish implications, it helped the forces of democracy. And he suggested the preposterous notion that because of it, maybe one day we'd work in the 'Big Bear,' the Soviet Union."

CHAPTER FIVE

Maintaining a Strong Foundation
The JDC in Israel

EARLY DURING Goldman's tenure as executive vice-president of the JDC, he and Jack D. Weiler, president of the organization, discussed the future of the JDC. "There was a perception that in the 1940s and 1950s JDC had been a Zionist organization, and since then it had become a social welfare organization on a global scale. Some of our board members preferred that JDC deal only with diaspora Jews, and to have the Jewish Agency, which was also funded by UJA, deal with Israel. Jack thought JDC should continue to do both, serve the diaspora and Israel, and I did, too. Actually, that belief was one of the reasons I was hired for the executive's job."

Sharpening the Joint's Jewish focus was not a universally agreed-upon goal to everyone in the upper hierarchy of the JDC. American Jews were becoming increasingly assimilated. Many JDC board members wanted the organization to continue to focus primarily on welfare needs, which were large enough to take up all of the organization's resources if so desired. But Goldman was personally committed to Israel as central to the Jewish world, to a vibrant and healthy diaspora, and to an emphasis on Jewish heritage and destiny as essential to any programs that American Jewry might conduct through the JDC.

"Ralph Goldman's vision of Jewish life is of an informed

Jewish life," says Dr. Seymour Epstein, former director of education for the JDC. "Jewish literacy is, for him, both a means and an end; if we're in the business of organized Jewish community work, for him the organized Jewish community is one that strives to create literate, cultured, and educated Jews, and on the way to that goal, does everything it can in its programming and its approach to Jewish life to create the possibilities for Jews to educate themselves. . . . I think for Ralph, like for myself and others who agree, the single greatest malaise of the Jewish people is ignorance of our own culture and our own heritage and our own literature."

When Goldman speaks about Israel, his deep love of the land and the people is apparent. Israel has long been a pivotal part of his own identity as a Jew, and he sees it as essential to the spiritual and cultural life of all Jews.

THE CHANGING ROLE OF THE JDC

Though some people asserted that thirty years after the birth of the State of Israel, the state ought to take care of its own business without major assistance from American Jews, Goldman believed that the idea of Israel had held the Jews together for five thousand years, and that the establishment of the state in 1948 had enabled Israel to become the wellspring from which all other Jewish communities could draw sustenance. Therefore, in Goldman's view, programs outside of Israel that dealt with heightening Jewishness must inseparably be intertwined with information about Israel; moreover, the future development of Israel must reciprocally be based on a heightening of all facets of Jewish spirituality, ritual, tradition, and culture, to inspire continued linkage with diaspora Jews.

Support for Goldman's increasing emphasis on these ideas grew from the JDC's 1975–76 self-study, which had grouped the organization's core values under two general categories, "preservationist values" and "developmental values."

Preservationist values had to do with ensuring the survival of Jewishness in all its manifestations—the strictly religious, the cultural, and the traditional. These values governed the JDC's welfare efforts, but they also mandated that the JDC outreach not neglect the spiritual, cultural, and Jewish-educational aspects of the aid given by the JDC to a far-flung community, even in circumstances where that aid necessarily had to concentrate on meeting physical needs.

Developmental values had to do with heightening the quality of Jewish social services and of Jewish life itself. These values governed the JDC's relationship with Israel during the important change embodied in the transition from the JDC as an entity that operated various programs to the JDC-Israel as an innovating social entrepreneurship, a transformation that Goldman had personally overseen. In the new configuration, developmental values were construed as mandating that, in addition to providing funds and materials, the JDC should guide individual recipients and communities toward self-sufficiency.

This notion suggested, the study recommended, and Goldman's personal philosophy insisted that in all of the JDC's programs, whether in Israel or in the diaspora, the JDC commit itself to time-limited endeavors. The JDC should be steadily decreasing its involvement in operating programs and increasing its generation of ideas, the providing of seed money, the development of manpower training and demonstration projects, and in many ways preparing for local funding and control of projects.

"JDC had a history of working with the most vulnerable and needy populations in Israel," Goldman recalls, and that history led it to recognizing two core populations that it dubbed "high-risk," because they were the least able to fend for themselves: the young and the old. Virtually alone in the family of nations, Israel—in significant measure through the efforts of the JDC— put special emphasis on these two sectors of its population. The challenge for the JDC, in its new configuration, was how to serve the needs of the young and the old in ways that were, as a memo put it, "society-building in nature, community-oriented, and addressing social imbalance." As the *Jerusalem Post* would shortly report, "The Joint Distribution Committee doesn't distribute any more. At least not in Israel. . . . The JDC has been increasingly concerned with not only doing good, but doing it wisely."

Goldman embedded the new principles as a set of criteria that all JDC projects in Israel must henceforth meet. Most projects would be strictly planned, and funded only for five years, with declining amounts of money given in each year, and they would have to include an "evaluative" component. Dr. Zvi Feine, the current chairman of ESHEL, says that these criteria ensured that JDC-sponsored programs "would never have the character of being imposed on a community from the outside."

Dr. Yitzhak Brick emphasizes the importance of Goldman's "five-years-and-out" idea. "Very few nonprofit organizations know how to operate in this manner," Dr. Brick says, "and they also do not know how to do their own long-term planning." He labels Goldman's insistence on doing one's own planning and getting out of projects quickly, while leaving the projects with a workable infrastructure, an example of Goldman being "a man of vision." Dr. Brick believes that people of vision usually exhibit just one of three different skills. "Either they are visionaries who can think ahead, or they are good at implementing somebody else's vision, or they have a great ability to convince others that something must be done. Ralph does all of these things."

HELPING THE AGING

One of Goldman's early accomplishments at the JDC had been the development of ESHEL, the Association for Planning and Developing Services for the Aged. As a visionary, Goldman could not permit ESHEL to stand still, and the JDC helped ESHEL continue to evolve in several ways. One focus was the development of pioneering day-care centers for the elderly in cities and in rural areas, particularly in the cooperative farming communities known as *moshavim*.

Many of the moshavim had been settled by the waves of immigrants who had arrived in Israel in the late 1940s; often, a community would be composed of people who had originally come from a single geographical area, such as Yemen. Their children and grandchildren might leave the *moshav* in the course of time, but the original settlers generally stayed put, and by the 1980s, thirty or more years after their arrival in Israel, many of them were elderly. A significant proportion of these people were vulnerable, because their families had scattered and were no longer able to care for them on a daily basis. In the day-care center program, frail elderly people were brought to the centers each day by bus, for meals, physical therapy, interaction with medical personnel, baths, laundry service, and other care. The existence of such centers enabled thousands of frail elderly to continue to reside in their own homes or in the communities where they had spent most of their lives, rather than becoming institutionalized.

The programs in three major cities saw ESHEL working in cooperation with municipal authorities to open special day-care centers for the mentally frail elderly, to work with hospitals in developing diagnostic services for them, and especially to expand neighborhood programs of sheltered housing for them. One particularly effective program, called the Jerusalem Project, provided advocacy resources and access to information to five different neighborhoods in Jerusalem. Israel's low rate of institutionalization of the elderly reflected the success of the "stay at home" theory.

BROOKDALE

Another focus of ESHEL's expansion was the Brookdale Institute of Gerontology and Adult Human Development, founded in 1974. It had initially been established to do research into the country's needs in terms of the aging, but the general concept of influencing society through research was applicable to many other areas. The need for such research was acute because, says current director Jack Habib, the government of Israel conducted "next to zero" research of its own, principally because it was "chronically strapped for funds and had to apply the funds it had to operating programs and meeting current crises."

Because the field of gerontology was so new in the mid-1970s, and there were so few institutions with adequate financial and governmental backing at work in it, Brookdale came in effect to function as a research institution and consulting resource for the entire world in the field of aging. In the late 1970s and early 1980s, the most important problem in the arena of the aging was how to allocate national resources, and the major issue was the relative balance between institutional and community services. One major product of Brookdale's first decade of operations was the landmark report, "Mapping of Long-Term Care Services for the Aged," which summarized all the available information on institutional and community services for the aged in Israel, giving policy makers the information they needed to decide what should be planned for the future. A direct result of this Brookdale study was the passage and implementation of the country's Long-Term Care Insurance Law.

In keeping with Goldman's emphasis on professional training, another major Brookdale-ESHEL project was the creation of a National Leadership Course for upper level management of field staff who worked with the aged. Providing all senior workers in a single field with the same sort of training and understandings of the needs of the population they serve, Habib contends, promoted a greater degree of professionalism among the governmental agency people responsible for housing, social security, and other services.

COMMUNITY CENTERS AND EDUCATION

During his tenure as chief executive officer, Goldman's efforts also influenced the JDC-Israel's work with the young. Continuing his long association with community center development, the JDC-Israel forged formal links to the Israel Association of Community Centers and through them created several fruitful programs. The community center–based preschool programs, urged into existence by Goldman in the early 1970s, were gradually taken over by Israel's Ministry of Education and Culture and absorbed into the ministry's ongoing programs. Complementing the emphasis on the young and the old, a five-year-plan jointly developed by the JDC and the Israel Association of Community Centers spurred what was termed a "quiet social revolution" through strengthening programs aimed at socially and economically disadvantaged adults.

Direct work with local communities was best exemplified by the Negev Project, in which the JDC's partners included the Ben-Gurion University, the Ministry of Health, and the health fund of the country's largest union, the Histadrut. At local clinics, the Negev Project offered to disadvantaged families care , particularly better mental and physical health care for infants and young children. The program was expanded yearly until it could serve some 300,000 people. Medical school graduates from the university working in the clinics were key personnel in helping these facilities ease the load on area hospitals. As more medical school graduates became available, the number of clinics was raised. Soon there were four in Beersheba, as well as others in newly developed towns and in a bedouin village.

Although the JDC operated no schools and was not in the business of education per se, many of the welfare, cultural, and rebuilding programs supported by the JDC in Israel and worldwide had educational components. In addition, about a quarter of the JDC's budget was devoted to assisting schools and other educational activities in more than thirty countries. Assistance went to schools operated by four major groups: two French groups, the Alliance Israelite Universelle and Ozar Hatorah; the Lubavitch organization; and ORT, the Organization for Rehabilitation Through Training.

Dozens of secular schools in France, and in North African countries such as Morocco and Syria, were operated by the Alliance Israelite, which also had some facilities in Israel. Its more religiously-oriented counterpart, the Ozar Hatorah, operated in the same French-speaking countries, offering religious instruction.

The Lubavitch organization, a worldwide Hasidic movement, operated schools in both French and Spanish speaking countries in North Africa. Also, during the Communist years,

the JDC quietly funded some of the Lubavitch underground educational efforts in the Soviet Union.

The ORT was the largest organization for which the JDC
supplied operating funds. It had schools and vocational training
facilities in such far-flung places as Bombay and South America.
In Bombay and other very poor places, ORT schools were accompanied by hostels in which the pupils could live while they
were being trained. Some four thousand ORT teaching personnel reached 100,000 students in twenty countries annually.
ORT's largest concentration of facilities was in Israel, where
more than a hundred centers operated, concentrating on the sizable educational task of bringing recent immigrants to the point
where they could better contribute as workers and citizens to
the country's progress.

The JDC-Israel continued its historic support for the operation of yeshivas in Israel. In forty of these, on a high-school level, a regular humanities program was combined with a religious
program and sophisticated computer sciences training.

PROFESSIONAL TRAINING

Under Goldman's impetus, the JDC continued to expand its support for the development of advanced community services manpower in Israel, in the expectation that better-educated
professionals would prove to be a key resource in moving society
forward. More than twenty programs were supported, from un-
dergraduate to doctoral level in the universities, and outside of the
university, to train paraprofessionals and to give continuing education to people already at work in the field. Whenever and wherever an individual or a group wanted to do an innovative project
that extended the ability of social workers to assist the vulnerable,
Goldman and the JDC were eager to assist; this was the way that
social work departments were started at hospitals in the Haifa area
and a graduate program for nurses set up in Tel Aviv.

Goldman continued to believe fervently in the necessity for
developing professionalism in all endeavors having to do with
social programming. His reasons were set out in a paper, "The

Role of the Professional in Developing and Shaping Jewish Communal Policies and Strategies." Although aimed principally at community workers in the diaspora, it had resonance for such workers in Israel. In Goldman's view, to keep alive a vision of the Jewish people as an *Am S'gula,* a people with a mission, required the assistance of Jewish communal workers. To counter the steady erosion of Jewish values and traditions, communal institutions and policies must be developed, then administered by a professional corps of trained and Jewishly committed social workers. The Jewish communal worker, Goldman wrote, must obtain a Jewish base of knowledge, and "must see himself as the guardian of Jewish continuity and as the exponent of a rich and illustrious tradition." The best professional, Goldman concludes, will be "a diplomat, a persuader, a negotiator of coalitions, an influencer of institutions and people who have the power to allocate resources."

Since the number of such well-trained Jewish communal workers was limited, Goldman promoted programs to produce more of them and to provide opportunities for the well trained to train others in the field. In a later article, Goldman advocated higher pay scales to attract the best and most idealistic of the next generation's Jewish youth, and, "equally as important . . . continued stimulation and opportunities for mental growth" on the job, in continuing-education studies and through exchange programs. Goldman believed the Jewish professional communal worker, as "the latter-day guardian of the Jewish heritage, should be as steeped in Jewish learning as the rabbi, teacher, or scholar."

EVALUATIONS

In later years, some in the JDC would come to believe that the training programs that Goldman championed had proliferated too greatly and needed to be reined in. There was also concern that some of the JDC's partnerships with the government had become rubber stamps for projects that the government wanted rather than what the JDC desired. In reaction, the JDC disbanded or modified several of its associations, and concentrated more on initiating ideas for new projects that the remaining associations would sponsor. It also began to work more with non-governmental partners, such as the Histadrut labor union and the Israeli Industrialists Association.

Perhaps the most cogent and productive of the critiques of this sort was aimed at Brookdale. "There needs to be a balance between meeting the agendas of agencies serving the aged and bringing new insights to the problems of the aged," a 1982 Brookdale internal report concluded, as the Institute, its work, and goals came under mounting criticism by the government and by the Institute's own funders. The difficulties stemmed from having a limited staff not able to tackle all the problems that needed to be addressed and from being pushed by government ministries to concentrate on the more immediate ones—the result of the burgeoning financial crisis in Israel—to the detriment of long-range planning.

The response was interesting: not to change Brookdale, but to go further with the Brookdale idea. Goldman points out that the issues Brookdale works on touch the concerns of four different government ministries and also have an impact on municipalities, the country's largest union, and its universities and hospitals, so the one institute had a multitude of masters to serve. The solution, Jack Habib recalls, was that "a Brookdale was needed for other health care issues, such as children's concerns, the health of immigrants."

Some people on the JDC board, dissatisfied with Brookdale, did not want to consider expansion of the institute. Rather, they favored drastically cutting back or eliminating JDC support for Brookdale because it was so expensive to maintain, or asking one of the universities to take over the institute. These prospects alarmed Goldman and the institute's first director, Dr. Israel Katz, who did not want Brookdale put in a position of relying too heavily on government funding for its work, since that might compromise its credibility as well as its ability to render independent evaluations of projects. An international panel was convoked to review Brookdale's work and its future paths. At the same time Goldman and Herbert Singer, a New York lawyer and philanthropist who had been one of Brookdale's founding fathers, sought and found donors to pledge enough money so that the Institute could survive and go forward even as JDC funding was reduced. The private endowment did a great deal toward enabling Brookdale to assure its independence, autonomy, and credibility.

In 1984, these efforts resulted in a new five-year agreement being signed by the parties, in the hiring of Habib as the new director, and in Brookdale's beginning to conduct more internally shaped research. In a 1983 report, Brookdale discovered that before the year 2000, there would be a 156 percent rise in the number of people over the age of seventy-five—a surge that the government had not counted on. Because of this, in 1984–85, Brookdale directed its resources into exploring the best means of organizing long-term care for the chronically ill; the role of informal family support for the elderly; redefining the role of the elderly in Israeli society; and improving the capacity of the government and private agencies to plan for and monitor services dealing with the elderly.

Goldman had long believed that Israel had a need for some sort of additional institution, perhaps along the lines of the Brookings Institution in Washington or the Hudson Institute in New York State, that could tackle the other great social issues facing Israeli society and lay out potential policy choices for those whose task it was to make decisions on these matters. He had first written a memo about such a need, and the possibility of funding such an institute. In 1969, and with backing from Lou Horowitz, Director-General of Operations in Geneva, and Edward Warburg, previous Chairman of the Board of the JDC for many years, he had obtained a 50,000 Israeli-pound budget allocation for such a project from the JDC. The money had not been used at the time, but the idea of an institute that could affect policy in Israel continued in the organization's memory and in the thoughts of Goldman.

Brookdale's approach had been to study a subject intensively, amass data, and only then to come up with findings and interpretations of the data that were above politics and were not identified with any party or creed. Israel's governing elite—the upper-rank civil servants and political leaders—accepted this approach and found it useful as guidance in many fields of health policy. Now Goldman wanted to adopt this approach to broader arenas.

The concept of a center for the study of social policy took off in the early 1980s, led by board members Singer, Katz, Goldman, and Professor Herman Stein. Such a center would have to be independent as well as nonpartisan and nonprofit, and it would have to recognize that social policies were inseparable from economic policies and realities. The center's objectives would have to include enriching the public debate as well as enlightening those who would ultimately make the decisions—the legislators in the Knesset—so that closed-door policy decisions would only happen after the public had a chance to learn about the issues and voice its opinions. The center itself would take no position on the issues that it studied, but it would present, explain, and analyze the implications of proposed solutions to problems. Using only a small core staff, the center would commission leading economists and academicians to study individual social issues. In 1982, such a center was created—the Center for Social Policy Studies (CSPS).

"One of the most important things the Center does is meet with all the ministers and with people from all the political parties to advise them of the Center's findings," says economist Arnon Gafni, former director of Israel's central bank and a consultant to the Center. Within a few years of its founding, the CSPS became an important institution in the governance of the country; its annual reviews of budgets and policies, as well as its individual reports on welfare, immigration, absorption, education, health, and social services became essential reading and resource material for legislators, academics, people in the media, and other informed citizens. Goldman muses, "If the budget of JDC were down to its last million dollars to give to a project, I'd give that million to CSPS and Brookdale Institute, with a small sum available as seed money for pilot projects, because that's where it would do the most good and have the most leverage."

CHAPTER SIX

Global Jewish Strategy, Step One

Aiding Soviet Jewry

T HE DREAM of reentering the Soviet Union and working with its approximately three million Jews was never far from the minds of Jewish leaders outside the Iron Curtain. To Goldman as to many others, reaching and assisting this particular group of brethren, the second-largest concentration of Jews in the diaspora, was the principal task of Jews on the democratic side of the Iron Curtain—it was a global Jewish problem and required, in answer, a global Jewish strategy, one that aimed to clarify and consolidate the positions, policies, and efforts of the international Jewish organizations concerned with the issues.

JEWS AND RUSSIA—AN HISTORICAL OVERVIEW

The tale of the Jews of Russia and of its smaller neighboring countries under Communist rule is long and tortuous. Jews had been persecuted under the czars of Russia for a thousand years before the pogroms of the latter part of the nineteenth century, which galvanized the migration of perhaps a million Russian Jews to other countries. In the revolution that brought the Communists to power in 1917, Jews formed an important segment of the elite, but their prominence was soon compromised by official governmental attitudes. The Communist state kept the JDC from working in Russia immediately after World War I, even though the Jews of Russia had suffered equally during the war and revolution with those in Western and Central Europe. The government of the USSR forbade allegiance by its citizens to any organized religion, and by the 1920s actively discriminated against Jews who continued to lead Jewish lives. Thousands of synagogues and Jewish educational facilities were closed. Soviet Jews were cut off from Jews elsewhere, and Zionism was forbidden.

After the death of Lenin in 1924, Stalin eliminated the Jewish-born Trotsky from the ruling troika and began purges to consolidate his hold as dictator and to get rid of Lenin's confederates, whom he considered current and future competitors for the top job. Many among the leaders he eliminated were Jews. The slaughter and exile that took place under Stalin at that time was on a very broad scale: 35,000 army men were executed by the secret police, who were then themselves purged, resulting in 100,000 additional deaths and the banishment to the gulag of between seven and fourteen million people. These larger-scale purges had a distinct anti-Semitic cast, sweeping proportionately more Jews than non-Jews from all walks of life, and reducing most Soviet Jews to poverty.

The anomalous bright spot in the relationship between the USSR and its Jews, in the 1920 and 1930s, was the Agro-Joint, by which the JDC provided the money to transport tens of thousands of Soviet Jews to Ukraine, and to equip, train, and outfit them as farmers. Both the Soviet government and the outside Jewish world pointed with pride to the positive effects of this program. But at the end of the 1930s, contemporaneous with the purges that eliminated the military and secret police cadres, Stalin shut down the Agro-Joint. Its hundreds of thousands of Jews scattered to the winds, many of them forced westward into the path of the Nazi juggernaut. The vast majority of those who had been Agro-Joint pioneers were never heard from again, killed in the Holocaust, or while serving in the ranks of the Soviet army, or in the despoliation and deprivation that accompanied the war in the USSR. Of the six million Jews murdered in the Holocaust, an estimated one and a half million were Soviet Jews.

THE POST-WAR CLIMATE IN THE USSR

After World War II, there were officially about three million Jews in the countries of the USSR, between one and two percent of the total population. An indication of Soviet Jews' worth to the state is that by 1947, their abilities had permitted them to rise again to positions of prominence. That year, Jews constituted almost 20 percent of the recipients of the Stalin Awards, annual national prizes in the fields of science, engineering, literature, and the arts. This was a much larger percentage than their share of the population would have predicted. Since Jews had been the most obvious victims of the Nazis, and since the Communists' emotional hold on the peoples of the USSR still had much to do with the government having fought the Nazis, there was a brief honeymoon period in the Soviet state's relations with Jews. This period was symbolized by the USSR being a staunch supporter of the establishment of the state of Israel. But that honeymoon never included in its embrace the USSR's own Jews, whose culture was consistently attacked and undermined by the government.

While the JDC was heroically working to assist the Jews of Europe who had survived the Holocaust, the organization was not officially permitted inside the Soviet Union, even though many Soviet Jews were suffering in like manner to their Eastern European brethren. Jewish life had been subjected to tremendous blows in Eastern Europe, but it had continued to exist there in varying degrees of strength from 1917 until the 1940s, when the Eastern bloc countries were taken over by Russian Communism. Conversely, in the Soviet Union, since 1917 the Jews had been constantly under the thumb of a regime that attacked and undermined their religious life, resulting in fewer Soviet Jews in the post–World War II period who could even remember a time when Jewish life had been vibrant in their homeland.

Conditions for Jews under Soviet Communist rule deterio-
rated even further in the late 1940s and early 1950s, the final
years of Josef Stalin. During the "Doctors' Plot" of January
1953, Stalin fantasized a conspiracy to take his life, led by Jewish
doctors who, it was alleged, were the recipients of JDC funds.
These doctors were also supposedly tied to Israel, a country increasingly viewed by Stalin as an accomplice of the Western
powers, the Cold War enemies of the USSR. According to
Yehoshua A. Gilboa's *The Black Years of Soviet Jewry, 1939–1953*,
the entire Soviet Jewish community was then reduced to a status
they themselves called "fifth-rate invalids," a term that referred
to the fifth entry in the internal identity card which all Soviet
citizens had to carry, an entry indicating the bearer's "nationali-
ty." Gilboa writes that being labeled in their identity cards as
Jews,

> almost entirely diminished the value of such attributes as ex-
> pert knowledge, capacity for work, excellent qualifications,
> and loyalty. The fifth entry requirement was applied indis-
> criminately, often claiming as its victims persons entirely di-
> vorced from Judaism from the religious, linguistic, cultural,
> social, or emotional aspects. In some respects the situation of
> the Jews had become worse than it had been under the Tsarist
> regime. . . . During Stalin's last five years the Jews were often
> confronted with a biological barrier, which even their repudi-
> ation of Judaism and assimilation did not enable them to break
> through.

Jews were removed from sensitive areas such as cities and
forced to outer areas where it was more difficult to make a living.
Jews who sought to use the laws regarding restitution of property seized by the Nazis were blocked. Jewish Communists who
wished to maintain their status—and their lives—began to echo
the Party line that Zionism was bad, linked to the evils of capitalism and cosmopolitanism, and that further emigration of Jews
from the Soviet Union to Israel must cease. Purges of Jews in the
top ranks of military and government organizations followed.

The situation cried out for response from the Jewish world

beyond the borders of the USSR, and the JDC was a leader in that response. Earlier, the JDC's establishment of the Société de Secours et d'Entr'Aide (SSE) in Geneva to carry on its work in the Soviet satellite countries was discussed. Two other major programs for trying to reach the Jews of the USSR between the early 1950s and the mid-1980s were the Lishka and Relief-in-Transit (RIT).

THE LISHKA

The Lishka began in 1952 as an initiative of the government of Israel in response to the spiraling anti-Semitism of the late Stalinist period. David Bartov, the Russian-born Israeli jurist who would eventually become the leader of Lishka, recalls that its operations began because of the alarming possibility that there could be the equivalent of another Holocaust, this time in Soviet-controlled countries. "The danger for Soviet Jews," Bartov says starkly, "was disappearance."

In 1952, Ben-Gurion summoned Shaul Avigur, a driving force in Aliyah Bet, the arm of the provisional government that had helped Jews from Europe emigrate to Israel by nonofficial means in the immediate postwar period. Avigur was sometimes known as Ben-Gurion's gray eminence, and in 1952 Ben-Gurion asked Avigur to form a new organization from the core of Aliyah Bet, which was then in the process of shutting down. The new secret organization was to aim at the Jews of the Soviet bloc. Its ultimate goal was to spur further *aliyah,* emigration to Israel, but until such an emigration occurred, its proximate goal was to keep the flame of Judaism alive within the Soviet Union.

Avigur was already a legend for his zeal and passion during the war of independence. Motke Yanai, who had been associated with Avigur in the army and who would work with him for many years in the new organization, recalls Avigur as a dedicated military man who turned his talents eagerly toward the new and subtler task of stimulating the emigration of Soviet Jews. The new organization headed by Avigur was known by various names, the most-used being the Lishka, understood as the

Liaison office of the Foreign Office, or the Adviser to the prime minister for Jewish Affairs in Eastern Europe. The Lishka reported directly to the prime minister, and its activities and budget remained secret for nearly forty years. Only recently, in the post-Communist era, have a few details about its operation been made public.

The Lishka had two aims: to encourage and enable the emigration of Russian and Eastern European Jews to Israel, and to function as the catalyst for Jewish reawakening in the Soviet Union. In large measure, and right from the beginning, the JDC provided funds for many programs that were, in effect, a continuation of a partnership between the state of Israel and the American organization that had worked well during and immediately after the war. A first grant of $20,000, issued on the instructions of Charles Jordan, was followed by forty years of much larger underwriting of the operations of the Lishka by the JDC. This direct, sustained partnership of the Lishka with the JDC also remained mostly hidden for forty years. Frequently, during that period, JDC leaders had to be discreet about the extent of the organization's cooperation with this arm of the State of Israel.

Goldman's friends Shaike Dan and Motke Yanai were among the first recruits to the Lishka. They served under Akiva Lewinsky, who had been involved in rescuing and bringing to Israel youth whose families had been lost in the Holocaust. Another early member of the Lishka was Nehemiah Levanon. In later life, Levanon has begun to tell stories about the Lishka.

A crucial story recounts what happened after a bomb exploded in the basement of the Soviet embassy in Tel Aviv in February of 1953. The Soviets recalled their emissaries and broke off diplomatic relations with Israel. Shortly, Levanon was posted to Stockholm and charged with finding routes for Jews from the USSR to come to Israel. And after Stalin died in March of 1953, when diplomatic relations between Israel and the USSR were restored, Levanon was posted to Moscow as an agricultural attaché to make the outreach to Soviet Jews directly. In recent years, he reconstructed his first impressions:

When we met the Jews, it was a terrible shock. A whole generation had emerged for whom being Jewish was nothing but a stigma. They had no language, no history, no knowledge about being Jewish—but they were still Jews. . . . At the beginning the main effort was for *aliyah*. But we were sufficiently humble to realize that it would be a long struggle to open the gates. . . . We had two challenges: to open the gates, and to get through to the Jews in any way possible with Hebrew and Jewish culture.

After two years of work in the embassy, Levanon was briefly detained by authorities while meeting with some local Jews in a Moscow apartment, then deported. Others continued the work, especially Israel's diplomats—some of whom did it willingly, others under protest. According to Bartov, diplomats stationed in the Soviet Union would spend most of their time working to meet Soviet Jews. The diplomats would leave them items such as Bibles, Hebrew grammars, and religious articles, whose purpose was to encourage them to continue some semblance of Jewish lives; they'd also leave other books, films, and tapes to counter the Soviet government's barrage of anti-Israel and anti-Semitic propaganda. Every Israeli official entering the Soviet Union, and even tourists from Israel (and some from other countries, including the United States), would come with baggage loaded down with books, calendars, Israeli newspapers, and other materials—all forbidden by Soviet law. "We would never spend more than one or two days a week in Moscow," Bartov recalls, "because we were always out somewhere in a smaller city, doing this work." As Chaim Potok detailed the operation in *The Gates of November: Chronicles of the Slepak Family*, these Israelis would travel throughout the Soviet Union,

> leaving behind them with seeming carelessness a Bible here, a periodical there, in a synagogue, an apartment, on a park bench, at a summer beach, as one might discard a newspaper after a train ride. Everywhere in the Soviet Union meeting anxious and forlorn Jews— in an old bazaar in Samarkand, a resort on the Black Sea, a synagogue in Lithuania, a village in

the Caucasus, a town in Georgia—often by chance and at times by design, enabling them to experience the presence of an Israeli, and witnessing in those Jews a sudden spark of astonishment, a rising buoyancy of spirit.

In exchange for these materials, the Israelis would seek the names and addresses of Jews and other information that would enable contact to be maintained. Levanon and others also continued Lishka work in Washington, New York, London, and other capitals of the west. In an interview, Levanon recalls that articulate politicians, more so than field operatives like Shaike and Motke, could "try and persuade friends in the State Department and on the Hill and [American] Jews that consistent pressure of public and political opinion in the West can have positive results and can make the Kremlin change its attitude toward the [Soviet] Jews and eventually open the doors for emigration."

Bartov contends that "without the JDC, I'm not sure if Lishka would have been able to reach its goals." He points out that most of the American and Israeli tourists who acted as proselytes for pro-Israel and Jewish life within the Soviet Union in the Lishka program never knew that the funding for their activities came from the Joint.

The JDC's cooperation with the Lishka, Goldman recalls, "was talked about only in general terms at the highest level of the JDC executive committee, and the real destination of the funds was never identified in the budget."

RIT: Relief-in-Transit

A second effort to aid Jews in Russia and its satellite countries was known as Relief-in-Transit, or RIT, because it had originally begun as an assistance program for Jews who were in transit from a place of danger to Israel. In 1952–53, when the JDC was kicked out of Eastern Europe, what had been an overt program had to go underground; Relief-in-Transit became monetary and material packages sent to sustain people behind the Iron Curtain. A letter in the JDC files, from Charles Jordan to Moses

Beckelman, in early 1953, states that the government of Israel had decided that henceforth "there could not be any records of the purpose for which expenditures are being made and that the JDC would have to be satisfied to spend its money without the kind of records that have been given us in the past . . . [because] it is considered that continuing to keep records on [recipients of aid] might endanger their lives."

The sending of packages into Soviet-controlled areas had actually begun during World War II. Akiva Kohane, a long-time JDC professional, had been part of a JDC-backed effort in Teheran to send relief packages across the border into Soviet Central Asia to aid Jews who had fled there from Poland and were cut off from other assistance and programs. The Teheran-based effort was run by a travel agency staffed by Zionist partisans. Many of the particulars of this program were repeated in later efforts. Clothing, food, and medicines were sent to specific persons at specific addresses, with postage and duties prepaid. Recipients could either use the materials in the packages or could resell the contents at relatively high prices and obtain cash with which to buy necessities. "Packages for relatives was a tradition among immigrants," Goldman points out. He tells the story of his own father scraping together enough money to send the occasional package from Boston to his own relatives in the Ukraine during the 1920s and 1930s.

In the post–World War II period, packages continued to be sent from Israel, and supposedly by Eastern Europeans who had become Israelis to their relatives "back home." The bulk of this work was funded by the JDC. But the program began to hit its stride in the 1950s, when the JDC was kicked out of Eastern Europe and when the Lishka was just beginning. The RIT package program expanded greatly as a partnership of the JDC and the state of Israel. Its packages were sent to a deliberately wide geographical area, in order to reach as many places as possible and to avoid the appearance of being directed only to places where Jews were concentrated. Some packages were transshipped from inside the satellite countries to particular recipients in Russia and Siberia, for instance, to prisoners and their families.

That most of the packages were able to get through to recipients was heartening, but the accomplishment was also a subject of curiosity. An Israeli official who made inquiries behind the Iron Curtain learned that the packages were being allowed to go through as part of a post-Stalin policy that encouraged a rise in the standard of living for Soviet and satellite-country people, which itself was permitted in order to deflect anger from the repressive policies of the governments. Motke Yanai, who with Shaike Dan was principally responsible for the operation of the package program to the USSR, thinks there was a more practical reason for Soviet cooperation: "The Russians made a lot of money from allowing the packages in," he points out, arguing that all of the fees for permitting passage of the packages went to the government. In addition, the Soviet state also benefited because the packages contained goods that were in short supply, goods that soon passed through the so-called "gray market" to land in the officially sanctioned shops that catered to higher-level government employees who had enough rubles (and the proper sanction) to buy Western goods. "Everybody knew the packages came from Jews, from the Joint, but nobody asked questions," Yanai insists. He maintains that the Soviet-bloc governments could easily have shut down the program at any time, and that their reluctance to do so is evidence that they needed the money and goods that the package program brought into their countries.

From a budget of $100,000 in 1951, the Eastern bloc RIT program reached more than $4 million in 1962. On the USSR list for RIT there were some 25,000 names—a very small fraction of the remaining several million Jews believed to be living there; in consequence, only about a thousand packages a month could be shipped from Israel. A 1963 JDC report suggests the inadequacy of what the package program was able to do in regard to the Jews in the USSR, and the frustration associated with it:

> Most of the families assisted in the U.S.S.R. are Orthodox and
> aged people. They generally are not eligible for social security,

since few can show a record of employment over a period of twenty-five years or longer. Furthermore, these people who were largely engaged in small businesses, or as shopkeepers, are considered remnants of bourgeois elements and are not in any case eligible for pension rights. The dependency of these older and religious Jews in the USSR on outside help is very great, and it is unfortunate that packages cannot be sent more frequently, and to all of the registered cases.

A typical letter from a Russian package recipient puts the relationship starkly: "In times of need children turn to their parents. You are our parents, taking the place of those who were wiped out by the Nazis." Jordan observed that the need of those "children" was for $160 a month in aid, and the JDC was able to send them, by various means, only $160 a year.

The 1967 war between Israel and its Arab neighbors brought immediate shifts in Soviet policy. Among them was a decision by the Soviets to no longer accept packages shipped into the USSR from Israel. Accordingly, the shipment points of the package program were relocated to a half-dozen cities in Europe where the USSR maintained commercial attachés who could issue licenses to send in packages. Yanai contends that the commercial shippers in such places as Denmark, Finland, England, and Switzerland did make some money on the packages, but not very much, and that they did business "with the understanding that they were doing humanitarian work." Even after the change to Western country shippers, Yanai says, the Soviet authorities and the Jewish recipients of the packages "knew very well that this was a Jewish and Israeli-originated operation. And what's more important, the government and the recipients gave these packages the name 'Joint *pecklach*'—Yiddish for packages."

Another result of the 1967 war was newly awakened interest in Israeli and Jewish affairs by some Jews inside the USSR, accompanied by protests of some Soviet Jews against the pro-Arab stance of their government. There was an increase in the number of Soviet Jews applying to emigrate to Israel. The term *refusenik* came into vogue, a term indicating Jews who were refused exit permits by the government and who were then dropped from their state-mandated jobs and became targets for governmental neglect. Unable to make a living because no one would employ them, these refuseniks became dependent on friends and relatives for food, clothing, and shelter.

Around this time, the part of the RIT program that originated in Israel became a separate, nonprofit Israeli organization known as the Society for Assistance to Needy Jews in the Diaspora. The package-sending program also became known as Azriel, which means "God is my help."

By 1972, through receipts for its packages, through names given by émigrés in Israel and in the United States, and through other means, Azriel had compiled a list of 70,000 current names and addresses of Jewish families. Such information was inordinately difficult to obtain because Soviet Jews had reason to believe that if their particulars were given to foreigners, the state would retaliate against them. When on a visit to northern Russia in 1972, a JDC executive office committee member offered to send a young man some Beethoven concerto recordings, the response from the young man was, "Never write me, never send me anything, you'll destroy my life."

Sander Levinson, a young Moldavian Jew who applied to go to Israel, lost his job as a blacksmith, and his wife her job as a music teacher. They were subsisting on packages until he was arrested and convicted for having his sister sell for him one of the articles in the package; he was sentenced to six years of hard labor for his offense. He and many others who suffered similar fates because they had wished to emigrate to Israel came to be known to Jewish organizations as "Prisoners of Zion."

The files of names and addresses were important not only to identify Jews in need of assistance but to gather documentation that could be used for the affidavits and personal invitations to join relatives, which Soviet Jews had to have in order to successfully apply for emigration. The Soviet government liked to appear as though it was a supporter of uniting families, so any emigrant who could say he or she was joining his or her family in Israel had a better chance of being allowed out of the USSR.

The JDC's card index had expanded rapidly. It included increasing numbers of activists, and of people imprisoned, fired from their jobs, or otherwise penalized for applying to emigrate. Accordingly, the JDC raised its budget for packages to $2 million a year in 1972. When as a condition of détente between the U.S. and the USSR, permission was given to 100,000 Soviet Jews to emigrate, there arose, in the opinion of Lishka director Nehemiah Levanon, an historic opportunity for the JDC and Azriel to do more, not less, than they had been doing. "We have to realize that with all the changes … millions of Soviet Jews are still cut off and isolated," he wrote the JDC. It was therefore important to recognize that

> Over and above their material value, the modest parcels . . . have an immense importance. They provide the moral support and encouragement for thousands of Jewish families. They are a constant reminder that the Soviet Jews are not left alone and that there is a warm-hearted and understanding Jewish people in the world, ready to help their brethren in the Soviet Union.

The JDC responded by almost doubling its allocation, to more than $3.6 million annually for the package program, about 12 percent of the JDC's total budget in 1976. In addition, the JDC partly financed package programs run separately by the Lubavitcher Chasidim organization, which sent parcels to its followers in the Soviet Union, and a similar program administered by the Association of Baltic Jews, headquartered outside of the Soviet Union, which sent packages to Jews living in the Baltic states that had become part of the USSR.

Jewish Emigration from the USSR and the "Drop-Out" Problem

Emigration from the Soviet Union ebbed and flowed. In 1973–74, discussion in both houses of Congress had resulted in the passage of what eventually became known as the Jackson-Vanik Freedom of Emigration Bill, which threatened to prevent the USSR from being awarded Most Favored Nation status and from receiving American loans so long as it continued to hamper free emigration. The Nixon Administration, and in particular Secretary of State Henry Kissinger, had opposed the bill, arguing that obstructing trade with the USSR would be bad for the United States and ultimately bad for Soviet Jews who wished to emigrate. American protests on behalf of freedom of emigration for Soviet Jews kept mounting, and this had resulted in the bill's passage and in the subsequent widening of the emigration gates in the USSR.

In what eventually became a mass exodus, during the next decade hundreds of thousands of Soviet Jews emigrated to Israel, their numbers so large that they changed both the character of the State of Israel and, to a lesser extent, the USSR that they left behind, draining it of some of its most productive citizens.

Goldman took up his duties as chief executive officer of the JDC in 1976, and though the JDC and all Jewish organizations in the West were thrilled at the recent loosening of the Soviet barriers to Jewish emigration, an important and difficult problem had cropped up in consequence. Thousands of Soviet Jews who had left the USSR with invitations to go to Israel, had decided to become dropouts, or *noshrim*, opting instead to emigrate to the United States, Canada, or other Western countries. More than one-third of the 13,000 who left the USSR for Israel in 1975 had ended up in the West. The dropout figure had jumped from 5 percent in 1973 to 20 percent in 1974. Goldman and his associates were alarmed because preliminary figures for 1976 indicated that the number of people who would leave the Soviet Union would be higher, and so would the percentage of dropouts. Akiva Kohane wrote Goldman on March 15, 1976, that in the month of February, for the first time ever, the percentage of dropouts to the West exceeded the percentage of those émigrés completing their journeys to Israel.

The State of Israel had gone to great efforts to find individual Soviet Jews, extend them invitations to emigrate, and make arrangements to transport and receive them; immigration was widely believed to be the lifeblood of Israel, and redirection of people exiting the Soviet Union to other destinations thinned that lifeblood. Also, the diverting of Soviet Jews to the West undermined the delicate balance of détente between the United States and the USSR that had resulted in spurring the Soviet government to permit Jews to rejoin their families in Israel. Since 1971, support for emigration of Soviet Jews had been codified into a United States Trade Reform Act that the Soviet government desperately wanted and into the SALT strategic arms limitation agreements between the two superpowers. Less than a thousand Soviet Jews per year were being given direct visas to emigrate to the United States, but emigration to Israel, considered family reunions, was seen by the Soviet government as a way to win the favor of the strong Jewish lobby in the United States. The USSR was ostensibly permitting Jews to emigrate to Israel in order to join their families under a government commitment to the Helsinki Final Act, which mandated signatory governments to enable the unification of families across national borders.

The diverting upset the Soviet government's balancing act in regard to the Middle East region. "The Arabs know," the Israeli diplomat Arie Lova Eliav wrote in 1974, that by opening the floodgates of emigration, "the Kremlin rulers . . . could double Israel's population within a short period of time. . . . The Soviets are making good use of this concealed weapon and . . . its presence is felt in every room where the Soviets conduct negotiations with the Arabs." But when fewer emigrants from the USSR began to end up in Israel—because they dropped out to go to the West—the Arabs became more able to shrug off Soviet pressure.

A third dimension of the problem: the wish of Soviet Jews to change their destination, once out of the USSR, presented a constellation of bureaucratic difficulties for American Jewish organizations assisting in the emigration.

Beyond these main problems were others that were more subtle: the dropouts were jeopardizing Jewish activism within the Soviet Union by implying that people agitating for exit visas to go to Israel were only doing so as a cover for escaping to the West. The rising number and percentage of dropouts gave Soviet authorities reason to put more pressure on Jews within the USSR. Last, there was a fear that if the number of dropouts rose, the Soviets would reduce or stop emigration because their rationale for emigration to Israel was repatriation and family reunion.

Jewish emigrants from the Soviet Union left Moscow by air to Vienna or on the "Chopin Express" train. In Vienna, they were met by the Jewish Agency; if they were destined for Israel, they received only minimal orientation before being readied for flights to Israel. It was upon the transmigrants' arrival in Vienna, however, that many of them announced a wish to go to the West, and opted to take a train to Rome where they were housed until such time as they could obtain refugee visas to the United States and the other Western countries. By long-standing arrangement dating back to the 1950s, the JDC shared the expenses of Jewish migrants who wanted to go to the West. "HIAS [the Hebrew Immigrant Aid Society of the United States] was treating the Soviet Jews as though they were refugees who had no place to go," Goldman recalls. Goldman argued that ever since the State of Israel was established and the "Law of Return" was passed, no Jew needed to be a refugee because that law guaranteed him asylum in Israel, which meant that he would technically never be a stateless refugee. Those who dropped out of the transmigrant program while holding an Israeli invitation and visa were making the entire visa program appear to the Soviets as a subterfuge, and their actions would endanger Jewish emigration. The JDC could not refuse to help transmigrants because they were Jews in need; but it wasn't happy about their decisions to abuse the Israeli *vysovs* (invitations) they had obtained.

Until the end of the 1973 war in the Middle East, the problem of dropouts had not existed. There had been virtually no dropouts from the emigration program. Only after that war had the number and percentage been steadily increasing, and in the late 1970s and early 1980s there was a fear that tens of thousands of Soviet Jews would congregate in Rome, pending their receiving visas from the United States and other Western countries. Of the Jewish transmigrants from the USSR who were temporarily housed in Rome, a 1975 report said 80 percent wanted to go to the United States. Most of those people had been sitting and waiting in Rome for at least six months in anticipation of receiving papers that would allow them to enter the United States. In Rome, the JDC operated facilities for the transmigrants under a contract with the United States Immigration and Naturalization Service. Quite suddenly in late March of 1976, Congress refused to appropriate the amount that the State Department had requested for this and for other programs, many of which involved Christian voluntary organizations. An intensive lobbying effort had to be mounted before the several million dollars owed to the JDC by the State Department could be approved by Congress (along with many other State Department obligations) and eventually paid.

Among the reasons given by potential dropouts for choosing the United States rather than Israel as a destination were that the United States had always been seen as the embodiment of freedom by Soviets, that life would be easier in the United States than in Israel, that they had relatives in the United States and not in Israel, that the climate in Israel was too hot for people used to colder lands, that in the USSR they had not been able to participate in Jewish life and thus felt themselves unprepared to exist fully as Jews in Israel, that they had too little information about Israel and had been told that it was a totalitarian country, and that they did not want to settle in Israel because it might mean becoming involved in a war.

There was an additional and very powerful reason for transmigrants to choose to go to the United States rather than to Israel: an outpouring of support from American-based agencies that, having spent years lobbying in the United States and in the USSR to permit Jews to leave the Soviet Union, now felt a positive inclination to assist the émigrés to come to the United States and to ease their integration into American society. The Los Angeles Jewish Federation reported spending over $1 million for resettling of Soviet Jews in that city in 1975. The New York Association of New Americans, using funds from the United Jewish Appeal, was able to give grants worth up to $3,500 for a family of four to those re-settling in New York

City. The facts about Americans' generosity toward the new immigrants were publicized, while the fact that the government of Israel actually spent the equivalent of ten times as much, about $35,000 for a family of four Soviet Jews to resettle in Israel, was not well known. "Freedom of choice" was a phrase that had many positive reverberations for Americans, and the notion that the Soviet Jews were exercising freedom of choice in deciding to come to the United States and not to Israel was an idea that drew wholehearted support from many American Jews.

There was also support for "freedom of choice" from some American-based Jewish philanthropic organizations, chief among them HIAS, which had been virtually dormant for years because Jewish immigration to the United States had slowed to a trickle in the 1960s. The challenge of assisting Soviet Jews in resettling in the United States had reawakened such organizations. As Dan Margalit, the Washington, D.C., correspondent for the Jerusalem newspaper *Ha'aretz*, reported in December of 1974,

> For many years, the Jewish communities [in America] did not have a real challenge. What is the Jewish challenge in America: to support the synagogue? To observe kashrut rituals? Now, the Russian immigration has brought life to the arteries of the Jewish institutions . . .

Margalit closed his article by saying that the government of Israel needed to convene a high-level conference with the presidents of American Jewish organizations to convince them that they must continue to spur the Soviet Jews who had left the Soviet Union with the help of Israel not to go to the United States.

A year and a half later, such a meeting took place. Goldman telephoned the leaders of two other American-based organizations about the problem and soon attended a conference among several leaders in a Cincinnati hotel room.

Among these parties, there was good agreement on the nature and dimensions of the problem, but little agreement on what could or should be done about it. The urgency of the situation was reinforced by new information coming out of the USSR that recent applicants for exit to Israel had been called into Soviet government offices, interrogated for hours about their "Israeli relatives," had their exit papers torn up, and had been forced to sign documents denouncing those relatives in Israel. There were also suggestions in the Israeli press that HIAS, the Jewish Agency, and the JDC were competing for the loyalty of the transmigrants, with the American-based organizations supposedly urging the Soviets to go to the United States rather than to Israel. Although the JDC wanted the transmigrants with Israeli *vysovs* to go only to Israel, the organization was already in the business of being a contractor to the United States government in housing the migrants who wished to go to the United States, so it was difficult for the JDC to adequately refute the charge.

JDC President Don Robinson, in Rome to view the situation, was amazed to go to the Sunday flea market and see Soviet transmigrants engaged in selling trinkets and souvenirs from Russia, not because they were penniless but rather to earn additional money to take to the United States. Robinson was saddened by this sight and conveyed to Goldman a sense of urgency to do something about the dropouts.

A SOLUTION TO THE DROPOUT PROBLEM

In June, Goldman and Akiva Kohane set out to personally explore the dimensions of the problem, accompanied by Goldman's son David, then a young law student. Among other tasks, they decided to accompany a group of dropouts on the train from Vienna to Rome. In response to a delicate political situation, the Austrian government had insisted that any such train taking Soviet transmigrants to another country be loaded in Vienna and not opened until its arrival in Rome. The train on which the Goldmans and Kohane traveled in the company of seventy-three Russians was sealed, and although fitted for passengers, it reminded many of the sealed cattle cars in which the Nazis transported Jews from their homes to concentration and extermination camps. The trip took twenty-three hours, and the train arrived in Rome on the eve of the Jewish holiday of Shavuoth. Goldman had noted that there "was no sense of holiday" at the hotel where the transmigrants had stayed, "no symbol or semblance of Jewishness." Moreover, compared to the emigrants from the USSR that Kohane recalled having seen in 1972 weeping with joy at being in Vienna on their way to Israel, the current crop of transmigrants "seemed just like ordinary travelers" and were "not excited about having landed in freedom." The lack of Jewish content in the welcome rankled Goldman as much as the emigrants' seemingly "nonchalant" attitude.

"On the train from Vienna to Rome we talked to seven heads of family and other members of the family units, representing thirty-three out of the seventy-three Russians en route," Goldman recalled. All but one of the families had received their *vysovs*, the Israeli invitations, at the request of previous dropouts who had learned how to manipulate the exit system. When the Goldmans reached Rome, they visited thirteen more heads of family units and learned that these would-be emigrants to the United States had sent in requests for *vysovs* for eighty-five further Soviet Jews still inside the USSR and expected that if exit permits were granted, none of those would actually emigrate to Israel but would instead try to go to the United States, Canada, or Australia.

Goldman's reaction to the situation was "motivated by Jewish compassion," comprised of equal measures of general compassion for all Jews, the wish to help the cause of Judaism, and the wish to strengthen Israel by means of new immigrants. He initiated action in three directions.

First, he importuned the American State Department to expedite the process of obtaining visas for those dropouts who were waiting for papers that would allow them into the United States. "It was costing the United States $1 million a month for the group," he recalls, "and besides, it was unfair to keep them in limbo for six months. This was just a matter of paperwork, and I thought it could be done more quickly." Eventually, prodded by Goldman and others, the State Department and the

Immigration and Naturalization Service (INS) managed to shorten the waiting time in Rome from seven to three months. These same groups, with Goldman in the lead, also lobbied the government to obtain more American visas for the transmigrants who were determined to become Americans.

Secondly, Goldman asked the education ministry in Israel to develop an informal education program for the Jews awaiting passage in Rome. He thought it was unjust that many children in Rome had been without schooling for periods as long as seven months. Goldman's earlier request to the Jewish Agency to provide the money had been turned down on the grounds that these Soviet Jews were going to the United States, not to Israel. "The education ministry also initially declined to set up schools for the same reasons," Goldman says. "I told them, 'These are *your* people, these are *my* people, and we have a responsibility to educate them as Jews.'" Goldman's reasoning struck a chord with a man of legendary compassion and imagination inside the government, Chaim Zippori, the director of Israel's community centers. Zippori became involved, and he and Goldman managed to change more official minds and to make an arrangement whereby the JDC subcontracted with the Ministry of Education and Culture and the Israel Community Centers Corporation to set up informal schools in the vicinity of Rome for transmigrant children and to set up educational courses for the adults. The objectives were three: socialization of the emigrants to assist them in rediscovering their Jewish roots, alleviation of stress and anxiety accompanying the transition from existing in a totalitarian system to living in a democratic system, and the encouragement of a favorable attitude toward Judaism and Israel. A survey found that more than one-third of the transmigrants participated in the Jewish education programs.

At the time, and continuing down to the present day, some Israelis harshly criticized the actions of the JDC in regard to the dropouts, charging that the JDC actively encouraged Soviet Jews to go to the United States rather than to Israel. "It was a reflection," Goldman says, "of the general public in Israel being unable to differentiate between JDC and HIAS; they didn't realize that we had different objectives and policies." The belief that the JDC was acting in other than the best interests of Israel was extremely hard to dislodge from public memory.

In order to interrupt the cycle of current dropouts providing the means for later Soviet emigrants to drop out after receiving Israeli *vysovs*, Goldman sent a personal message through his son David to the government of Israel that it ought not to send *vysovs* to the eighty-five people in the USSR whose names had been provided by the current dropouts, but that during this period of détente HIAS should initiate a program of invitations for United States family reunions, as the government of Israel did. The Israel government response was that they could only agree if such American invitations were issued. Otherwise, it would be immoral for them not to send Israeli invitations. HIAS, however, was not prepared to undertake this route because the Israeli visa already had a record of success.

DEVELOPING A GLOBAL JEWISH STRATEGY

In the third and perhaps the most important action, Goldman suggested to Yitzhak Rabin, the prime minister of Israel, that he appoint a committee to review the entire matter, consisting of high-level representatives from the prime minister's office, the Foreign Office, the JDC, the Jewish Agency, HIAS, and other broad-focus organizations that were working with the transmigrants. "We had a problem that was facing the entire Jewish world," Goldman remembers, "and what I had in mind was that the leadership should develop principles and policies to address that problem, ones that would reflect all of the issues, all of our concerns, and would carve up and allocate our responsibilities. Later on, I began to call this sort of response a 'global Jewish strategy.'" The most responsible leaders recognized, as did Goldman, that from the late 1930s and through the 1950s, ad hoc global strategies had been developed by the philanthropic agencies in response to important and threatening matters, but after the crises spawned by World War II had resolved, coordination of response among the philanthropic agencies and the government of Israel had dissipated. Now it was time, in Goldman's view, to reinvigorate the idea.

Precisely how to do so and what the implications of developing a global Jewish strategy might entail were not yet clear to Goldman in mid-1976. In later years, he was able to articulate what he meant. "I don't believe that it is possible today to have a Jewish policy that will be run by American Jewry as they see fit and by Israeli Jewry as they see fit. There is one Jewish people . . . [and] there are problems of the entire Jewish people which the representatives of the Israeli government and the leadership of the Jewish people in the diaspora must discuss together and try to find solutions."

In the instance of the dropouts, in July of 1976 Goldman's suggestion to the prime minister that a top-level committee be convened and set on the course of making a global strategy was immediately implemented. Representatives of American and Israeli organizations convened in Geneva, with Goldman and Levanon (of the Lishka) as coordinators. The meeting had been preceded by an extraordinary conclave of all the American-based organizations, who among themselves had agreed on a co-ordinated program that became the agenda of the conference. The essence of the plan was to encourage transmigrants with *vysovs* to Israel to go only to Israel. Toward that end, the government of Israel would be urged to revise the issuance of *vysovs* to Soviet Jews with the understanding that the papers would be used solely to emigrate to Israel. At the same time, the American organizations would lobby the American government for more directly issued visas, and would also curtail or replace current practices that in effect encouraged transmigrants not to continue on to Israel but to be diverted to other countries. A more disciplined approach to which agency would do what tasks was to be established and put into practice.

No firm decisions on these large policy changes were immediately made, but they were placed under active consideration. A "committee of eight," consisting of four Israelis and four Americans, was impaneled by the prime minister and charged with meeting monthly to help resolve the problem.

Addressing the gathering, the prime minister emphasized two points: (1) that the increasing number and percentage of dropouts endangered future emigration to Israel and needed to be reversed, so that more Soviet Jews could leave the USSR to make *aliyah* to Israel; and (2) that while an emigrating Jew always had a right to freedom of choice as to his or her final destination, Israeli and American Jewish organizations did not have a moral responsibility to aid a person who had an Israeli *vysov* if he or she was not en route to Israel. Jewish emigration should not appear as anti-government but rather as a humanitarian act of repatriation.

The conferees agreed with these positions, but the prospects of attempting to ensure that those with Israeli *vysovs* actually went to Israel rather than elsewhere, and of possibly curtailing aid to dropouts, did not sit well with many organizations—particularly in the United States, where the slogan of "freedom of choice" became a battle cry. The JDC worked with the dropouts only after they got a written release from the Jewish Agency representing the government of Israel. According to a report in the *Washington Post,* the proposal to end aid to emigrating Soviet Jews with Israeli *vysovs* who were choosing to go to other Western countries was developing into "a bitter and emotional controversy."

The committee of eight was enlarged to include organizations dealing specifically with Soviet Jews and became a committee of ten. Although this body reached no decision on a recommendation for a policy change by Israel, it cohered around changes in the care of transmigrants in Vienna and Rome.

By mid-September 1976, President Gerald Ford was able to tell a meeting of the B'nai B'rith in Washington that he was working with Soviet Communist Party Secretary Leonid Brezhnev on restoring Soviet Jewish emigration to the United States to the levels it had reached prior to the 1973 war—an action that would provide more Soviet Jews with visas to the United States, which would help alleviate the problem of dropouts who held Israeli *vysovs*. On the other hand, Austrian Chancellor Bruno Kreisky stated explicitly to foreign reporters that "Whoever comes to Austria to emigrate elsewhere will not only be admitted, but we watch also that his right to choose the country to which he wants to go should be respected." Kreisky announced that he opposed any attempt by Israeli or American Jewish agencies to limit the movement or destination of the transmigrants.

Shortly, there were reports in the press suggesting that a rift had grown up between the American Jewish organizations and the government of Israel on the dropout issue. Public pressure to do nothing that would restrict the emigration of Soviet Jews—to whatever destination—continued unabated and delayed the setting of a date on which any new policy could take effect. Changes in governments in Washington and Jerusalem, with the election of Jimmy Carter to the American presidency and of Menachem Begin as prime minister of Israel, along with other factors, prevented for the next six months any implementation of a new policy on dropouts.

By mid-1977, the culminating effect of simply considering the instigation of a new policy, of pressure in the United States to issue additional visas to come to America, of the changes implemented by HIAS, the JDC, and the Jewish Agency in processing transmigrants in Vienna and Rome, and of moves toward peace in the Middle East by Egypt and Israel, began to ease the dropout trend. While in the first half of 1977, 50 percent of the transmigrants dropped out, in the second half of the year, more than 50 percent were opting to continue on to Israel. The dip was only temporary, however, and the total number of people awaiting resettlement in Italy continued to increase, to the point where the JDC was continually caring for approximately five thousand transmigrants; as one bunch would leave for the United States, just as many new Soviet Jews would arrive in Rome, needing food, clothing, shelter, and education. The difficulties of dealing with the dropouts and of the JDC operating facilities to assist them in Vienna and Rome until American entry visas could be obtained for them persisted for another decade. On the positive side, the notion of attempting to articulate and coordinate a global Jewish strategy in response to a problem that touched upon all the Jews of the world was importantly established.

CHAPTER SEVEN

Global Jewish Strategy, Step Two
Helping the World

WHILE THE WORK in Israel and in Eastern Europe proceeded apace, the next step in Goldman's elaboration of a global Jewish strategy came in response to crises in Iran and Ethiopia.

Goldman and the JDC were beginning to recognize a recurring difficulty of coordinating various humanitarian groups' efforts: the near-impossibility of holding agencies other than their own to a coordinated agenda. Despite the best intentions and a continuing effort, Goldman couldn't get the many other Jewish organizations to work together.

Part of the problem was the attitudes of the Jews in the diaspora toward Israel: in the future, it would no longer be a matter of unquestioning obedience. Therefore, while Jews would probably remain solidly united in their commitment to Israel, the relationship between Israel and the diaspora would have to become more mature—to become a relationship of mutual aid, and not of giving and receiving. Mutuality of concern would have to spur Israel and the philanthropic agencies to develop better coordinated Jewish strategies on such broad issues as the continued viability of Israel, the religious-cultural state of the diaspora, the defense of Jewish rights in the diaspora, and the achieving of financial independence of Israel from the diaspora, while simultaneously establishing an interdependence between the two entities. Goldman believed that interdependence and maturity of outlook must be the goals of the JDC.

UNREST IN IRAN

The need for the JDC and other Jewish aid organizations to work together became acutely evident during the late 1970s, during the fall of the Shah and the ascension of the Ayatollah Khomeini. For decades, the JDC had been working in Iran, where a Jewish population of about 80,000 made it one of the ten largest Jewish communities in the world. A small minority in a primarily Moslem country, Iranian Jews were well entrenched; some were wealthy and many were in Iran's burgeoning middle class, although the majority were poor. Only a few held significant government positions. Their Iranian Jewish relatives in New York and Los Angeles had also become relatively well-off. Fifty thousand Jews lived in Teheran and could trace their ancestry back to 700 B.C.E., when the Babylonian king forcibly settled a group of Jews in the area.

When Goldman visited Iran in 1973, Shah Mohammed Reza Pahlavi was at the height of his power, buying Phantom jets and one quarter of the equity of the Krupp industrial empire in Germany, and he affected deliberate benevolence toward the Jews in his country.

On that trip to Iran, Goldman found an entrenched JDC program badly in need of realignment. The schools being supported with JDC money were a mixed bag, some serving the very poor, others the middle class; Goldman's position was that the middle class should not be subsidized, only the poor. There were similar overreaching problems having to do with a large "free lunch" program, the medical clinics, and a JDC-supported Jewish hospital that was serving as many Moslems as Jews. Goldman wanted responsibility for these programs to be "revised so as to answer the needs of the poor and disadvantaged while those who can afford it pay for their share." Goldman concluded from his visit that there was great potential for the

Iranian Jewish community to sustain itself and take care of its more vulnerable members, and that the JDC, while helping the community to do so, must drastically change the ways in which JDC funds were being used in Iran.

Needing a new staff member to oversee the Teheran office of the JDC, Goldman found a likely candidate in Michael Schneider, who was then working in London for the Jewish Welfare Board. Born in South Africa, Schneider describes his deep involvement in the anti-apartheid campaign as "mother's milk," on the front lines of guerilla operations such as sabotage and smuggling people out of the country. Goldman thought Schneider was a perfect fit for the job, "Someone who knew how to sacrifice in the service of his ideal." For Schneider, the JDC's offer meant, as he later wrote, "a chance to get out of a gray suit after twelve years in the same organization," and a chance to work with Goldman, who in conversations over a period of months "introduced me to a global Jewish vision, of a world in need of repair, of communities in need of succor and restoration." Schneider was thrilled by the prospect of raising the level of what he was able to accomplish, but because of paperwork difficulties and other problems, could not take up his post in Teheran until August of 1978.

When Schneider arrived in Teheran, he found a country moving toward upheaval. Watching television in his hotel's lobby on the first day of the Moslem holy month of Ramadan, which was also Iran's Constitution Day, Schneider heard the Shah say that in response to the discontent he was taking some measures to liberalize the country, including scheduling free elections in the near future, more freedom of the press, and an openness to opposing views. These remarks did not sit well with native Iranian hotel guests and staff, and Schneider felt distinctly uneasy. A month later, huge crowds of silently protesting fundamentalists marching in the streets, some flagellating themselves, impressed Schneider by their "utter and absolute discipline." Although the CIA and Israel's Foreign Office did not believe that Khomeini, exiled leader of the Shiite Moslems, could return and overthrow the Shah, Schneider concluded just the opposite.

While Schneider went about streamlining and reducing the JDC-sponsored activities, antigovernment Iranians demonstrated and police fired bullets into crowds. In the wider world, U.S. President Jimmy Carter, Egyptian President Anwar Sadat, and Israeli Prime Minister Menachem Begin met at Camp David to try for peace in the Middle East. By November, after massive strikes in the oil fields and at the universities in Iran, Schneider had his family flew to safety in Israel. Delegations of Iranian Jewish leaders began to confide that they were exploring emigration possibilities.

In New York, after almost daily telephone conversations with Schneider, Goldman recognized that piecemeal efforts by groups such as Lubavitch and Agudat Israel to bring small numbers of Iranian Jews out of the country—well-meaning though they might be—might seriously harm the Iranian Jewish community, and he decided that only a concerted and organized effort by the world Jewish community could avoid the destruction of the Iranian Jews. Such a program, he wrote, would require "the submergence of organizational interests to the broader interests of global Jewry." While some groups had already begun efforts of their own, others had not because they insisted that even if Khomeini successfully made a revolution, it would not endanger Iran's Jews. The JDC was also being criticized for not doing enough to rescue Iranian Jews.

Schneider closed the JDC office, sent the staff home, and operated from the Hilton Hotel in Teheran, trying to maintain the JDC's projects by telephone contact. In late November, Khomeini called for a month of bloodletting, and the Shah attempted to head off revolution by having Shapour Bakhtiar, a trusted associate, form a civilian government.

That December in New York, Goldman convened an interagency group that included people from the government of Israel, ostensibly so that the JDC could present information from Schneider and others about the situation in Iran but really to have the group consider what could and should be done to help the Iranian Jews. "Some people inside the JDC questioned why we had to take the lead in this sort of coordination, but I felt that it needed to be done, and we had the best and most complete information about Iran." The assassination of an American oil executive in Iran on December 23, 1978, was an unmistakable signal to foreigners to leave the country.

Schneider and Goldman spoke daily during this period, using a bit of code to confuse any wiretappers; they avoided mentioning names of people or even initials. "The man who had been in Iran but was now in Europe" was Khomeini, "a cousin" was an Israeli official. Schneider believed that anti-Semitic posters and slogans on the walls were balanced by Khomeini's personal assurance to a friend that minority groups would not be persecuted when he returned. Goldman reported to his superiors Schneider's tale of despairing comments from the Israeli ambassador, and his description of a removal of a Jewish family done so openly that it provoked reaction from the surrounding Moslem community. By mid-January of 1979, while 15,000 Iranian Jews had left the country, 65,000 remained. On January 16, 1979, the Shah fled Iran.

Schneider traveled to Israel in an attempt to urge the government and the Jewish Agency to prepare to extract Iranian Jews from danger; he returned to Teheran in time to watch Khomeini's triumphant arrival on February 1, along with three million people in the streets. That day was "euphoric," but the next day, "reality set in" as Schneider realized that the revolution would be one of "retribution and revenge." He reported by phone to Goldman that, "There is still some possibility of a peaceful transition, but it's getting smaller." Nonetheless, the Iranian Jewish community leaders continued to oppose any mass extraction of people by Israeli or diaspora agencies. The community's appreciation of danger was so low that parents delayed sending their children out of the country until they could decide whether to send them to religious or secular schools. Schneider had difficulty convincing them that Khomeini's benevolence toward minorities might quickly fade. A three-week wait for visas to the United States or to Israel, and the lack of passports among the less wealthy, were added difficulties. So was the awareness by poor Iranian Jews—picked up from Israeli sources and broadcast on Iranian radio—that some Jews were fleeing Iran when others were unable to escape.

Finally, what "absolutely terrified" the local Jewish leaders, Schneider reported to Goldman, were direct attacks in mid-February. The Israeli Embassy in Teheran was trashed, the El Al airline became unable to fly into or out of the city, and street fighting erupted in Eshratabad, the lower-middle-class Jewish area. "I really think we're the only Jewish operating unit at the moment," Schneider reported in a phone call. Minutes later, the Hilton Hotel was attacked. Schneider took cover in a bathroom while shots riddled his room. Soldiers stripped him of the money he was carrying, and he was held by the mob for eight hours, only barely escaping with his life. Schneider phoned Goldman to say that the attacks on the hotels were a sign that everyone not in sympathy with the revolution must leave the country. Schneider started to do so, but still concerned with the many thousands of less well-to-do Iranian Jews who could not get out, Schneider authorized the burning of local JDC records, knowing that in some Communist countries such lists of locals who assisted the JDC had been used as the basis for reprisals against them after the JDC had been forced to close its offices.

A Coordinated Rescue Effort

Goldman stepped up his efforts to have concerted actions taken by the larger philanthropic and governmental agencies. While rescue measures were being discussed, the leaders of the Jewish Agency in Israel sent Goldman a telegram asserting that only their agency would deal with that issue.

Incensed, Goldman prepared a return telegram, saying "no one has a monopoly on rescue." And to be certain that the prime minister was aware of what the Jewish Agency was trying to do, Goldman recalls, "I asked the Israeli consulate to send this cable to the Jewish Agency in code, because I knew that the prime minister was given copies of coded cables." The cable was sent, and the Jewish Agency backed off a bit. In the late spring of 1979, Goldman added to the agenda of an already-scheduled summit meeting on the dropouts in Rome, the topic of Iran, in an attempt, as he later put it, "to bring about a confrontation on the issue on the part of world Jewish leadership."

At a first meeting at which only the American agencies participated, they agreed that the JDC and HIAS would not extend any formal assistance to the Iranian Jews for leaving their country. Extracting them from Iran and getting them to Israel was the province of the government of Israel and of the Jewish Agency—although the latter expressed to Goldman its reluctance to have other organizations assist in this task

In Jerusalem for another round of meetings, Goldman confronted Raphael Kotlowitz, leader of the Jewish Agency Immigration Department, about the need for action. Pronouncing himself "sufficiently shaken" by Goldman's facts and arguments, Kotlowitz said he needed to confer with Prime Minister Begin. When he did so and returned to tell the conference on June 28 that the JDC and HIAS should continue to do nothing at all in regard to Iran, Goldman and Don Robinson were dissatisfied. The next day, at a meeting of American lay leaders with Prime Minister Begin, Robinson raised the issue of Iran, and it became clear that Begin wanted the JDC and HIAS to act, as well as the Jewish Agency.

Schneider and Goldman then met privately with Begin. They decided that the JDC would assume financial responsibility for needy Iranian Jews fleeing the country (through Turkey, Afghanistan, or Pakistan) who chose to go to the West rather than to Israel. They further agreed that the government of Israel, or the Jewish Agency, would assume the costs for Iranian Jews exiting the country who wished to go to Israel.

This agreement broke the logjam, and on July 3, the earlier decision of the council was reversed. The JDC, HIAS, and all other agencies began to work: the Jewish Agency handled all departures of Jews from Iran, a multi-agency team tried to steer most of those fleeing to Israel, and the Jewish Agency took care of all those who wanted to go to Israel while the JDC and HIAS cared for those who opted for other destinations, principally the United States, Great Britain, Canada, and France.

Goldman's position was that dealing with emigration to Israel was a worldwide Jewish responsibility for which philanthropic funds should be used, but that family members of those who wanted to emigrate had the first responsibility for meeting their transportation costs. Shortly, he put pressure on successful Iranian Jewish communities in New York and Los Angeles to help their brethren who wished to come to the United States rather than to make *aliyah* to Israel. This effort bore fruit, but not enough to cover the expenses of everyone who wanted to emigrate to the United States. Goldman asked another American-based initiative, the Hebrew Free Loan Society, to chip in and loan money to individuals going to the United States if they couldn't obtain it elsewhere. "Initially, the Hebrew Free Loan Society said no, because they were concerned that the Iranians wouldn't pay back the loans and their return loan rate would fall, but we persuaded them. Hebrew Free Loan put up $1.6 million, got almost all of it back in good order, and helped resettle thousands of Iranian Jews in the West. If the JDC had had to pay for the costs, UJA would have had to raise $10.6 million, since JDC received only 15 percent of UJA income."

During the crisis in Iran, Goldman and Schneider developed a close working relationship. "From that day on," Goldman reminisces, "I was certain that Michael should be my successor." Toward that end, over the next eight years he would ask Schneider to take on various assignments to season him. "He gave me things to do that were always slightly beyond my reach," Schneider recalls, "and I relished them."

A Burgeoning Crisis in Ethiopia

The next assignment Goldman asked Schneider to take on was in Ethiopia. Here was a new opportunity to further develop a strategy so that Jewish organizations involved in these issues would work toward a common good and present a unified position. The country was then under the control of Marxist, antireligious rulers. Settlements of people who claimed to be Jewish existed in the far reaches of Ethiopia, in Gondar; their rites and traditions were out of the Old Testament, and while some among the rabbinate in Israel did not want to accept them as being Jewish, many other Jews in Israel and in the United States were willing to do so. The most recent Ethiopian census, which asked people historical questions to determine their background, reported 29,000 Ethiopians claiming to be Jewish. They called themselves Beta-Israel, and held the deep belief that one day they would be "redeemed" by returning to Israel.

JDC was operating modestly in Ethiopia through a long-established ORT program. That program was one of the casualties during the 1978 "Red Terror," in which thousands were killed in factional warfare and in a conflict pitting neighboring Somalia against Ethiopia. The ORT was asked to leave Ethiopia but managed to stay by shifting the sponsorship of its work to non-Jewish entities such as the United States Agency for International Development (USAID) program. Because the Western countries and Israel were perceived as siding with Somalia, after a comment from Foreign Minister Moshe Dayan to the effect that Israel was helping Ethiopian Jews leave that country, Haim Halachmi, who had been running the small, unpublicized family-reunion program for the State of Israel as well as a JDC program whereby money orders were sent to families in distress, was told by the Ethiopian foreign ministry that there would be no further cooperation with Israel. "So we had to find another way to bring the people [to Israel]," Halachmi recalled in an interview. "In the same period the population here pressed on us, saying that their relatives are in danger, have nothing to eat, they have nothing, etc., etc. So I applied to Ralph Goldman."

After consultation between Halachmi and Goldman, the JDC set up the *sa'ad* (welfare) program, in which Americans ostensibly sent packages and money orders to relatives in Ethiopia who were clearly suffering because of their Jewishness. The packages were sent through a coordinating office that Halachmi maintained in Israel. As revealed by a 1979 letter to the JDC, the cases were acute:

Mr. Tackla Achenedar, the chief clerk of ORT in Gondar, was killed. Mr. Mesignau Dassa, a teacher, was killed. Four teachers that have been to Israel were arrested. Gedalia Uria, Asenaku Sandaka, Assefa Geta, and Tadessa Bayuch already for more than a month and a half have been in prison. Abraham Kehat escaped. Nobody knows his whereabouts. Akive Ben Baruch (son of the chief priest) may be arrested any day. There are six young fellows that used to work in Mekorot (Israel water company) in ORT and they disappeared. The situation is daily deteriorating. . . . Hence, we the members of the community and the country are appealing with a big cry for your urgent help in order to help save the four teachers on whose neck there is lying a sharp sword before the last ray of hope is extinguished . . .

Money was sent to assist the four teachers; but as Halachmi recalls, "Everyone in Ethiopia wanted to be a Jew then, because everyone knew that when a letter comes from the United States, there is a money order in it. So we were very careful, and it was very, very difficult to decide who [was] Jewish and who [was] not Jewish."

While people left behind in the northern sections of Ethiopia became more and more impoverished, a quarter of a million Ethiopians crossed the border in the Sudan and took refuge there against the ravages of war. A small percentage of the refugees in the Sudan were Jews who wanted to go to Israel. But the Sudan was technically at war with Israel.

"By this time, there were a lot of organizations getting involved," Goldman recalls. HIAS was assisting some refugees in the Sudan, various Israel government agencies were attempting to maneuver, and the American Association for Ethiopian Jews (AAEJ), led by Goldman's former teacher and close friend, Graenum Berger, was agitating for all to do more. Berger's organization had been assisting in the *sa'ad* program.

As the situation in Ethiopia and in the Sudan continued to deteriorate, Goldman's relationship with Berger, and Goldman's wish to have all the Jewish organizations involved in Ethiopia working together in a coordinated way, came in conflict with

Goldman's position as a confidante of the government of Israel. "I was in Geneva when I received a call telling me that twenty-three Ethiopian Jews had arrived in Jerusalem after being rescued by the government; but Berger, who was visiting Jerusalem that day didn't get a similar call." Kept in the dark, Berger stepped up his verbal attacks on the government of Israel for not doing enough for the Ethiopian Jews, accusing the state of not being interested in these particular Jews because they were black Africans.

At a luncheon in New York, Goldman told Yehuda Avner, an assistant to Prime Minister Begin, in regard to Ethiopian Jews, "If you don't do more, you'll lose my support," Goldman recalls. Trying to convince Goldman that the government was doing all it could but that there were dangers in publicizing their efforts, Avner told of meeting secretly in Addis Ababa with Haile Mariam Mengistu, the Ethiopian leader, and having seen eighteen photographs on the wall of his office, seventeen with X-marks over their faces. Goldman understood the need to keep the Israeli support efforts from the press, lest some people be placed in danger, but insisted that it was important to inform those like Berger who could be trusted to understand and to keep the information confidential.

At Goldman's suggestion, Avner brought together leading advocates for Ethiopian Jewry. Regrettably, Berger could not come to the meeting. Prime Minister Begin confided some of the government's secret attempts to assist Ethiopian Jews and told the conferees of a letter he had given to President Carter asking the president to use his good offices to pressure Mengistu to permit Ethiopian Jews to be airlifted to Israel. Avner stopped Begin from circulating the letter itself, suggesting that "only Ralph can read it."

Suspicion and jockeying for turf within the Jewish philanthropic and assistance community working to help Ethiopians abated somewhat, but did not disappear.

After the ORT organization was kicked out of Ethiopia, the United States State Department told Goldman that the JDC would never be able to work in Ethiopia, but Goldman decided

to try to get in anyway. Direct talks between the Ethiopian government and the JDC produced permission for the organization
to send in relief supplies and to establish a medical clinic in
Gondar, where some 400,000 people were at risk because of a
prolonged drought, so long as these programs were nonsectarian, serving non-Jews as well as Jews. Shortly, seventy tons of relief supplies, valued at $500,000, were sent, and the clinic
program began, under some guidance from Michael Schneider
and later by Manlio Dell'Arricia who had previously worked for
the JDC in Italy with the Soviet transmigrants. The medical
program was operated in the field by Dr. Ted Myers of San
Francisco, a physician with multiple specialties who volun-
teered, with his wife, Peggy, for this work. "This was the beginning of our association with the Myers," Goldman recalls,
pointing out their continuing work with the JDC in Eastern
Europe, the formerly Communist state, and in the Middle East,
down to the present day.

"For Ethiopia, I gave Michael Schneider and Ted Myers two
sets of stationery each," Goldman recalls. "One set had 'Jewish'
in the name of the organization and the other didn't, and I told
them to use whichever set did the most good." Similarly, for
Halachmi's work, Goldman obtained blank letters of invitation
to emigrate to the United States from NYANA, the New York
Association for New Americans, because the word "Jewish" did
not appear in the organization's name; once the Ethiopian Jews
were flown to Greece, they were rerouted to Israel. Much of
Halachmi's work was funded directly or indirectly by the JDC.
"For example," Halachmi recalls, "when I sent emissaries to look
for a certain part of the [Jewish] population which was separated
from Gondar and Tigre in the East of the country . . . I presented the bill to the JDC and they paid without any problem."

By agreement with the Ethiopian government, the JDC-
funded medical program and a JDC-USAID agricultural recovery program were nonsectarian but targeted Gondar, an area of
Ethiopia where the Jewish population was concentrated. Despite
the programs' success and the assistance rendered by other agencies in the mid-1980s, conditions continued to deteriorate as

famine increased the terrible toll that the continued war exacted on Ethiopia. Therefore, the discreet money order program to Jews continued.

In those years, some Ethiopian Jews succeeded in trekking through unfamiliar territory at night—150 miles over deserts and nearly impassable highlands, encountering bandits and guides who took all of their belongings and money in exchange for allowing them to pass into the Sudan, where they found a bare, disease-ridden existence in the refugee camps. Between 1980 and 1984, Israel was able to repatriate a total of four thousand Ethiopian Jews, but by mid-1984 some ten thousand remained in the Sudanese camps. Moreover, since it was the younger and healthier Ethiopian Jews who had made the trek to Sudan, the population of Jews left behind in the Gondar were more vulnerable and more in need of outside help than ever before.

American-based Jewish organizations like the JDC and the Association of Ethiopian Jews (AEJ) were having difficulties operating under their own names in the Sudanese camps. So after Ted Meyers had made a fact-finding trip there, Goldman arranged for the JDC to pay the Israel-based Jewish Agency to care for the Ethiopians in the camps—$642,000, or $8 per person per month.

Internal sniping between the AAEJ, the government of Israel, the Jewish Agency, and various other organizations continued, with Goldman unable to reconcile their differences or achieve greater coordination of efforts. Over the summer of 1984, an estimated two thousand Ethiopian Jews perished along the way to the camps in the Sudan or in them, together with tens of thousands of Ethiopian refugees who were not Jewish. Clamor in the world press mounted for Israel and the wealthy American Jewish community to "do something." An op-ed article in *The New York Times*, also printed in the *International Herald Tribune*, accused Israel and organizations like the JDC of "fiddling" while Ethiopian Jews were dying. Goldman reported to a JDC board meeting that "As these articles criticizing the State of Israel, and others, including us of course, appear, those of us who have the responsibility for carrying out the work are faced with a dilemma. Do we try to answer the press on the various charges, or must we continue to try to do the best, and not respond to the charges publicly?" His answer was not to respond publicly to the accusations but to encourage the various organizations and state agencies to keep the "functional liaisons working" to accomplish the task at hand, succoring Jews in the Sudanese camps as well as in Ethiopia.

Goldman agonized over his inability to keep the several organizations focused on those tasks. In addition, he had to keep secret new information that had come to him—information about a massive government of Israel plan for the rescue of the Ethiopian Jews in the Sudan. Under pressure from American Jewish circles to take further actions in the camps in Sudan, he felt he could not do so for fear of jeopardizing the impending rescue. Arye Dulzin, Chairman of the Jewish Agency, was in the same situation but felt impelled at a congress in Canada to release to advocates for Ethiopian Jews details of the still-secret airlift that was about to begin.

On November 21, 1984, the government of Israel, with the help of the United States State Department, started an airlift of Ethiopian Jews to Israel. The original name given it by the government of Israel was *Gur Aryeh Yehuda*, the lion of Judah's cub, but a week after it began it was renamed "Operation Moses" by the UJA, which undertook a $60 million fund-raising effort in support of the airlift and the subsequent absorption program for Ethiopian Jews in Israel. After ferrying to Israel seven thousand Ethiopian Jews, the operation was abruptly halted in January of 1985, when the Sudanese government withdrew its cooperation in reaction to a press report about the clandestine operation.

In later years, JDC involvement with the Jews of Ethiopia would continue, through programs conducted in Ethiopia after the organization had once again been permitted into the country directly. Some of these programs included Operation Solomon in 1991 (a rescue follow-up to Operation Moses), and the sustained work with the absorption of Ethiopian Jews into the social fabric of Israel.

Humanitarian Relief Efforts and the "Open Mailbox" Campaigns Worldwide

Another level in the enlargement of Goldman's purview of a global Jewish strategy developed in response to a series of disasters that did not involve the Jews as victims. For Goldman, taking Judaism seriously has always meant extending aid, on many levels, to anyone who needed help, whatever their background.

In 1978, an emissary from the Catholic Relief Services (CRS) came to Goldman with an idea for an "interfaith hunger appeal" in which Catholics, Protestants, and Jews would join. "The United Jewish Appeal had been approached and did not want to participate," Goldman recalls, "but I thought that a philanthropic organization like ours ought to get involved. This was less of a relief effort than an educational one." The Church World Service, a Protestant group, joined the CRS and the JDC in this effort; later, Lutheran World Relief became the fourth partner in the Interfaith Hunger Appeal (IHA). Through the 1980s, the IHA grew in size, attracting substantial corporate contributions, as well as individual ones to its "lunchless luncheon" programs held in major cities.

The idea of a joint effort among several religious agencies, but one in which Jews could participate and be identified as Jews rather than as anonymous donors, had resonance with Goldman's increasing view of what Jewish philanthropy could and should attempt to accomplish. He also understood the symbolic value of having people open up the newspaper and see that Jews were involved in humanitarian efforts. In the ensuing decades, the JDC would frequently act in concert with Catholic Relief Services and other agencies on various projects.

During October and November of 1979, tens of thousands of starving Cambodians arrived at the border with Thailand, seeking asylum and aid. Stories of their plight moved people in many countries. The world community, acting through the United Nations High Commissioner for Refugees, set up camps to assist the Cambodians, and individuals and organizations sought ways to contribute to the effort to succor those who had survived the "killing fields" of Pol Pot and the Khmer Rouge. The JDC made an immediate contribution of $10,000 to the emergency feeding program.

"The JDC, as an organization, had always donated money to nonsectarian disaster relief, though not a lot," Goldman recalls. "But with the Cambodian situation, there were American Jews who wanted very much to contribute and who wanted to do it as Jews. They preferred doing so to donating through the Red Cross or some other international organization." However, when Goldman brought the idea of donating to nonsectarian relief through the JDC to the executive steering committee, some members thought that for the JDC to do more than offer a modest contribution would be wrong because a larger effort would detract from the JDC's main work, which all present agreed must continue unhindered. "But I was getting pressure from local federations to do something," Goldman recalls. "Many more people outside the board reasoned that what had happened in Cambodia was a genocide, and that Jews should always be on record as fighting genocide." Goldman points out that in 1979, times had changed enough to permit Jews to identify themselves as Jews and to take actions because of that identity. In that regard, he recalls bumping into Brooklyn Congressman Stephen Solarz at an airport around this time and chatting with him about what Solarz was able to accomplish in Congress, versus what an earlier Brooklyn Jewish congressman, Emmanuel Celler, had been able to do during his heyday, between the 1930s and the 1950s. Solarz was able to address more, and to identify his actions and advocacy with his Jewish background and concerns; therefore, Goldman felt, the JDC was justified in acting in the same way.

"What I came up with for Cambodian relief was an 'open-mailbox' campaign. We let it be known that JDC was opening a special mailbox for contributions earmarked for Cambodian relief, to provide a venue for those of our supporters who wanted their contributions to the cause identified as having come from Jews. We asked that earmarked contributions be over and above the donor's contributions to the UJA, from which JDC derived its regular budget." Goldman also expended some of the JDC's own budget in this effort by absorbing the overhead costs involved in the efforts, and by sending staff members to the camps in Thailand to identify which among the many needs of the refugees the JDC could help fill. After the visit, the staff recommended that the JDC participate in an educational program at the main holding center, teaching nine thousand children between the ages of six and eleven, many of whom had not been in a classroom in the previous five years.

"In less than a year, the open-mailbox program took in more than $320,000, which went straight to the refugee effort," Goldman points out. The strength of the donations, the even-handed way in which the needs were evaluated, and the way the newly donated money was spent convinced the doubters on the board that having the JDC contribute to the relief of the victims of another tragedy was a valuable and proper extension of Jewish philanthropy.

"After that," Goldman recalls, "the pattern was established. So when there was an earthquake near Naples in 1980, I just called up our office and instructed the staff to open a new mailbox, specifically for the victims of that disaster."

From then on, open-mailbox campaigns became a feature of JDC actions, used to succor victims of the war in Lebanon, and of the great famine in Ethiopia in the mid-1980s, a cause to which Jews contributed—through the JDC—over $2 million. "One donor started with giving $50,000 for Ethiopian famine relief and later escalated to giving many millions of dollars directly to JDC because he said he was impressed that a Jewish organization would be involved in a cause in which Jews themselves weren't the victims."

An opportunity for the ultimate assistance in this regard arose as a result of the escalation of Israel's war on its attackers, which spilled over into Lebanon in early June of 1982. Within a week, Goldman convened a high-level meeting of representatives of the leading American Jewish philanthropic organizations, to whom he disseminated a memo of broad compassion that proposed a "people-to-people, ecumenical, humanitarian enterprise," a rehabilitation of the population in Lebanon to "bring about a stable and strong Lebanese government." The initiative ought not to come from Israel, Goldman recommended, but from the United States. It should take the form of a $500 million to $1 billion fund whose contributors would include voluntary agencies and governments, with Israel agreeing to participate at a later, appropriate moment with a contribution of $100 million. "It is an act in which diaspora Jewry, and especially American Jewry, [can] participate, and might reduce the self-flagellation on the part of some of the critics, and may also neutralize some of the anti-Israel backlash anticipated in America." Pointing out the necessity of separating emergency relief from long-term rehabilitation, Goldman emphasized the need to plan for long-term projects in a way that would be "sufficiently imaginative in scope of participation and resources" to achieve the desired objectives. Toward these ends, the JDC immediately offered a $100,000 contribution.

This was a grand, humanitarian vision, and it involved the JDC acting as a Jewish organization leading a completely non-political relief and development effort aimed at assisting all civilians in need, regardless of religion, politics, or national affiliation. Among its remarkable aspects was that it was being proposed by the JDC, an organization having a history of a long and intimate partnership with Israel, one of the main combatants in the Lebanon war.

Shortly, in response to direct requests from the Lebanese officials in Tyre and Sidon, the JDC purchased mattresses, cookware and eating kits, and other materials for the comfort of families, and by early July, had turned these over to Lebanese officials for distribution. The JDC also arranged for the transport of twenty tons of used clothing collected in Jerusalem to sites in Lebanon. Additional supplies for other families under the care of Catholic charities were also purchased and delivered by the JDC, which was able at first to operate in Lebanon more easily than other agencies because the government of Israel implicitly trusted the JDC and let its trucks through Israeli lines. After the initial emergency passed, the JDC participated in campaigns to inoculate South Lebanese children against polio and dysentery, and in other work to remove rubble and rebuild communities and hospitals.

Goldman visited the relief efforts, which operated in cooperation with such disparate agencies as the Lebanese Ministries of Social Welfare and of Health, the Israeli Ministry of Social Welfare, the United Nation's relief agency, Caritas (Catholic relief), the Tyre and Sidon municipalities, and the Lebanese Red Cross. By early 1983, the amount of cash and supplies donated had surpassed $2 million, an amount larger than that raised and distributed by more broadly based Christian and nonsectarian based agencies.

The earthquakes in Mexico in September 1985, and a volcanic eruption in Chile in December 1985, occasioned additional development of the open-mailbox campaigns. The Mexican Jewish community asked the JDC to open such a mailbox for Mexico, in conjunction with its own efforts to raise money within the country to deal with the disaster; within two months, the mailbox had collected $600,000 from American Jews to go with the $1.8 million raised by Mexican Jews. In Chile, the JDC's open-mailbox collections contributed to a rebuilding effort spearheaded by Israelis and led by humanitarian and peace activist Abie Nathan.

RETIREMENT, BUT NOT DEPARTURE

When Goldman turned seventy in 1984, he decided that it was time to retire; however, for Goldman retirement meant stepping down as executive vice-president but continuing to work full time for the organization. He kept an office at JDC headquarters in New York and spent much time in Israel and traveling. Actually, Goldman retired twice. In 1986, he was called out of his first retirement to become executive vice-president while a search for his new successor was underway. At the end of 1987, when Michael Schneider was selected—as Goldman had hoped—he retired again. The second time, too, it would be a full-time working retirement.

Retirement freed Goldman from some responsibilities, but not from those larger tasks mandated by his understanding of international Jewish concerns. "When I retired for the first time in 1985," he recalls, "one of the things I did was form an institute to study the recovery of community property by Jewish communities."

Throughout Europe and the Moslem countries, buildings that had once been owned by Jewish communities had been seized by the state, or had simply been taken over when the Jewish populations were killed or emigrated. "My idea was that communities could sue to get these properties back, if not to use them for their original purposes, then to sell them and apply the money to support current programs." Several formerly communist Eastern bloc countries agreed to property reclamation, and so did many of the CIS states; it was estimated that two thousand pieces of communal property had been taken from Jewish communities during the seventy years of the Soviet Union.

When dealing with the recovery of community property, the assumption was that the property would be restored to the local community and not to outside bodies. Therefore, there were three different steps to follow: prepare an inventory of Jewish communal properties, assemble documentation for legal ownership, and encourage the local Jewish community to sell the properties and use the income for their own needs.

Another seminal contribution to an understanding of global Jewish perspective came in the form of an entity called the International Development Program (IDP). Back in the late 1970s, the US AID program of the United States State Department had approached the JDC to set up a consortium of Jewish agencies to do relief and medical work in Africa. Goldman initially agreed to have the JDC participate on a limited basis, because he "didn't want to stretch the staff" to be more deeply involved. But after the open-mailbox campaigns for Ethiopians in 1986, when the State Department asked the JDC to take over its program of relief in Africa, Goldman believed that it could be done with existing JDC resources. He founded the IDP, a JDC-operated entity that received money from the American government and employed experts, most of them Israelis, in relief and medical clinic programs in sub-Saharan Africa. One of Goldman's objectives in fashioning the IDP was to employ experts from Israel to work in countries whose governments often had not officially recognized the state of Israel. IDP operations in sub-Saharan Africa were so successful that other IDP projects were shortly undertaken in virtually every corner of the lesser-developed world, for instance in El Salvador, China, and Morocco, and later in such varied regions as Sarajevo, Hungary, and the Palestinian sectors of the West Bank and Gaza.

The IDP's stated objectives were "to demonstrate Jewish humanitarianism; to cooperate with resident Jewish communities; to utilize technical assistance; and to provide a Jewish presence in the Third World." Here was a realizing of the trilateralism concept that Goldman had begun to elucidate in the 1970s, now brought to bear on problems far beyond its original purview. And it was not only the United States that provided the diaspora-community third leg of the triangle. For as the JDC-IDP evolved, it became the vehicle for such projects as those in Zimbabwe and Botswana, for which the Danish Jewish community was an active partner, obtaining money from the Danish government to complement that obtained from the American government. JDC-IDP also found ingenious solutions, as in the collaboration between Alpha Omega, the international Jewish dental fraternity, with the dental facilities of the Universities of Casablanca and Rabat, and the Moroccan ministry of health, to create and operate a mobile dental clinic for children in rural Morocco.

As a second type of project, the IDP program established its own procedures for recovery and rehabilitation programs in connection with occasional natural or man-made disasters, ranging from earthquake in Armenia to famine in Somalia and the civil war in Rwanda. "When the genocide began in Rwanda and also in Yugoslavia, we were able to combine an open-mailbox campaign with the usual health and educational work that the IDP was doing, to provide a greater degree of assistance than would have been possible in the past," Schneider states.

More recently, after the Middle East peace accords were signed, the IDP has been at work in several Moslem countries and in Palestinian-controlled territories, working with American funds and experts from Israel and other countries.

1 ꝑ *Taken in 1919, one of the earliest photos in the JDC archives shows organization leaders overseeing the first postwar shipment of kosher meat to starving Jews in Poland.*

2 ɤ *A JDC-supported kindergarten in Poland in the 1920s.*

3 ɤ *Between 1924 and 1938, Agro-Joint helped nearly 300,000 Jews establish new farm settlements in the Ukraine and the Crimea in an attempt to alleviate starvation and help secure Soviet Jews their full rights as "productive" citizens.*

4 ♭ *May 1946. Herb Katzki with Holocaust survivors, who are departing from Bremerhaven, Germany, for New York on the first DP immigrant ship, S. S. Marine Flasher. Katzki served the JDC for more than fifty years. His last position was Associate Executive Vice President.*

5 ₰ Helen and Ralph Goldman,
August, 1942.

6 ❧ *Washington, DC, 1951. The four aides to Israeli Premier David Ben-Gurion conferring during Ben-Gurion's first visit to the United States as Prime Minister. L. to R.: Colonel Nechemia Argov, Goldman, Teddy Kollek, Zvi Zinder.*

7 ❧ *Ben-Gurion and Goldman.*

8 ⸶ *Kfar Shmaryahu, Israel, 1970. The wedding of Goldman's daughter Judy was attended by then-retired Prime Minister of Israel, David Ben-Gurion. L. to R.: Helen Goldman, David Ben-Gurion, Naomi Goldman (in the back), Judy Goldman, Ralph Goldman, David Goldman.*

9 ⸶ *Ralph and Helen Goldman with dog Sabra and daughter Dede (Naomi), on leave from her military service during the Yom Kippur War.*

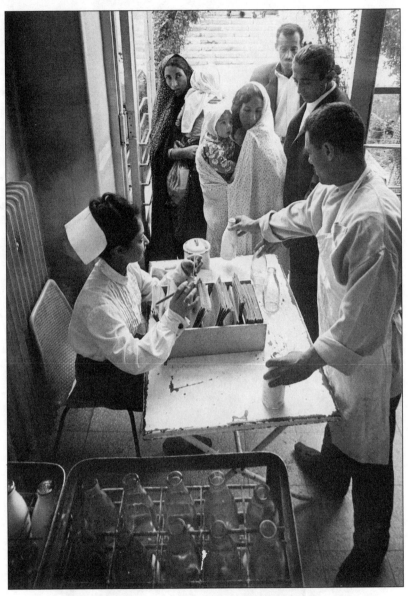

10 ❧ *Tehran, Iran, 1968. Milk distribution at the Jewish community hospital in Tehran, as part of a mother-child program. JDC was helping 21,000 of the country's Jewish population of 80,000.*

11 ♭ *In Israel, the JDC funded a project to enable access for physically challenged people to visit public places of interest. Violinist Yitzhak Perlman inaugurated the access mechanism at the newly excavated tunnels around the Western Wall in Jerusalem.*

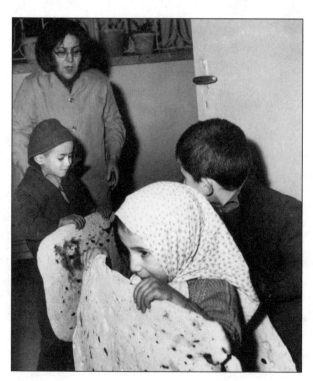

12 ♭ *Iran, February 1972. Children in a JDC kindergarten in Iran practicing the Passover ritual, from baking their own matzah to conducting their own seder.*

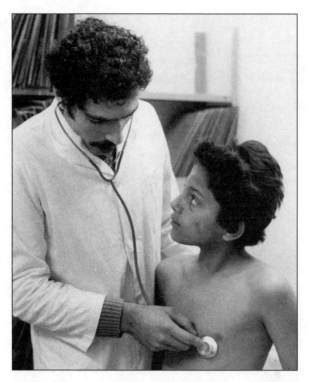

13 ᛘ *Rahav, Israel, 1983. Health clinic in a Bedouin village, one of eleven clinics included in Project Negev, funded by the JDC.*

14 ᛘ *Goldman visiting a program for the Druze in Israel and meeting with Sheik Amin Tarif, the spiritual leader of the Druze, 1967.*

15 ᛘ *A newly arrived immigrant from the Soviet Union practicing his old vocation of basket-weaving in his new home in Israel.*

16 ⚭ *Goldman initiated the Mailbox Campaign for JDC Non-Sectarian and International Development Programs in disaster areas. The first such program was in Cambodia in 1980; children received food and tutoring after the floods that devastated wide regions throughout the country.*

17 ⚭ *1984. JDC staff members Jerry Spitzer (right) and Manlio Dell'Ariccia (middle) distribute clothing in famine-devastated Ethiopia.*

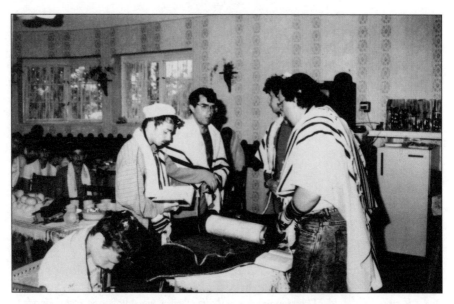

18 ❧ *Since 1988, the JDC has taken advantage of new opportunities to increase its involvement in the cultural, religious, and educational aspects of Jewish life throughout Eastern Europe. Pictured here are Jewish high school students in Hungary attending religious services as part of a summer camp program.*

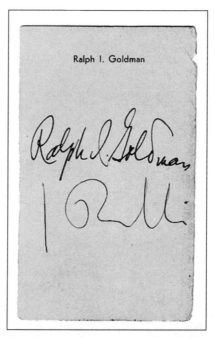

Ralph I. Goldman

19/20 ⊱ Warsaw, Poland, 1981. When the formal agreement did not arrive in time for their meeting, Ralph and the Polish minister Kuberski signed a piece of paper from Ralph's notepad. The signatures symbolized that the whole contract depended on good faith (above). This enabled the JDC to return to Poland, and a formal signing ceremony was later held in Warsaw (below).

21 ❦ *Bucharest, Romania, 1987. Heinz Eppler, President of JDC, and Ralph Goldman, Executive Vice President, leading a mission to Romania, then under the dicatatorship of Nicolae Ceausescu. They are shown with their host, Chief Rabbi Moses Rosen, and his wife, Amalya.*

22 ❦ *Louis Zorensky, in whom the JDC found a stalwart champion of its Israel programs and a wise counsel on global affairs.*

23 ⸱ *Zagreb, Yugoslavia, 1972. Passover supplies being unloaded
in front of the Jewish Community Center.*

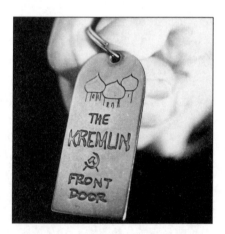

24 ⸱ *The key ring given to
Goldman in commemoration of his
famous principle: "The JDC
will return to Russia only through
the front door."*

25 ❧ *Jerusalem, 1986. Ralph Goldman and long-time mayor of Jerusalem, Teddy Kollek.*

26 ❧ *Tchaikovsky Hall, Moscow, May 1989. The first public concert of Jewish music in decades, organized by JDC. Tickets went for 6 rubles and were scalped for 42 rubles ($63). L. to R.: Cantor Yosef Malovany, Goldman, Conductor Constatine Krimetz.*

27 ᛘ *Jerusalem, 1991. A meeting of the original JDC Soviet Union team brought together the JDC team with the legendary Israeli hero, Shaike Dan. Sitting L. to R: Motke Yanai, Shaike Dan, Michael Schneider, Stanley Abramovitz, David Harman. Standing L. to R.: Amir Shaviv, Ralph Goldman, Asher Ostrin, Seymour Epstein toasting with a bottle of Russian vodka.*

28 ᛘ *Ralph's son David, Minister and Charge d'Affaires of the Israel Embassy in Buenos Aires, who was killed in the terrorist bombing of the embassy on March 17, 1992.*

29 ᛘ *Beit David, a cultural center in the Lauder/JDC International Summer Camp in Szarvas, Hungary. The center is named after the late David Ben-Rafael, Goldman's son.*

CHAPTER EIGHT

Opening Doors

The JDC in Eastern Europe, 1979–1983

WHILE THE JDC was engaged with Jewish communities in Iran, Ethiopia, and Morocco, it also kept its focus on Eastern Europe. The peril of the Jewish communities of Communist Eastern Europe remained urgent; there was also a sense that the JDC would have to deal with the communities in satellite countries in a way that was satisfactory to the Communist governments before being permitted to assist the much larger Jewish population in the heart of the Soviet Union.

The fear was that the Jewish communities of Eastern Europe might vanish when the last of the survivors of the Holocaust died. Moreover, if the communities did somehow sustain themselves by adding new members, they might be unable to maintain a Jewish identity composed of both religious and cultural elements, a palpable danger since these communities were growing steadily more secular as time went on. While anti-Semitism had progressively quieted since the uproar of the era of the "Doctors' Plot," it still existed, erupting in yearly, and sometimes monthly flare-ups. Examples of anti-Semitism could be found in occasional Eastern European magazine and newspaper articles quoting the "Protocols of the Elders of Zion" or repeating the Nazis' theme of Jewish capitalism conspiring to take over the world. Many anti-Semitic outbursts were printed in official Communist party publications and represented a clear danger for Jewish communities in Yugoslavia, Czechoslovakia, Poland, and Bulgaria.

What the JDC could bring to these Jewish communities, in addition to the welfare support they were already providing through the SSE, was attention and linkage with the rest of the Jewish world. Through the JDC, the Eastern European Jewish communities could be assured that they were not alone or forgotten by their brethren. And through the JDC's attention, it was hoped, those communities would be comforted, and the few that had a large enough critical mass of population might be energized.

There is a Talmudic saying that "A door that closes does not reopen so easily." The doors of most of the Eastern European countries had been closed on the JDC for many years. A reopening of the doors to Romania and Hungary had been accomplished, but the JDC's reentry to countries such as Czechoslovakia, Poland, and Bulgaria was not going to happen as easily. "We were already doing things in these countries 'through the back door,' you could say. But I wanted the JDC to return to these countries through a wide-open front door—by invitation of the government," Goldman recalls.

Initiatives in Czechoslovakia

A side door to Czechoslovakia was opened slightly for the JDC by Dr. Lavoslav Kadelburg of Yugoslavia. One of Kadelburg's many activities was serving as the main Yugoslavian member of the European Council of Jewish Communities. Set up after World War II by the JDC and supported by it since that time, the European Council held annual meetings in locations such as Paris, Vienna, and Geneva. By the late 1970s, these meetings had become an important venue in which representatives of Jewish communities from countries that no longer permitted the JDC to operate directly on their soil could talk with those who did have direct contact with the JDC. In September of

1980, Dr. Kadelburg was invited to visit Czechoslovakia and to talk to officials there about the JDC, whose return to Hungary had already been accomplished. After Kadelburg's visit, he telephoned the JDC and shortly thereafter met Goldman at a European Council meeting. Kadelburg's main information was that the Jewish community in Czechoslovakia, as well as Dr. Karel Hruza of the government's Secretariat for Church Affairs, was interested in renewing direct contact with the JDC.

"Prague may have been almost as Jewish as New York City," Henry Taub points out. Before World War II, Jews had been integral to Czechoslovakian life, responsible for between 30–45 percent of all invested capital in the country, and perhaps even more deeply involved in the country's cultural life. There had been 315,000 Jews in Czechoslovakia prior to the war. Afterward, about 40,000 remained alive. In the immediate postwar period, the JDC had spent eight or nine million dollars in the country, in addition to aiding about 19,000 Czech and Slovak Jews to emigrate to Israel, and 7,000 to other countries. Czechoslovakia had been supportive of Israel at this time, even providing some military matériel to the infant Jewish state during the battles of the late 1940s.

Then, in January of 1950, the atmosphere changed to reflect the new Soviet anti-Israel stance. The Czech government ordered the JDC's Prague office closed, and the JDC was forced to leave the country. In November of 1951, fourteen high-ranking members of the Czech Communist Party were arrested; eleven of them, including the general secretary, Rudolph Slansky, were Jewish. At their trial a year later, the prosecutor said, "If we realize the true meaning of bourgeois nationalism from which the international Zionist organizations [develop] . . . we understand why Rudolph Slansky finds himself a prisoner in court." The prosecution also alleged during the trial that the JDC had conducted "espionage, sabotage, shady currency transfers, black marketing, and smuggling . . . with the pretext that it was engaging in welfare work." Eight of the eleven Jews on trial were judged guilty and were subsequently hanged. In echoes of the Slansky trial, dozens of Jews were arrested and held for periods as long as several years without being charged with crimes, until released later in the 1950s by a general amnesty.

After the Slansky trial period, however, the Czechoslovakian government did permit the SSE to send in money and render other assistance to the country's dwindling Jewish population. This assistance continued even through the months in 1968 when Czechoslovakia was invaded by the USSR and a less liberal government replaced the one that had allowed the SSE to continue to operate. After the crackdown of 1968, about 3,400 Jews emigrated to Israel.

Having been absent from direct work in Czechoslovakia for thirty years, the JDC was eager to return to direct work there. Some sixteen Jewish communities, scattered throughout the country, were the focal point for about 6,000 Jews; estimates put the actual number of Jews in Czechoslovakia at double that number since there were as many "unregistered" Jews as those who openly acknowledged their religion. A newsletter published abroad by Jews originally from Czechoslovakia identified the reason that many Czech Jews continued to hide their Jewishness:

> Even the most assiduous student of the personal columns published in 'Vestnik,' the Czech-language monthly of the Jewish community in Czechoslovakia, will fail to find any references to births, although even in Czechoslovakia, young Jewish people of whom there are admittedly not many, add to their families from time to time. It appears, however, that the parents of new arrivals fail to advise the community, obviously out of fear that their identification with the Jewish community will be to their and their children's disadvantage.

Goldman and the lay leaders were determined to return to direct work in Czechoslovakia only if the JDC's entry could be through the front door—that is, in response to an official government invitation. And against all odds, such an invitation was extended in 1980.

Before proceeding further, Goldman called on Robert Barry, the deputy assistant secretary for European affairs in the United

States State Department, to discuss the potential opening. Barry was surprised at the Czechoslovakian overture to the JDC because he described United States–Czechoslovakia relations as quite poor, mainly because the United States continued to hold $400 million of Czechoslovakian gold as security for American, French, and British claims against the Czechoslovak state. These claims dated back to the postwar period, when many industries, including those owned by foreigners, had been nationalized. Most Favored Nation status for Czechoslovakia was considered out of the question until the claims and gold issue were resolved. Moreover, a bill then being considered by Congress would authorize the United States to seize the gold, sell it, and use the interest to pay the United States claims, but continue to hold the capital for eventual return to the Czechoslovakians—who considered this bill a potential disaster. Barry speculated that for the Czechoslovaks to approach the JDC at this perilous time might be part of a carrot-and-stick approach—offering something to an American organization with one hand while continuing to fight the American government with the other. But because there was still an important unresolved issue between the two countries, the State Department felt it best that this time—unlike the JDC's approach to Hungary in which State was quite involved—the JDC ought to follow up the overture on its own.

On the eve of a meeting with the Czechoslovakians in mid-January of 1981 in Vienna, Goldman discussed strategy with Maître Haymann, Ted Feder, Akiva Kohane, and Shaike Dan; the gracious Haymann was eager to have the SSE step aside as of the next monthly allocation to be sent to the Czechs so that a de facto arrangement would be in place even before a de jure agreement with the Czechoslovakian government had been made.

Later that same day, Goldman and Kohane sat down with the representatives of the Council of Jewish Religious Communities of the Czechoslovak Socialist Republic: Dr. Dezider Galsky, the president; Bohumil Heller, the vice president; and Artur Radvansky, the general secretary. The conversation was mostly conducted in German. It was a very emotional meeting for both sides, since it would end the isolation from the Jewish world that the Czechoslovaks had felt since 1952, the time of the Slansky trial in Prague. Despite the community's urgent need for support, Galsky said, they came to the JDC not as *betler* (beggars) but as *bruder* (brothers). Goldman responded warmly to this theme, and to the drafted letter of invitation that the community was prepared to send, since it expressed the consent of the government to the arrangement. The Czechoslovaks said that they wanted the JDC's return to be unpublicized, since, as Galsky pointed out, "Czechoslovakia was getting dollars from Libya," whose government was anti-Israel and anti-Jewish.

Even though other rather frank statements were made by the representatives of the Czech Jewish community, Goldman and his colleagues believed that each of the three men was required to report back to a different official of the government about the behavior of the others. "But we always assumed that anything we said in such a meeting would be reported to the government anyway, so we acted accordingly," Goldman remembered; all the men were careful to refrain from saying anything that could return to haunt them.

A JDC visit to Prague was arranged for mid–February 1981. Despite the Czechs' request that there be no publicity, an item about the government's invitation to the "long-banned United States Jewish organization to reopen its Prague office" appeared in *Newsweek* in late January, most likely planted by the Czechoslovak government itself. The article also mentioned that Czechoslovakia was seeking Most Favored Nation status from the United States. Soon after, Goldman and JDC President Henry Taub, accompanied by their wives and joined by Dr. Kadelburg, went to Prague for formal meetings.

Going into Czechoslovakia, Goldman felt a greater sense of apprehension and responsibility than he had on entering any other Eastern European country. The source of both the anxiety and the added obligation were the same: the unsolved 1967 murder of his predecessor, Charles Jordan, in Prague. Goldman and Taub pointedly asked to be taken for a walk on the bank of the Vlatava River—the place where Jordan's body had been found fourteen years earlier. There "in a brief service . . . to a hero of the American Jewish community," as Taub later put it in a report, they said *kaddish,* the prayer for the dead. When they did not return to their hotel on time, their wives suffered moments of panic and fright, thinking that the worst might have happened to them. Goldman in particular felt that he had a responsibility to bring up the matter of the murder of Jordan with the highest Czechoslovakian official he would encounter, to demonstrate that the JDC had not forgotten the event and still awaited an official accounting of it from the government.

After a formal dinner with several government officials, Goldman and Taub did what some among their hosts (and among those back home in the United States) had pleaded with them *not* to do: they raised the Jordan matter in a private moment with the ranking minister, Dr. Karel Hruza. As Taub remembered the meeting, "We were very persistent in letting him know that the Jewish community was still very much aggrieved by this; that if there was any information—we did not accuse him of withholding information or not acting fairly—but if he would be helpful in locating information that would help us understand what had happened, it would put the issue to rest." Hruza did not take offense and agreed to look into the matter and report back to the JDC about it. However, the report never came.

As evidence that no offense was taken, the JDC was officially invited to return to Czechoslovakia; Goldman used the JDC contract with Hungary as a template for the Czechoslovakian accord. Since the three representatives of the Jewish community in Czechoslovakia who Goldman had met in Vienna were all Czechs, the JDC had to be careful to also seek out the Slovak Jewish communities. "I remember meeting the president of the Slovakian Jewish community," Henry Taub recalls; the man said to him in Yiddish, "'If you want to see a Jew, you have to come to Bratislava,' meaning that on the Czech side the Jews were highly assimilated and probably had forgotten their roots."

Actually, none of the Jews in Czechoslovakia spoke Hebrew. Thus Goldman was quite surprised that at the state Jewish museum, for the first time in the country, he was able to communicate in Hebrew with the museum's director, a non-Jew. The museum had been founded in 1906 after the demolition of the ancient Prague ghetto, but many of the objects currently in the museum had been stolen by the Nazis from Jews elsewhere; the Nazis had amassed them here with the intention of making a "Museum of the Perfidious Jew and the Extinct Race." Goldman was moved to find among the items the robe of Rabbi Shlomo Molcho, a kabbalistic scholar of the early sixteenth century who believed he was the messiah and had a large following in many countries.

Goldman believed that this museum, Franz Kafka's home, the seven-hundred-year-old Alte-Neue synagogue, and other places of Jewish interest were maintained by the government with an eye toward attracting more Jewish tourists from the West and to demonstrate to the outside Jewish world that Czechoslovakia was not anti-Semitic. "There was a belief in all these Eastern European countries that JDC, and American Jews in general, wielded a lot of influence in Washington, and with CBS and NBC, which they think are controlled by Jews," Goldman recalls. "They thought we had much more power than we do, and no protestations to the contrary from us could convince them otherwise."

PLANS TO REENTER EASTERN EUROPE

Once the JDC was officially in a country and in direct touch with its Jewish communities, JDC professionals were able to go in and perform their own assessments of the communities' needs, and by their expertise help the people in the country improve the delivery of services. By being there as often as every few weeks, they were also able to learn more about what the communities required or desired. "Also," Goldman points out, "when you call or write and say you will be in Prague or in Budapest three weeks from now and will stay for three days, you are able to push to have arrangements made and meetings held that might not take place if you were not on the spot." The increased attention by JDC country directors and staff did not generally result in raising the amounts spent on welfare activities because these needs were already being met. In Hungary, the direct involvement of the JDC brought requests for more materials with which to start kindergartens; in Czechoslovakia, there were requests for more religious articles.

Most important, according to Goldman, was that "our being there, in Hungary and Czechoslovakia and the other Eastern European countries, made it possible for a new generation of Jews to link up with others." Participating in regional meetings and having personal ties with Israel and with American Jews through the JDC, Goldman sums up, gave to young Jews in Eastern Europe "a sense of belonging" that was vital to the renewal of their communities.

The ultimate ideal of the JDC was to bring a country's Jewish communities to the point of being self-sustaining. The model was the Jewish community of France. While in the immediate aftermath of World War II, French Jews required enormous amounts of welfare and spiritual assistance, by the 1960s the communities were vital enough and had become home to enough people of wealth and commitment that France's Jewish community could gradually take over all of the programs formerly funded and administered by the JDC. The JDC could then direct its resources into other communities whose needs were more pressing.

It was obvious that any revival in Eastern Europe would take a good deal of time, perhaps more time than the twenty years that France's renewal had required, and such a revival might fall short of the goal because there were not enough Jews in any single country to provide the necessary critical mass for a true revival. Goldman nonetheless continually urged the Eastern European communities in the direction of being self-sustaining. "It is the JDC's philosophy that local communities must participate in some way in their own support, and develop their own local resources for supplying that support," he insists. In several Eastern European countries, that philosophy translated into the JDC assisting a community by helping it import *matzot* from abroad that could then be resold and the profits used to underwrite the community's share of the cost of a program.

After the reentries to Hungary and Czechoslovakia had been accomplished and publicized, even outsiders began to ask the obvious question. "I recall a late evening session at the King David Hotel in Jerusalem in February 1981, after we had landed in Israel from Czechoslovakia. A friend of Henry Taub's was so excited by our tales of what had happened, that he said to us, 'And the Soviet Union—when?' The next morning, Henry Taub told me that he couldn't sleep the night before, because he'd been thinking and dreaming about that next step." But it was still not yet the moment to try to open the door to the big prize, the Soviet Union.

A TOEHOLD IN POLAND

There had been three million Jews in Poland before the onset of World War II, the largest Jewish population in Eastern Europe and a significant fraction of Poland's total population. Polish Jewry suffered greatly in the Holocaust: of the six million killed, more than two million were Polish Jews. After the war Poland had perhaps 150,000 Jews, half of whom soon emigrated to Israel or to Western countries that were more tolerant of Jews. Nearly 40,000 more Polish Jews emigrated after 1968, when anti-Semitism surfaced in tandem with crackdowns on liberalism throughout the Soviet bloc. In 1980, an elder of the Jewish community estimated that 5,000 or 6,000 people lived openly as Jews in Poland, and there were perhaps another 10,000 who were "lost in the shadows," that is, refusing to acknowledge their Jewish identities because of fear of reprisals or the need to stress Communism over religious beliefs to get ahead in the state-run enterprises and government posts. The decimation of Jewish life in Poland had been near-total, its character symbolized by the fact that there had not been a bar mitzvah in Poland in the previous twenty years.

The small number of remaining Polish Jews was organized in two groups, the Communist-led Kulturverband and the more independent Union of Jewish Religious Congregations. The groups had been somewhat at odds over the years, but there were signs in November of 1980 of a thaw between them, occasioned both by the growing political upheaval in the country—the democratic labor movement, Solidarity, and its leader, Lech Walesa, had come to the fore in September of that year—and by the obvious need to succor aged Jews and to care for Jewish cemeteries and antiquities. In January of 1981, an official of the Union of Jewish Religious Congregations called Akiva Kohane to say that he would be attending a World Jewish Congress meeting in Jerusalem, that the Polish Minister of Cults would also be in Jerusalem at that time, and that the official wanted to initiate a meeting there between the minister, the representatives of Polish Jewry, and the JDC.

On their way to Jerusalem, the Jewish Union men stopped in Vienna, where Goldman, Kohane, and Feder met them.

"It happened to be the same day that I'd met the Czech representatives, and the contrast could not be more striking," Goldman recalls. As he put it in a note to the files, despite both communities existing under Communist rule and feeling oppressed as Jews, "The Czechs seem proud and hopeful of a community that will continue to exist for some years. This was not the sense one had in the case of Poland—a community that is living in the past . . . with little hope for the future." Goldman fervently hoped that if he eventually did visit Poland he would not find things to be as bad as all previous reports had led him to fear. He told the Polish representatives that because of scheduling problems, he could not meet Minister Jerzy Kuberski in Jerusalem the following week. "This was really an excuse," Goldman recalls. "I preferred to meet the minister in Poland, and I wanted an invitation to do so."

At the Jerusalem meeting, however, representatives from the Kulturverband, who also attended, repeated to other Jewish leaders the desire of both Polish organizations to have the Joint come to Poland, and conveyed to the JDC that the Kulturverband was acting on the authority of the government. Akiva Kohane saw this as a thinly veiled attempt by the Communist-dominated organization to edge out other Polish Jewish organizations so that the Kulturverband alone would be the connection to the JDC should the JDC return to Poland. The next day, an invitation of sorts arrived from the Polish Office of Religious Denominations, but it was for a JDC representative to attend a ceremony of laying a wreath of flowers at the Monument of the Ghetto Uprising, not an invitation to resume direct programs. Nonetheless, the invitation was seen as the equivalent to getting a foot in the door, and so it was accepted with alacrity.

As spring yielded to summer of 1981, the political situation in Poland grew more complex and potentially dangerous. General Wojciech Jaruzelski had become the president, and though he was seen as a moderate, he was still a Soviet-trained military man who had to be wary of a Soviet invasion to restore full dominance to the Communists. Liberals won out over hard-liners, while the threat of a Soviet invasion hung over both factions. It was in this strained atmosphere that Goldman, Taub, and Kohane visited Poland on behalf of the JDC in July of 1981. Later, Goldman and Taub would describe the trip to the JDC executive committee as painful. "The people in Poland live on the razor's edge," Taub told them after returning to the United States. With the Solidarity revolution ongoing, "tremendous forces" were at play; inflation was spiraling, with food prices expected to jump from 80 to 100 percent in the coming year, and shortages of many commodities were already evident. "The lines for such things as milk, cigarettes, and gasoline," Taub said, might be "tolerable during warm weather, but no one knew that was going to happen when it got cold." Along the eastern border of the country, Soviet forces held military exercises.

During the visit, the JDC contingent met with Minister of Religious Affairs, Jerzy Kuberski, whose message was that the government was well-disposed toward the JDC's return and would sign an agreement modeled on the one between the JDC and Hungary. Kuberski was an unusual man for a government minister: he was president of a private organization that honored the memory of Janusz Korczak, a physician, author, and educator who had willingly accompanied the children under his care to Treblinka and shared their fate. Kuberski would shortly make public statements lambasting postwar anti-Semitism and lauding the thousand years of contributions by Jews to Polish history and culture.

The JDC party visited the Jewish cemetery in Warsaw. Overgrown, it seemed to have been unattended since World War II. Yet it was the final resting place of people so internationally prominent that the visitors recognized their names. "It was like walking through an American Indian graveyard [in a land] where no Indians exist anymore but you see some evidence of their type of civilization," Taub later said; he and Goldman were incensed when an official pledged to clean up the cemetery not because that would honor the Jews buried there, but rather because the headstones and monuments were fine examples of Polish craftsmanship.

Goldman was equally struck by the area known as Mila 18, the heart of the former Warsaw ghetto. "All that remains is a square with some crumbling structures. It was as if nothing had happened there, in the heart of the ghetto which had been a center of thriving Jewish life before the war." Only a dilapidated monument identified the place.

Lodz had been home to 300,000 Jews and was the site of the largest Jewish cemetery in Poland; when the JDC delegation visited it, they found workers debating the number of Jews buried in unmarked graves—one said 20,000, another, 40,000.

En route to Auschwitz, the JDC-assigned car needed gas, and the group of visitors was forced to wait in a line of two hundred cars, an experience that vividly illustrated the shortages the Poles were enduring. At the notorious death camp of Auschwitz, Goldman recalls, he saw "the white powder of burnt bones, still sparkling, as if, thirty-five years after the Holocaust, the dust was still alive, giving light." While there was a Jewish museum and seventeen huts to give a sense of what the infamous concentration camp had been like, Goldman was angered that none of the identifications or explanatory texts were printed in Hebrew; this, he knew, was not the fault of the Polish government but of the anti-Zionist faction of Poland's Jews who had had the task of writing the exhibition's explanatory text.

One thing the JDC officials did not do in Poland was meet with the group of forty Jewish students who had formed themselves into a somewhat radical clique; since these students were not members of either the Union of Jewish Congregations or of the various organizations in the Kulturverband, and since the JDC's policy was to only deal with groups recognized by the governments of these Eastern European countries, Kohane considered that meeting with such young firebrands was potentially damaging to the JDC's official relationship to Poland. But Goldman was nonetheless attracted by their youth and by their insistence on being perceived as Jewish in a society where burying that identity was still the route to success, and he lamented that they couldn't reach out to them.

Returning home, Goldman and Taub could not but conclude that the situation in Poland was worse than they had expected and that a swift reentry into Poland by the JDC was essential. The JDC had recently taken over the direct transmission of money from the SSE, but a formal government agreement was needed; without one, the explosiveness of the political situation might fatally delay the JDC's abilities to further assist Poland's Jews.

The Czech Jews have a blessing pronounced when a man takes up a high office: *bakol mikol kol,* may you be the right man in the right place at the right time. That was precisely what could have been said of Goldman when he began his mission to Poland on December 12, 1981.

Had Goldman not been in the air en route to Warsaw on a LOT Polish Airways flight from New York when martial law was declared at midnight, December 12–13, 1981, it is likely he would never have been able to enter Poland at all; Akiva Kohane, who had been scheduled to fly from Geneva to Warsaw to meet him (and to be his translator when talking with the

Poles), had his flight canceled as Poland was suddenly sealed off to all outsiders.

Arriving mid-morning and walking down the steps of the plane, Goldman saw two soldiers with guns but was not alarmed; rather, as he put it in a later memo, "I felt rather good to see soldiers on the field . . . for me as a traveler they represented no concern; on the contrary, I felt more secure." He was met shortly thereafter by Tadeusz Dusik, vice-minister of Religious Affairs, and by the leaders of the Union of Jewish Religious Congregations and the Kulturverband. They told him in Yiddish, "We are in a war emergency." Only slowly did Goldman figure out that war had not been declared, just martial law. Dusik seemed embarrassed by a guard's insistence that Goldman find his own bags and open them for inspection, but Goldman made light of that, having already decided that the best course was to "show no concern" and go ahead with the planned ceremonies. As they left the airport, they had to pass through numerous checkpoints, and when they arrived at the hotel they found its main door closed and had to enter through a side portal. The dining room was closed for the emergency, but was opened solely for Goldman, Dusik, and the Polish Jewish leaders.

Just then, Polish military units were breaking Solidarity strikes throughout the country, jailing the union's leaders, including Walesa, and curtailing "anti-Soviet" activity. In the process, seven people died and hundreds more were injured.

At the hotel, all the parties seemed to want an agreement signed, but there were difficulties: most of the material was in Polish, with rough English translations, and because Kohane's flight had been cancelled, Goldman did not have a JDC translator available. Since so much would depend on the precise wording of the document, Goldman pored over the documents, meticulously comparing the Polish original, the English translation, and his copy of the Hungarian agreement—which his associate, Sherry Meltzer Hyman, had packed for him "just in case it was needed." He went to the American embassy to send a message home that he was proceeding with his duties "normally." "I felt quite safe and not concerned for my safety—at least not consciously," Goldman recalled, but he wanted his family not to worry. He also sent a message to Akiva Kohane.

At the embassy, Goldman was fortunate to find as the chargé d'affaires a man whom he had previously met when he had been stationed in Hungary—Herbert Wilgis. The chargé did not think this was a good time to sign an agreement, since the United States government was considering whether to cut off aid to Poland and whether to forbid aid to Poland from voluntary agencies. Wilgis said he wanted to ask Washington's opinion on the matter. Alarm bells went off in Goldman's head and reminded him of the old Yiddish expression, *"fregen a shaileh is traif*—if you ask a rabbi for a formal ruling on the question of whether the meat is kosher or not kosher, the chances are that the rabbi will respond that it is not kosher." In other words, Goldman did not want the question asked, because he assumed that if it were asked at all, the answer would have to be "no."

At this moment, and throughout this tense period, Goldman felt extremely conscious of the responsibility he bore and determined not to let anything deter him from demonstrating to Poland's Jews that their brethren in other countries cared about them and would continue to succor them. In the hotel, Goldman spent a restless night trying to reconcile differing versions of the agreement and making sure they gave the JDC enough latitude to act as it saw fit. "I was on a humanitarian mission and felt that as an ambassador of the Jewish people, I was representing people, not representing governments."

He decided to sign the agreement even though he had not been able to finish comparing the translation with the Polish original, because, he reasoned, it was better to have Kuberski's signature on a paper than not to have it.

At meetings that morning with the Jewish community leadership, even old-line Stalinists let Goldman know how upset they had become because a socialist, labor-oriented government had used military force against the working class. Debates started, reminding Goldman of the ideological clashes of his youth, between socialists and communists. He discerned beneath the passion of the debaters real fears "that they, too, might be hauled off, and possibly detained or arrested," and mentally noted that the participants were speaking, in part, for the microphones that all had to assume were hidden in the walls. Beyond these fears, too, he sensed "the fear of a dark cold winter" to come, without food, without coal, without medicines. Weeks later, it would be learned that Jews were being pulled out of queues for scarce goods and accused by non-Jews of stockpiling for sale on the black market. Polish radio stations broadcast anti-Semitic stories, such as that Jews were in the vanguard of Solidarity and pursuing a Zionist agenda by trying to dismember the country.

A formal lunch with Kuberski was held; the sale of alcohol had been banned, so Goldman and others brought miniatures from hotel room bars with which to make the toasts. But the documents did not arrive from the translator, and by five in the afternoon the minister needed to leave for another appointment. Although everyone else in the room seemed nervous, Goldman calmly pulled out of his pocket a yellow slip with his name printed on it and said to Kuberski, "We don't need the documents. Here, you sign this piece of paper, I'll sign it, and as far as we're concerned, this blank piece of paper is our agreement. It is all based on goodwill between us, anyway." Kuberski agreed and declared that the document was signed.

Kuberski was ready to go back to his office and to sign the document the next day, but Dusik suggested that they wait a few minutes, and shortly thereafter a courier arrived with the formal documents and a photographer to record the moment. At the ceremony, Goldman added icing to the cake by announcing to Kuberski that the JDC was establishing an annual Korczak Award in the amount of $2,500; the minister pronounced himself moved.

THE LAST DOOR BUT ONE:
THE JDC IN BULGARIA

The JDC's attempt to reenter Bulgaria, the last of the important Eastern European countries in the Communist bloc that were not actually republics within the USSR, "was due to my persistence," Goldman says. He wanted to be able to say that the JDC opened every door there was to open in Eastern Europe. But there was also a need: the JDC knew that Yugoslavians had tried to assist their Jewish brethren in Bulgaria on their own, that there had been inquiries to the JDC from Bulgarian Jews now and then, and that Bulgarian Jews had expressed to Yugoslavian emissaries an interest in studying Hebrew.

In the spring of 1981, Goldman contacted Dr. Kadelburg and started discussions with him about Bulgaria. In the fall of 1981, Goldman received word back from Kadelburg that a JDC visit to Sofia would be welcomed, but Goldman felt that he must complete the JDC's entry into Poland before addressing the Bulgarians. By the end of 1981, the reentry to Poland had been accomplished and he was ready to deal with Bulgaria in the spring of 1982.

Before World War II, Bulgaria had had a substantial Jewish community, and in the immediate postwar period 45,000 Bulgarian Jews had emigrated to Israel, where by the 1980s they constituted an important and well-established group. An estimated 5,000 Jews remained in Bulgaria, but they were isolated from the other Eastern European Jewish communities since Bulgaria's Jewish organizations were not members of the European Jewish Council, even though such other hard-line countries as East Germany permitted their Jewish groups to join that council. American Jews were aware that during World War II, Bulgaria had refused to turn over any of its Jews to the Nazis, which enabled those Jews to survive the war; the Congress of the United States had even passed a resolution commending Bulgaria for that action. But when 250 Bulgarian-American Jews traveled to Sofia to present the Bulgarian government with a copy of that resolution in July of 1981, the government had not welcomed them and cancelled some of the events that were to have taken place during their visit. Bulgaria was known to want Most Favored Nation status, but the United States did not look favorably on the request at that point.

Traveling with Dr. Kadelburg, Goldman was met at the

airport by Dr. Salvator Israel, the ranking officer of the Sofia Synagogue and of the Central Jewish Religious Council, and his son Marcel, an engineer. Goldman was delighted to find that he could converse in Hebrew with Dr. Israel, a physician and the historian of the Bulgarian Jewish community. There was no official car to transport them to a hotel, so "We traveled by streetcar," Goldman recalls, "and my hotel room was no more spacious or comfortable than a cubbyhole in a kibbutz, though I was told it was the best hotel in Sofia." On a walk through the city he was startled to find supermarket shelves reasonably well stocked, even with foreign items such as lemons selling at a fair price; this seemed odd when compared to the obviously depressed economic situation of the city in general. Goldman was concerned that the absence of ceremony and comfort in his welcome indicated a lack of government support for his visit; indeed, he had started his trip with no meetings with government officials on the schedule. Now, however, one meeting had been arranged, with the assistance of Barry, who had recently taken the post of United States ambassador to Sofia.

At a luncheon to discuss strategy for the next day's meeting with the government, Dr. Israel told Goldman that the government might not remember the JDC's assistance to Bulgaria right after the war, when it set up a series of agricultural cooperatives and then gave them as a gift to the country. Goldman and Dr. Israel met the next day with Deputy Foreign Minister Lybomir Popov, who spoke English well, having served as ambassador to the United States for a total of nine years. The conversation was mostly pleasantries, with Goldman offering little and Popov saying the Jewish community's needs were already being met. "The issue," Goldman recalls, "was how to reenter the country—with what sort of program. Would they permit us to do the same things we were doing with Hungary, Czechoslovakia, Yugoslavia? Dr. Israel knew that the government wanted to attract tourists, and so he pushed the idea that the JDC be permitted to bring in kosher meat. Popov responded, 'When there is peace between Israel and the Arabs, we'll consider kosher meat.'"

As in Poland, there were two Jewish group clusters in

Bulgaria, Dr. Israel's group that administered the Sofia syna-gogue, and another that was secular-cultural and had strong Communist ties. The latter was led by Dr. Yosef Astrukov, one of three Jewish members of the parliament. "I had to navigate between the groups," Goldman remembers. One result of his visit, he was happy to see, was that Astrukov and Israel—both physicians and committed Jews, though heads of rival organiza-tions—began to communicate more often and more readily.

As Goldman did in every visit he made, he attended services in the local synagogue. Sofia's synagogue was venerable, beauti-ful, and huge, with room for twelve hundred worshippers, though only a relative handful of people could be found for a service. Dr. Israel's group, unable to maintain the synagogue by itself, had recently agreed to have the government renovate the synagogue in exchange for it being used as a concert hall when-ever it was not in use for religious ceremonies. On an inner wall of the synagogue, Goldman recognized a name in a tapestry: Canetti. He wondered if this person was related to Elias Canetti, winner of the 1981 Nobel Prize for literature, and later found out it was the author's cousin.

On his visit, Goldman met two young government scientists in their thirties with wives and children who had studied Hebrew in Budapest and with Dr. Israel, and who wanted to be-come cantor-rabbis. Ted Feder, director of the JDC office in Geneva, had previously met them in Romania, where they had also gone for study. They spoke German and English in addition to passable Hebrew, and Feder had been fascinated by them, es-pecially, he wrote, "when one realized they were practically giv-ing up their jobs, so they said, in order to embark on Jewish communal work." Goldman was heartened to talk to them, and the JDC later provided fellowships for them to continue their studies abroad.

In a memo to the files about this trip, Goldman wrote that he could not "help but marvel at some of the inner strengths" of the Bulgarian Jews, holding onto their Jewishness in a commu-nity on the verge of aging out of existence; and as for the two young men, he was delighted to assist them, because, he had to admit, "It's difficult to fathom what motivates them to continue their Jewishness."

A JDC limited program of religious and cultural supplies was arranged for Bulgaria, but it had to be administered for the JDC by Dr. Kadelburg since the government did not want to have direct contact with the JDC. Ever the optimist, Goldman saw this arrangement as the positive extension of his trilaterilism concept. In Latin America, the three legs were the local community, Israel, and the United States; in Bulgaria, the local community would depend not on the United States Jewish community so much as on its Yugoslavian and Hungarian neighbors, and on Israel.

AN ALBANIAN WINDOW

The small country of Albania had not even been in the JDC's plans for reentering Eastern Europe, because of all the Communist countries it was perhaps the most shuttered and isolated from outsiders; it adhered more to the Chinese than to the Russian style of Communism. But in July of 1983, Goldman heard from the JDC's representative in Greece, Lidya Ashkenazi, that an Albanian Jew then living in Brooklyn, New York, had recently visited Albania and reported to her about a community of some three hundred Jews, of whom precisely twenty-three needed assistance. There was no prospect of anyone from the JDC entering the country to even check on the condition of those requesting assistance. Still, Goldman decided to try to reach and help them. Goldman recognized that there was a chance of the entire matter being a confidence scheme to extract money from the JDC for a fictitious purpose, but then again, the total amount to be spent was relatively small, and so he reasoned that this was a risk that must be borne. Goldman learned that the Brooklyn-based Albanian Jew was petrified to speak of his brethren, "scared of the consequences for himself and the Jews in Albania. Whatever chance JDC was taking was small in comparison to the chance he [Cohen] was taking in confiding in the JDC." After receiving a set of names and addresses from the Brooklyn man, Goldman and Kohane arranged with a Swiss company headquartered in Zurich—not the SSE—to send small amounts of money, monthly, to the twenty-three Albanians. "There was never a report back as to whether the money had reached or aided them," Goldman recalls. "But that didn't bother me, because at least we had tried to help when help was requested."

With this last arrangement, the JDC's return to the satellite countries of Eastern Europe was complete. Through one maneuver or another, through the force of Goldman's character and his elucidation of the JDC's firm principles, and by having patience and being willing to work through channels, all the doors had been opened.

In later years, Goldman could look back and see that the results of the JDC's reentry to Eastern Europe in the 1979–1983 period were mixed. "We had the most success in Hungary," he opines. He judges the programs in Czechoslovakia and Poland as helpful, enabling their institutions to become a bit more vital, giving a new generation something to work with.

In this regard, he recalls what a breakthrough it was when the devaluation of the Hungarian currency brought about a crisis meeting with Miklos in Paris. "The devaluation would mean that Hungary would lose about $200,000 from the JDC, and Miklos wanted to restore that. He offered all sorts of things and finally suggested we ought to spend more on Jewish education—that is, on a nonwelfare program, and on education, something that was usually reserved only for the government to administer." Goldman had been wanting to boost Jewish education for years, and had been blocked from doing so in all of the Eastern European countries, even Romania. So he jumped at the opportunity to support real renewal in Hungary by educating a new generation of Jews in their religion and culture.

And he regretted all over again not having reached out to the forty student mavericks in Poland. Goldman knew more than ever that galvanizing the young was the key to sustained renewal of Jewish life in the decimated communities of Eastern Europe. There were lessons here to learn from when the moment came to directly approach the USSR. That moment had not yet arrived. But until it did, the JDC would continue to try to reach the millions of Jews within the USSR by means of the ingenious Package Program.

CHAPTER NINE

Packages of Hope
The Azriel Package Program Continues—and Flourishes

P ACKAGES sent by Azriel, the JDC's package program, provided a tremendous opportunity to reach and assist Soviet
Jews who were under fire from the Soviet authorities because
they had expressed the desire to emigrate, and also those who
would never be able to emigrate but who wanted to live as Jews
within the Soviet Union. "I considered the plight of the Soviet
Jews the Number One issue for Jewish people around the
world," Goldman states. "I knew we were going to have to increase our support dramatically, because we had to do more to
reach the Soviet Jews."

Increased Israeli efforts to "get more people out of the Soviet
Union," Goldman reported to the JDC Executive Committee
in 1977 "has a bearing on our package program—because we are
being requested to send in more and more packages. *Vysovs* are
reaching some 480 communities, which means that more and
more people in the Soviet Union have to be reached with packages as well."

THE PACKAGE PROGRAM: A QUIET SUCCESS

A sampling of some of the name-cards in the file of package recipients from the Azriel program showed that the profile of

recipients was changing. Packages were now being sent principally to those under the age of fifty-five and to people who were
in one way or another being hurt by the Soviet authorities for
their beliefs. There were twice as many people in the card file as
there were packages being sent each year, so the need for expansion was obvious. The greater the Communist government's
pressure on Soviet Jews, the larger the need for packages to be
sent in to assist the targets of the pressure. At a time when each
Jew who sought to emigrate had to amass a 900 ruble required
exit fee—an amount equal to an average person's yearly salary
and very difficult to accumulate in a system where most people
were barely able to pay their overhead expenses—to be able to
sell a fake fur coat from an Azriel package for 450 rubles positively affected a Jew's ability to emigrate. Internally in the JDC,
Goldman sought to improve the package program, which had
begun in June 1953. By 1977, the $4 million-a-year package
program was then shipping some 22,000 packages a year in
twenty different package variants, according to the ages of the
recipients, the season of the year, and other factors. Recipients
were able to sell the contents of the packages in the Soviet
Union for between $16 million and $32 million. This multiple
was far in excess of what it was possible to obtain by directly
sending dollars into the Soviet Union.

Goldman sought improvement in three ways: by broadening
the distribution and effect of the packages "to let the maximum
number of people know that these packages were arriving, that
we hadn't forgotten the Soviet Jews"; secondly, by sending in
the most appropriate materials, those that could be resold for the
highest price; and thirdly, by lowering the cost of the packages,
"getting more bang for the buck."

To accomplish some of these purposes, Goldman began what
he called Operation Inventory and asked the help of a recent recruit to the JDC board, Heinz Eppler, the principal owner and
CEO of a chain of 250 retail clothing stores, whose talents and
connections matched very well with the task at hand.

Eppler looked at the clothing items in the packages and noted that many of them had come from such distinguished retailers

as the London firm of Marks & Spencer, purchased at only modestly discounted prices—"$22 for a pair of blue jeans," Eppler recalls. Goldman decided to see if surplus merchandise could be donated, free of charge, and approached a Boston friend who manufactured raincoats and who agreed to give his surplus coats. But not all available surplus merchandise was appropriate to put into a package for Russians. Motke Yanai turned down an offering from an upscale men's wear manufacturer, telling Goldman, "That stuff is more for Shaike," a playful dig at his friend's well-known fine tastes.

Goldman asked Eppler to go abroad to evaluate the workings of the package program, and to come back with a plan for upgrading it. Eppler had no idea what he would find, and was a bit skeptical when he first encountered Shaike Dan and Motke Yanai with their secretive, eclectic habits. Eppler recalls landing with his wife Ruthe in Copenhagen without having made prior arrangements with the representative of Azriel. Yanai telephoned them at their hotel, then refused to leave a number where they could reach him; the next day, Yanai took them to visit a package shipping facility, where he showed a passport with an assumed name.

Dan told Eppler that he would like to be able to send twice as many packages as were currently being shipped; Eppler recognized that it would be nearly impossible to obtain twice as much donated merchandise as they were now getting, and so he asked Shaike for a more specific shopping list. It included 50,000 pairs of blue jeans and 45,000 fake fur coats, along with shoes, sweaters, and assorted cold weather gear. The list was reasonable from Eppler's point of view, and he was impressed with the overall efficiency of the Azriel operations. But he recognized that Operation Inventory was going to have to be selective, because what retailers like Korvette's and Kmart were willing to donate was not necessarily what was needed. As Eppler put it, "You can't use pink hot pants in Moscow in December."

Shortly, Eppler came to a conclusion which he today believes Goldman had already reached but had wanted him to deduce for himself: that the package program ought to manufacture the apparel it needed in order to bring down the cost of the goods it was sending into the Soviet Union. With Maurice Cohen, founder of the Boston retailer Lechmere Sales, as cochair of his committee, Eppler invited high officers of American merchandising concerns, and of the unions that represented their employees, on a trip to Israel to see the workings of Azriel and the Lishka. They, too, were impressed, and agreed to cooperate with the plan to specially manufacture merchandise for the package program. The manufacturers agreed to have their factories work at low cost on raw materials that the JDC would provide, while the heads of the unions obtained agreement from their members who worked in those factories to accept reduced wages for making the particular items that would be sent in the packages. The committee further raised the value and effectiveness of the packages by soliciting surplus inventory of such important items as shoes, most of which came through the efforts of Herbert Schiff, leader of the Shoe Corporation of America.

"When I told Shaike we were going to take over supply, he didn't trust me; he thought maybe I was trying to make some money from the program," Eppler recalls. "Frankly, I initially thought the same about him. But we eventually got past that, trusted each other, became good friends." Eppler and his associates found a way to obtain blue jeans for $3 a pair, found an Auschwitz survivor who would make fake fur coats for $16 apiece—half the previous price—and bought sweaters at low cost in Italy and the Far East and reshipped them.

Other JDC executives recall Eppler's enthusiasm for the cause as a major contributing factor to the success of this effort. Eppler himself points to the precision of his Israeli compatriots about the merchandise, for instance as reflected in a memo in the files: "With reference to the 10,000 fake fur coats, Motke Yanai indicated that he did not wish to have any fake Persian lamb, seal, leopard, etc.; that he preferred long hairs and that a maximum of 2,000 (preferably 1,500) should be produced from the mink pieces available." Also at Yanai's insistence, Eppler and the manufacturer agreed to buy back any "unsatisfactory" fur coats delivered to Europe.

The fake fur coats and other goods were first shipped to Eppler's company warehouse in New Jersey. There they were warehoused and readied for transport in containers to the distribution points, where they would be transferred into packages for the individual addressees. The value of the material goods and other contributions to the RIT program would eventually reach $5 million dollars a year and all of it above and beyond the budget for RIT provided through regular donations to the UJA. When one American federation wanted to deduct the $50,000 worth of goods contributed from the amount of money it had pledged to raise for the UJA, Goldman recognized the difficulties this would present, and sent the federation a curt message, "Recognition, yes; credit, no."

As a result of the new measures introduced by Goldman, Eppler, and Cohen, costs for the package program materials dropped considerably, not only from the use of donated and manufactured merchandise, but also because such things as warehousing costs were absorbed. These measures permitted the number of packages sent to skyrocket without significantly raising the cost of the program, until twice as many packages were being assembled and sent for the same amount of money. Eventually, the number of packages would reach 84,000 a year.

Similar measures to increase the quality of the contents also increased the street resale value of the packages, so that one package could support a recipient family for several months. As Maurice Cohen reported to the JDC executive board, the real meaning of the package to the recipient varied: "Sometimes it means the difference between life and death, sometimes it means a ticket to freedom, sometimes a subsidy or the only means of maintaining themselves for six months."

Another side result of the package program was closer cooperation between the JDC and the Lishka, the Israeli government liaison bureau for dealing with the Soviet Union and Eastern Europe, whose importance Eppler recognized as being crucial to assisting the the Soviet Jews. Through this cooperation, in the years to come, the Lishka would secretly operate as many as forty Talmud Torah schools, to teach Hebrew and other concomitants of the Jewish faith with materials purchased and clandestinely sent into the USSR by the JDC.

From time to time, there were crises for the package program. In the late 1970s, for the first time in the memory of Akiva Kohane, who had worked with packages to Russia since 1944, the Soviet Union refused to deliver packages from abroad to recipients. Most people believed the Soviet action was to counter the Carter Administration's pressure on the USSR to correct human rights abuses. In this action, and a later, similar one in the 1980s, the Soviets arbitrarily raised the duties on some goods between 200 and 1500 percent–(the highest rise was on the most desirable item, jeans); raised other duties on goods while the packages were in transit (so that a package would not be able to clear customs, even though duties on most of its items had been prepaid); destroyed more than 25,000 packages of matzot that had cost more than $400,000; and delivered the remaining matzot only after Passover, the holiday for which it was required. Other food and clothing packages were returned to the senders, thereby forcing the JDC to spend extra money to redeem them.

In the American Jewish community there were internal debates about whether or not to publicize such losses and expose the Soviets to ridicule and censure in the world press; it was soon decided that to publicize the stoppage would jeopardize the package program, which needed to continue despite any obstacles. Moreover, the action of the Soviets appeared not to be aimed solely at Jewish-origin packages. Other religious- and secular-based organizations sending parcels to other ethnic groups in the Soviet Union were also finding their duties raised, and their packages destroyed or returned. Word of the Soviet interference with mail from the United States did find its way into Congressional hearings, but Congress could do little to alleviate the situation.

Frequently during these years, the secrecy with which the JDC was compelled to operate its package program made it appear to outsiders that the JDC was not doing very much for Soviet Jewry, and brought the organization denunciation from other American groups dedicated to assisting Soviet Jews. Some of these attacks were ignored; others were answered quietly in personal appeals to their leaders. When the magnitude of the program was revealed to them—at the peak, sustaining perhaps a quarter-million individuals and families, and costing the JDC as much as one-quarter of its entire annual budget—the criticisms were muted.

That the packages sent to Jewish recipients were particular thorns in the side of the Soviet government was apparent from articles in the Communist press, such as this typical one from the newspaper *Sovetskaya Moldavia*:

> Subversive anti-Soviet organizations in the West do not spare any expense—they finance the cost of the goods as well as the customs duties or other taxes. The addressee finds out what the contents of the parcel are from a typed list. . . . One characteristic of this postal operation has become apparent—the number of parcels increased sharply after 1980, a year in which, as we know, the number of Jews wishing to leave the USSR to Israel and other capitalist countries declined steadily. The purpose of this operation is clear: to create a false impression of Jewish "prosperity" in the "promised land" among the Soviet citizens who receive such gifts. . . . Would it not be better to forward this "assistance" to at least some of the 40 million poor Americans, more than half of whom live in constant hunger?

The newspaper *Sovetskaya Belorussia* reported in a lengthy article castigating the JDC that a Soviet academic, V. Bolshakov, had determined that three-quarters of the JDC's budget was spent on "anti-Soviet and anti-Communist activity and to subsidize the Zionist secret service." To achieve what the newspaper characterized as espionage goals, "the basic means have been bribery and presents in the form of packages of foodstuffs and other materials." *Izvestia* declared that Zionism had always seen socialism as its "mortal enemy," and opined that Zionism had fomented subversive activity not only against the Soviet government but against Soviet Jews, attempting to "undermine the friendship of the [disparate] peoples of the USSR" Since 1975, when the USSR first sponsored in the United Nations a resolution equating Zionism with racism, inside their own borders the Soviets even took to equating Zionism with Nazism.

The government also devoted its energies to convincing its more highly assimilated Jews that they should put distance between themselves and those who wished to emigrate to Israel. This message was conveyed clearly at the trial of Yosef Begun, a Soviet scientist who had applied to emigrate. He was tried for conducting a course in Hebrew after he had been fired from his job and convicted of being a parasite on the state. Former Soviet citizens who arrived in the West during this period documented a whole host of official anti-Semitic actions taken in the guise of anti-Zionism, from the demotion and ostracism of Jews in government posts to the confiscating of bibles and the suppression of worship opportunities. Perhaps the best-documented anti-Semitic action was in education: the number of Jews admitted to universities dropped by 40 percent in seven years. Fields that had been almost dominated by Jews, such as physics and engineering, were successively closed to new Jewish applicants. In the 1940s, for instance, 30 percent of the students in the mathematics department at Moscow State University had been Jews; by 1972, the figure had dropped to a token 1 percent. Two Jews who were about to graduate—Boris Ulyanovsky and Anatoly Sharansky, both known as outstanding students—were told that their exam marks were substandard and they would not be permitted to graduate. A few years afterward, both men were convicted of anti-Soviet activities connected to their wish to emigrate to Israel and were sent to Siberia.

Decades later, David Bartov estimated that "90 percent of all the people who received packages [in the Soviet Union] eventually emigrated to Israel." They did not do so all at once, or even over a period of just a few years, but it was a fulfillment of a prophecy articulated by Ben-Gurion in the 1950s, at the height of the Cold War, when it seemed as though the Soviet colossus would endure forever. Ben-Gurion predicted that eventually a million or more Soviet Jews would emigrate to Israel, and an equal number would remain in the USSR and belong to rein-vigorated Jewish communities; he also predicted the eventual demise of Communism—very few people believed him on ei-ther count. Bartov recalls that early on in days of the Lishka and the package program, some Israeli government ministers dis-missed as a "dream" the idea of an eventual large emigration from the Soviet Union. But the steady accumulation of materi-als sent in to the USSR by the JDC and brought in by the Lishka officials and Jewish tourists from many countries were a major factor in building up a body of Jews who wanted to emigrate to Israel and could envision the possibility of successfully doing so.

A secret survey of more than twelve hundred Soviet Jews, conducted with great difficulty in the Soviet Union toward the end of the 1970s by a Soviet physicist before he emigrated to Israel and by Soviet anthropologist Mikhail Chlenov (a leader of the Jewish underground, who remained in the USSR), found that interest in Jewish affairs had picked up even among those who were not thinking of emigrating to the West. For instance, 93 percent of those who would not list their children officially as Jews if they did not have to, did want to buy and have books on Jewish history, and 89 percent of those Jews who opposed emi-gration also wanted to buy such books and make them available to their children.

By the 1980s, Jewish prayer shawls were being worn by young people at synagogue services, where before there had been virtually none available. Books in Hebrew circulated through the underground; an important one was a Russian translation of Leon Uris's novel *Exodus*, which was printed on thin paper in small type so it could be easily concealed. As JDC's director of Jewish Education, Dr. Seymour Epstein, recalls, "This was the book that made thousands upon thousands of [Soviet] Jews become aware of their pride, their national her-itage, etc., and of their link to the State of Israel. . . . When you send out books, you are never sure what is going to happen to them. In all education work, the product is not as visible as, let's say, in social welfare. But in this particular case, these books brought back tens of thousands of Jews to the Jewish people."

Many Soviet Jews who read the JDC-funded books emigrated, while others were inspired to become more active in Jewish affairs inside the Soviet Union.

In this time, Bartov recalls, through the combined efforts of the Lishka visits program, the JDC-funded Azriel package program, and the information provided by recent immigrants to Israel from the Soviet Union, the file containing the names, addresses, and particulars about Jews in the USSR grew to nearly a million names. If emigration from the Soviet Union increased, as expected, Israel would experience problems in absorbing the influx. Bartov knew that the information in the Lishka files would enable the government to best help the newcomers and wanted a large computer to be able to deal with that information, but that computer cost a half-million dollars. "The government of Israel didn't believe even at that time that there could be a million émigrés," Bartov remembers, "and they didn't think we needed a computer to deal with them. Only the JDC understood." By then, Heinz Eppler had become president of the JDC, and he convinced the organization to allocate the $500,000 to buy a computer for loan use by the Lishka. "The computer permitted us to get ready for potential émigrés up to two years in advance of the time they were able to leave the Soviet Union and come to Israel," Bartov asserts. "This made it possible to plan and better carry out their assimilation into Israeli society."

FREEDOM FOR RANSOM

The trust that Shaike Dan and Motke Yanai increasingly reposed in Heinz Eppler, as well as in their longer-term friend Ralph Goldman, came to fruition in another, even more clandestine operation to help beleaguered Eastern European Jews in the 1980s, an operation that had roots as far back as the 1950s: arranging the emigration of Jews from Romania to Israel by buying their freedom, head by head.

This was done by the Lishka with money from the Jewish Agency and the JDC—despite general disapproval of such a practice in the West. For instance, when the Soviet Union passed a "diploma tax" on applicants for emigration who had received advanced degrees in the USSR—ranging up to $20,000 for Ph.D.s—Americans were outraged not only at the charges, but also at the implied attempt to extort money from American Jews to pay them. In *Diaspora: An Inquiry into the Contemporary Jewish World*, Howard M. Sachar wrote that these "staggering ransoms were far more than the Jewish Agency could provide, even with its access to Western Jewish funds. Nor would the Agency have acquiesced in the payment of this blackmail, had money been available." Not so: in the modern Communist period, if Jews in Eastern Europe and the USSR could be ransomed in a way that was not made public, the government of Israel and the JDC were willing to pay the prices requested.

Yanai recalls that he and Dan initially made contact with the Romanian secret police and arranged for the emigration of specified numbers of Romanian Jews to Israel each year, in exchange for payment to the secret police of several thousand dollars apiece. There were premiums exacted for Jews with special expertise or advanced degrees. It was never possible for Yanai or Dan to ascertain whether or not part of the payments were going into the hands or bank accounts of dictator Nicolae Ceaucescu, but they believed the dictator had to have known about the operation. Arrangements were made one year at a time, and the price also varied from year to year depending on the desperateness of Romania's economic situation, the exchange rate, and international political realities. Because Romania was closely allied with some Moslem countries, at certain points in time the program had to be less overt than at others.

Once or twice a year, Yanai recalls, he would take cash into Romania in a suitcase. Traveling on an Israeli diplomatic passport, he would say that the suitcase was a diplomatic pouch that could not be opened or questioned. The largest amount conveyed in this way was a half-million dollars. When he delivered the cash to a member of the secret police, the man looked at the suitcase and said, "Next time, bring Samsonite."

In the 1970s, according to an intelligence advisor to

Ceaucescu who defected to the West, Ion Mihal Pacepa, the cash-for-emigrants program was expanded to encompass the repatriation of ethnic Germans to West Germany—which handed over cash, just as Israel had. Pacepa quotes the dictator as frequently saying that "Oil, Jews, and Germans are our most important export commodities."

In the mid-1980s, Shaike Dan requested from Eppler additional funds (beyond what he had obtained from the Jewish Agency) to pay for the emigration of Jews from Romania. "Shaike asked JDC for $3 million, saying he could buy the freedom of a thousand more Jews with it," Eppler recalls. I told him we'd find the money, but that unless a thousand extra Jews emigrated, the deal was off." Dan agreed that if his "friends," as he styled them, would not let out a thousand more Romanian Jews, they would get nothing. However, at the end of the year, only about eight hundred extra Jews had been allowed to emigrate. "I chided Shaike about this," Eppler recalls. "He said that the reason for the shortfall was slow processing by the Israel embassy, but that he needed something for his friends so they would continue the process. We settled on $250,000. Later, Shaike reported back that he told the Romanians it was a matter of 'honor among thieves,' and they had accepted that explanation." Goldman and Eppler were pleased that they had assured the lives and futures of nearly a thousand Romanian Jews in Israel for about $300 per person. In the several decades that the money-per-person operation ran, the bulk of Romania's Jews were extracted and resettled in Israel, where today they and their descendants account for nearly one-tenth of the population. Moreover, the need to keep the operation running enabled Romania to maintain diplomatic relations with Israel even when other satellite countries severed them—even at a time, Pacepa asserts, when Ceaucescu considered Palestinian leader Yassir Arafat to be his best friend, and cooperated in assassination attempts on Israelis and in the terrorist attacks on Israel by Abu Nidal. Regularly scheduled flights between Bucharest and Tel Aviv by El Al and the Romanian national airline also served the purposes of wider Jewish emigration, as Romania permitted Jews from other countries in eastern Europe, including the USSR, to travel to Romania and then take planes to their final destination, Israel.

CHAPTER TEN

Through the Kremlin's Front Door
Reentering the USSR

A T THE CHORAL Synagogue in downtown Bucharest, Heinz Eppler and Goldman scanned the packed house during a special concert featuring Canadian and American cantors singing Jewish liturgical and traditional music. Goldman nudged Eppler, pointing out that in the balcony were several Russian officials, watching and enjoying the music as much as the Romanians. "Someday we'll do this in the USSR," Eppler whispered to Goldman, who nodded. Goldman took out the little pocket notebook that went with him everywhere and showed Eppler a recent note he himself had written: it displayed precisely the same sentiment, the wish to one day have the JDC sponsor a magnificent cantorial concert in Moscow.

THE VIEW FROM THE PLATEAU

When Goldman reached the mandatory retirement age of seventy at the end of 1984, he wrote a one-hundred-page memorandum to Eppler, then the president of the JDC, outlining the accomplishments of the JDC during Goldman's nine years as its chief executive. While the memo celebrated the return of the JDC to Eastern Europe, it had little to say about the hope of fulfilling the dream of working directly with the millions of Jews who still resided in the Soviet Union, perhaps because for those Jews emigration had become increasingly circumscribed. And while the package program was reaching tens of thousands of Soviet Jews, millions more were not being adequately reached. Through the work of the Lishka, the Lubavitch, and other third parties, there were JDC-funded Talmud Torahs in every major and many minor cities in the Soviet Union, as well as two JDC-funded Jewish summer camps. Books printed and translated with JDC funds—books that previously had to be smuggled in one by one—were being shipped in by bulk lots, including those that discussed Israel in realistic terms, and Hebrew grammars. But it seemed as though a plateau had been reached in regard to what the JDC was able to do in the USSR from a distance, and that the JDC would continue to be constrained only to working from the outside, looking in.

When, after less than a year of retirement, Goldman was re-called in 1986, the long and winding path to the JDC's reentry to the Soviet Union took a decisive and positive turn. At a breakfast meeting in New York on October 29, 1986, Goldman was deliberately seated next to Konstantin Kharchev, Chairman of the Council of Religious Affairs of the Soviet Union.

"I had meticulously followed a rule in regard to working with Eastern European governments," Goldman recalls. "I would not permit any of the professional staff of the JDC to be associated in public with advocacy issues or groups relating to Soviet emigration, and I tried to discourage the lay leadership from such associations, too. But when an opportunity arose for Heinz Eppler and me to meet Kharchev at a breakfast of Jewish leadership concerned with Soviet Jewry, I decided to make the most of the opportunity." The host of the breakfast was Rabbi Arthur Schneier, head of the Appeal to Conscience Foundation; Schneier initially wanted Eppler, as president of the JDC, to be seated at the minister's table.

Eppler recalls, "I had a hunch that Ralph, who had much more experience in diplomacy, would get on better with the minister, and insisted that Ralph take the chair."

"I sat next to Kharchev," Goldman later wrote in a debriefing memo to the files, "and proceeded to tell him about the JDC." Goldman did so in a specific order, first mentioning the work in Moslem countries and Ethiopia before introducing the subject of Eastern Europe. He referred to his discussions with the Czech Minister of Cults, a conservative, before discussing those with Miklos, the liberal minister from Hungary, and his liberal ministerial counterpart in Poland. "I finally led up to our hope that we could visit the USSR. He said we should do so."

Goldman explained that he hoped they would be invited to the USSR, and that if they were, they would want to meet there with the minister and also with Jewish religious leaders. In return, Kharchev told Goldman that his job was as a defender and protector of minorities, and that there were vast differences between the roles of religions inside the Soviet Union and in the United States; for instance, while moral values were taught by American churches, in the Soviet Union, moral values were represented and conveyed by the Communist Party alone. Kharchev described the difficulty of permitting Soviet Jews to emigrate as a political problem, not a religious one, and implied that religious matters were more amenable to being solved and that religious believers ought to have their needs met. This last statement was a comment on an arrangement that Kharchev had just agreed to with Schneier for the rabbi's group to send kosher meat from Romania into the USSR.

Goldman promised to write to Kharchev, and shortly did so, reiterating that the JDC would be pleased to make an official visit to the Soviet Union if invited. When an answer arrived from Kharchev, it was ambiguous—it wasn't clear whether it was an invitation, and Goldman turned to Rabbi Schneier and to David Bartov for interpretation. Both men "felt the answer was not negative." Part of the reason for optimism was that for the past year, Soviet President Mikhail Gorbachev had been making apparent his wish to reform the Soviet system in the direction of *glasnost,* or openness. As one result of this openness, poet Andrei Voznesensky had been permitted to publish a poem lambasting those who had desecrated the mass grave of Jews shot by the Nazis in the Crimea in 1941 and also criticizing the officials who tolerated the desecration, implying that both were anti-Semitic acts. As another result, the Soviet Union was speeding up its review process for applications for emigration to Israel. Although the Soviets had permitted less than a thousand Jews to emigrate to Israel in 1986, the lowest number in a decade, it did release from prison (in a supposed exchange of spies with the West), the famed Jewish dissident Anatoly Sharansky, who then joined his family in Israel.

On the other hand, Gorbachev's program was not all positive for "minority groups" such as Jews. In the past, public demonstrations against anti-Semitic activities had been permitted, but a new law promulgated under Gorbachev forbade any unauthorized demonstrations, with transgressions punishable by one-year prison terms for the leaders.

"It was a very strange period," Kharchev later recalled in an interview with the JDC. "Because on the one hand, Gorbachev was trying to show all foreign authorities that he was a very good man . . . but on the second hand he was a [Communist] Party leader, and the Party slogan was not any religions, OK?" Kharchev said that there was a "contradiction" between the "freedoms" guaranteed by the Soviet constitution, which could include religious freedom, and "Party rules, class practice," which forbade religious practices and organizations. He expressed the difficulty by analogy, confessing that before he had been appointed to his post, he had never read the Bible, and "after this I open the Bible—night, yes, but day, only Lenin." He recalled that he had grown up in an orphanage, his mother's and father's identity a mystery, but possibly among those who had been killed during the Stalinist purges of 1937, and that "my education was like good religious education, right for God—but for Communist God."

WORKING TOWARD A LEVEL OF COMFORT

During the summer, Goldman received word from the Soviet embassy in Washington that Andreii Parastayev, a high-ranking diplomat, would meet with him in New York to discuss an eventual visit by the JDC to the Soviet Union. Meeting Parastayev in New York, Goldman asked the diplomat, "Do you know of the Joint?" and Parastayev replied, with a smile, "Yes— it is an organization of spies." When Goldman laughed in return, they were off to a good start.

As Parstayev recalled in a later interview, he was soon "captivated" by Goldman, "because Goldman understood the delicacy of our affairs better than any United States State Department official, including all the Secretaries of State, I had ever worked with." Parastayev also characterized Goldman as "a great teacher," who would answer any and all questions having to do with Jews, Jewish history, and the like. Goldman's straightforward answers to all sorts of questions, even when truthful answers could have been embarrassing, led Parastayev to reject the conclusion of material in the Soviet files that had blamed the Joint's exit from the USSR in 1938 on the JDC, rather than on Stalin.

Shortly, Parastayev "felt very comfortable with the concept of the Joint going back to the Soviet Union," but knew that others in Moscow "did not share my level of comfort," and so took things a step at a time, first writing home to friends in the International Department of the Communist Party that Goldman was potentially useful to the Soviet Union and that continuing talks with him would be helpful. These friends "were very professional, sober-minded and realistic people who were open-minded and cautiously supportive in presenting this to the bosses upstairs. Eventually I was told it was OK to maintain contact with Ralph." He recalled that "these were strange times in the Soviet Union. If I hadn't taken precautions not to compromise myself, the whole affair [of the JDC's reentry to the Soviet Union] could have been compromised and without doubt would have fallen apart."

After receiving approval from Moscow for the next step, Parastayev met Goldman at the Jockey Club in New York for lunch, on the day after Rosh Hashanah, in September of 1987. At the lunch, Parastayev greeted Goldman with Hebrew greetings for the new year. This, Goldman recalls, was a sign that "something was up." The Russian told Goldman of his intention to advise Moscow to invite Goldman and the JDC to the Soviet Union for an "exploratory visit." Parastayev later recalled that this was a "very large" and "unorthodox" step for him, but one that was "made easier because I had every confidence in Ralph."

The warm relationship that developed with Parastayev over the course of these meetings in Washington and New York, Goldman believes, was the key to the eventual extending of a formal invitation for the Joint to pay an official visit to the Soviet Union.

It was the opening to Soviet Jewry that Goldman had hoped for and worked for diligently over the course of many years, painstakingly proving the JDC's trustworthiness and reliability through carefully-crafted programs in Communist-bloc countries, by the impartial and determinedly nonpolitical nature of the JDC's operations, and in a sense through adherence to Goldman's tenet that pursuing such openings were essential.

As Kharchev would later recall, the JDC had a "history [of a] very good organization helping simple men, simple people," which he learned about from Soviet files and from conversations with leaders such as Adolf Shayevich, the chief rabbi of the Soviet Union. This reputation convinced him to issue the invitation—an offer, he suggested, that was "not good for my career," since, despite glasnost, issuing it was a daring thing to do.

The invitation to return came at a particularly resonant time for the JDC, fifty years after the organization had been expelled from the Soviet Union in 1938, and at a particularly poignant time for Goldman, who had scheduled his second and final retirement for January 31, 1988, when he would yield the post of executive vice-president to the man he had long groomed to be his successor, Michael Schneider.

"We had a JDC board meeting coming up in two days," Goldman remembers about the December invitation, "but I decided not to announce the invitation to the USSR at the meeting, for two reasons. First, I thought that if any announcement came, the Soviet government should make it. Second, Gorbachev was arriving in Washington, D.C., the next week, and about a quarter-million people were going to protest him there, agitating for the release of Soviet Jews; I didn't want to upset the protest plans by giving the Soviets a way to say they were being good to the Jews by inviting in the JDC. So I kept the invitation quiet for a while." That week, as well, Goldman received a letter from the president of the UJA, castigating him and the JDC for not doing enough to publicize the work the organization had done in regard to the Soviet Union. Goldman was tempted to refute this letter by letting the UJA in on the secret, but decided that his larger responsibility was "to keep my mouth shut for the time being." As important, the invitation was only that, an invitation to visit and get acquainted; it did not carry with it any definitive promise to permit the JDC to operate within the Soviet Union, and there was a distinct possibility that even after a visit, nothing of substance would materialize.

Michael Schneider was delighted with the invitation, and would accompany Goldman to the Soviet Union, along with Heinz and Ruthe Eppler, Manuel Dupkin, the chairman of the Eastern European area committee of the JDC board, and Dupkin's wife Carol. In their discussions, Goldman, Schneider, and Eppler determined that even after Goldman retired, he would remain an integral member of the JDC team dealing with the Soviet Union.

In an internal memo, Goldman noted that the invitation had been accepted in the spirit of "dealing with Jewish issues from a global perspective," and of following the pattern earlier established in Eastern Europe: working with the government and only with those Jewish community organizations that "have the blessing of the authorities." In a later note for circulation to other Jewish organizations, Eppler emphasized that "The special role we have chosen for ourselves does not always permit us the luxury of choosing those people with whom we do business."

TESTING AND BEING TESTED

As Goldman prepared to travel to Moscow in January of 1988, he remembered some things that Ben-Gurion had long ago said about the Soviet Union and about Soviet Jews, and went back in the literature to find them. In the 1950s, Ben-Gurion had predicted that one day Israel would contain four million people. That prediction was linked to his dream of mass emigration from the Soviet Union. In 1958, Ben-Gurion declared, "There is no other solution for Russian Jewry but *aliyah,* although I assume that a great part—maybe half—will not come. But this *aliyah* will give us [Israel] the power to realize . . . two great objectives: a new society, and a large scientific center." In another interview several years later, Ben-Gurion predicted the eventual emigration of one to one-and-a-half-million Soviet Jews to Israel. Asked by *Look* magazine in 1961 to gaze a quarter-century ahead, Ben-Gurion prophesied, "The Cold War will be the legacy of the past. The internal pressure of the intelligentsia, which incessantly grows in Russia, for more freedom, and the pressure of the masses for raising the standard of living, may bring about democratization of the Soviet Union during the next quarter-century." That democratization, and the pressures Ben-Gurion had identified, were intensifying rapidly in January of 1988, and although the Cold War was not yet over, it had already faded considerably, allowing more and more interchange between East and West with every passing day.

In Moscow, the small JDC group was met at the airport by the chief rabbi of the Soviet Union, Adolf Shayevich. They were given VIP treatment—government black limousines permitted to travel in lanes reserved for the mighty, suites at hotels, interpreters who spoke perfect English. They were whisked to an immediate appointment with Kharchev, and in the minister's office were met by a number of other people; among them Goldman recognized Samuel Zivs, a Jewish law professor. "I thought this was the end," Goldman remembers, because he knew who Zivs was, even though the others in his group did not: the deputy chairman of an anti-Zionist group. Goldman feared that if word got back to the United States and Israel that the JDC had met with Zivs, there might be adverse consequences.

Kharchev laid out what they would do and whom they would see during the week. "We had little opportunity to review the itinerary," Eppler recalls, "and we didn't recognize most of the names on the list. But we'd decided that this was the time for them to get to know us, and we'd let them call the tune." For instance, they were scheduled to meet with people who had something to do with emigration—a group that the JDC would have preferred to avoid, because the JDC had nothing to do with emigration—but they chose not to object to that meeting in order not to change the program that Kharchev had set.

The JDC delegation succeeded in avoiding meetings with *refuseniks*, or dissident groups. They were also very careful in what they said and where they said it, since they could not help concluding that their helpful interpreter had the clout of a KGB agent—when he flashed his badge, tickets to the opera and ballet materialized, places on planes were changed, traffic was rerouted—and that their behavior was continually being evaluated by their Soviet hosts. "Despite some stories in the press, that said we were being allowed back into the Soviet Union, we had the definite impression that the decision to work with the JDC had not yet been made," Eppler remembers, "and we didn't want to give Kharchev or anybody else a reason to say 'no' to us." In the December 1987, meeting in Washington between Gorbachev and Reagan, for instance, the Soviet leader had flatly refused Reagan's request that he permit open emigration of Soviet Jews to Israel or to the United States; for the JDC group to give any indication in Moscow, a month later, that the JDC's future actions might encourage such emigration would surely injure the possibility of being able to set up programs within the USSR. Another topic, not quite forbidden but a minefield to be carefully trod, was education; it was against the law to teach religion to groups, and children could only be taught religion by their families.

Some individuals and groups that the JDC met on this trip were later to be important to its efforts in the USSR. These included the men connected to the Choral Synagogue in Moscow and the similarly-named synagogue in Leningrad, and a leading academician, Yevgeny P. Velikhov. Chief Rabbi Shayevich, who had met them at the airport, was the leader of the Moscow

Choral Synagogue, and Vladimir Pliss was the cantor—or, as he styled himself, the choral director. In Leningrad, to which they made a one-day visit, the principals were Rabbi Efim Levitis and community leader Gregory Grossman. The JDC leaders had assumed that such men associated with the main synagogues would be important to them. But they were pleasantly surprised to meet Velikhov, chief of the World Laboratory at the Academy of Sciences, whose task it was to bring world culture to the USSR. Goldman was excited to meet a scientist of Velikhov's stature and significance, a man who represented what Gorbachev was trying to do through perestroika and who was actively trying to reach out to the West. A warm relationship developed between the Soviet academician and Goldman, one that would later prove useful to the JDC in many areas, as Velikhov opened many doors and facilitated the birth of programs that the JDC was pleased to support.

The JDC group had asked to make one change in the program: to see the Jewish Collection at the Hermitage in Leningrad. They were told this would be nearly impossible to do, yet on their visit to Leningrad the doors of that collection were opened to them, so they could view objects that had been secreted away from Western visitors for nearly seventy years. Also in Leningrad, the visitors discovered thousands of Jewish books in the attic of the Choral Synagogue, a reflection of the substantial Jewish cultural heritage of the city.

Most of the JDC visit, however, was given over to what the Soviets wanted them to see and to people who wanted to tell the JDC something or to test the JDC's commitment. Officials of the Russian Orthodox Church wanted the visiting Jews to know that all religions were being tolerated in the Soviet Union. Ministerial representatives of departments lateral to Kharchev, such as that of Humanitarian and Cultural Affairs, wanted the visitors to understand that Yiddish theater and other cultural manifestations of Judaism were encouraged in the Soviet Union.

At every opportunity, the members of the JDC delegation tried to convey what the JDC had been doing in Eastern Europe as a model for what might be done in the USSR. Eppler stressed several themes: "I said that our mission was to help assure that Jewish people could live openly as Jews wherever they wished to. Naturally, I wanted them to believe that what we wanted to do wouldn't hurt them, and that our clout might help them in Washington. I also told them that we'd bring in dollars and tourists, as we were already doing in Hungary, Poland, Czechoslovakia, and Romania. And I also strongly implied that the American Jewish community had great influence with our national government."

As they were whisked from place to place in Moscow, along the city's broad avenues, the JDC visitors could not help but notice the long lines in front of many food and clothing shops; with the advent of some capitalist competition in the Soviet Union had come shortages as Soviet supplies shut down, unable to compete in the more open marketplace.

The most significant test of the JDC group's commitment and fortitude came at a meeting of the "Soviet Peace Foundation," held in the home of Colonel General David Dragunsky, the foundation's chief—a man known as virtually the last Jewish ranking army official in the USSR. One member of the foundation was the chief of cooperative farms, another was a high government official, a third the leader of a theater—as the introductions proceeded around the room, it was clear that everyone there was a prominent Soviet Jew. "The message was: 'See how the Jews prosper in the Soviet Union; we don't need any outside help,'" Eppler recalls. It was clear to Goldman and the others from the JDC that these were the anti-Zionists who had publicly opposed Jewish emigration to Israel, just the people they had not wanted to encounter or confront. "We'd been set up," Eppler insists, perhaps by someone higher in the hierarchy than Kharchev. That feeling grew as Dragunsky asked Eppler to tell them—since Soviet Jews had everything they needed—why the JDC had come to Moscow.

"I stood up and said we'd come to reach out to Jews, to learn from you, and to teach you from our culture," Eppler recalls.

"What kind of Jew are you?" the group leader asked. "You don't even speak Yiddish. What can you teach us?"

Eppler "took his abuse and sat down," but Goldman rose to inform the group that the language of modern Jews was no longer Yiddish but Hebrew.

That these Jews knew neither language was made amply clear when they were entertained by a female opera singer intoning *Yiddische Mama*. "Tears rolled down her face during the performance," Eppler remembers, "but afterwards, when Ralph spoke to her in Yiddish, it was clear that she didn't understand the language at all."

After this and similar tests, the JDC group might have despaired, but the last day of the trip restored their spirits. During a sabbath service at the Choral Synagogue, Minister Kharchev sat on the *bimah* (podium) with Eppler and Goldman—an important positive sign. Then Goldman was asked to address the congregation.

"I had thought about it, and since I didn't speak Russian, and my message would have to be translated anyway, I decided it was very important for me to speak in Hebrew, especially after that meeting with the Peace Foundation," Goldman remembers. "Hebrew was a no-no in Russia in those days," Eppler points out. "People had been jailed for teaching it, and it was the language of Israel, and that was another sore subject." Goldman's speech in Hebrew was translated by Rabbi Shayevich into Russian for the crowd. After the service, there was a Sabbath dinner in a back room, with the rabbi, the cantor, and the government officials. "Someone had told Kharchev about the Agro-Joint, and he asked about reviving this," Eppler recalls; "I told him that our mission had changed, we were no longer doing things like that." Then another official mentioned the possibility of the JDC funding a state theater and of cultural exchanges wherein the Yiddish theaters and musical groups would visit the United States. Goldman demurred, saying that he no longer wanted to do these things, either.

Nothing was decided then and there, but the discussion had begun, and Goldman, Eppler, Schneider, and Dupkin left this last dinner with the feeling that something positive would come out of this preliminary visit to the Soviet Union. When they boarded the plane for Zurich the next morning, it was with assurances that future visits could be made to determine the nature and shape of the relationship between the JDC, the Jewish communities of the Soviet Union, and the appropriate government ministries.

THE REAL WORK COMMENCES

In the interim before a second trip to the Soviet Union, Goldman put considerable thought into trying to decide what the focus of the JDC's expected return to the Soviet Union would be. He determined that it would be the synagogues, in particular the Moscow Choral Synagogue, seat of the chief rabbi of the Soviet Union who was a formal appointee of the government. The notion of focusing on the synagogue was not universally admired or agreed to by others concerned with Soviet Jewry, who believed, as Goldman put it in a later memo, that the JDC should not do business with what some of them called "the KGB of synagogues." They thought the JDC ought to work with community-based organizations. Even close friends for whom Goldman had the utmost respect and who had spent long years working in the Soviet Union, believed that starting with the synagogue was the wrong approach, as did stalwarts of the Jewish underground in the USSR and leaders of other international Jewish organizations. Goldman was adamant. Aside from the pragmatic aspects of working with and through the synagogue that was closely connected to the Ministry of Religion, Goldman deemed it important to do, because of his "belief and conviction that Jewish communal life in the diaspora . . . cannot afford to minimize the significance of the one institution that has been so central in the long history of Jewry—the synagogue."

Contemporary with the planning for this historic trip, Goldman realized another part of his dream for revivifying Jewish life in the diaspora and in Israel itself, by convincing the JDC board to support the work of one of Israel's leading charismatic rabbis and scholars, Rabbi Adin Steinsaltz. Born in 1937 to

200 ⊦ I Seek My Brethren

parents Steinsaltz characterizes as "anti-religious," he began serious religious study on his own at the age of fourteen, and by the
age of twenty-eight, in 1965, had begun his modern commentary on the 2.5 million word Babylonian Talmud, a task equivalent to that undertaken in the eleventh century by the renowned
commentator Rashi.

Through his teachings, social criticism, and radio and television broadcasts, Steinsaltz became famous in Israel, which
helped create an appetite for his multivolume Talmudic commentaries. "The Talmud is a compendium of millennia of
Jewish experience and the focus of Jewish learnedness,"
Goldman says, "but it needed modernization so that current
generations could benefit from it. Rabbi Steinsaltz has made it
possible for us not to lose this great source of Jewish historical
experience and learning."

By the mid-1980s, Steinsaltz's work was broadly popular in
Israel, with waiting lists to purchase new volumes as they were
published. Nonetheless, Steinsaltz's institute claimed an annual
deficit of $360,000. For years Goldman had written memos and
letters decrying how "unfortunate" it was that "this great genius
has to spend a lot of his time in fund raising and lecturing abroad
when he should really be devoting his time to scholarly work."
After soul-searching and reflection on how best to aid
Steinsaltz's work, in 1988, Goldman persuaded a subcommittee
of the JDC board, and then the full board, to allocate $400,000
to underwrite the Hebrew-language edition of the Steinsaltz
Talmud. "What clinched the argument was the Talmud that the
United States Army had produced with JDC's help in the late
1940s for the Jews in the Displaced Persons camps," Goldman
remembers. "If JDC could support the republication of the
Talmud at that time, when we had so many other pressing matters vying for our resources, then we should be able to do it in
the modern era. The board agreed." JDC support for the
Steinsaltz Talmud assured the continuance of the project thereafter. As it happened, this support was offered at the same time
that Steinsaltz was arranging for an English-language edition of
the Talmud commentaries to be published in the United States.

"In a way, it was the closing of a circle," Goldman observes, "bringing the products of a modern Israeli rabbi's thoughts about these important Jewish books to the largest diaspora audience, the English-speaking Jews of the United States." For Goldman, personally, it was also a way of expressing his support for a spiritual leader of modern Judaism, one whose broad outlook and Jewish-oriented goals resonated with his own.

Goldman decided he would take some of the Hebrew versions of the Steinsaltz Talmud to the Soviet Union as gifts when he next visited. That official reentry trip kept getting put off, and the JDC began to wonder whether at the last minute the Soviet government would find some excuse not to allow the organization's official return. Also, there was no real increase in the number of Soviet Jews being permitted to emigrate to Israel.

But in July of 1988, Eppler, Schneider, and JDC executive Amir Shaviv were in Bucharest and received a provocative signal. It came at a six-hour lunch honoring the fortieth anniversary of Rabbi Moses Rosen as chief rabbi of Romania. Among the thirty speakers was Rabbi Shayevich from the Soviet Union.

A reserved and quietly humorous man who was not a Talmudic scholar but had great respect for them, Shayevich had been trained in Budapest in the 1970s, and little notes about him had been appearing in the JDC files since then as he worked his way toward succeeding the former holder of the chief rabbi position. He was respected by some, including Goldman, as a man who represented the effort to keep Judaism on the map of the USSR during difficult times, but he was also vilified by the Jewish underground in the Soviet Union for having been a tool of the government; articles in Israeli newspapers, quoting Soviet Jews now in Israel, named him as an agent of the KGB. Many in the West believed that Shayevich had been no more than a bureaucrat doing an ordinary job, comparing him unfavorably with the charismatic Rabbi Rosen of Romania, whose personal intervention with a dictator in a Communist environment had kept Judaism alive in that country.

On the dais in Bucharest, Shayevich concluded his speech with the words, "When we say our prayers, 'Next year in

Jerusalem' are those empty words? No, no, no! We mean it seriously and hope to see it in our times."

Eppler, Schneider, and Shaviv were agog at the apparently positive sign being given by the Chief Rabbi of the Soviet Union. But they couldn't be sure about it; as Eppler mused, "He either delivered a significant message on behalf of the Kremlin—or he did it without permission and will be shipped to Siberia when he goes home." Shaviv found Shayevich in the crowd and asked for clarification. "The rabbi was somewhat uncomfortable," Shaviv recalls, "but he assured me he meant business and was positive that the gates would open soon and Jews would be permitted to emigrate from the USSR." Later that evening, in a crowded reception at Rabbi Rosen's home, Eppler decided to be even more direct. With Shaviv translating his words into Hebrew, Eppler told the surprised chief rabbi of the USSR, "You have a once-in-a-lifetime opportunity to be a great Jewish leader. Either do the right Jewish thing and become a great leader like Rabbi Rosen, or you will miss the opportunity." Shayevich responded politely with a few sentences, then melted into the crowd.

But two days later, as Eppler, Schneider, and Shaviv visited a JDC transit station in Rome, they learned from questioning the new transmigrants that they had had to wait only a short while before being allowed to leave the USSR. It became apparent that something in Soviet emigration policy was changing—and for the better. Shayevich's signal had been real.

In October of 1988, after many months of planning, last-minute hitches, and uncertainty as to what could be accomplished, Goldman and his wife, Helen, set off for Moscow.

Where the January visit had been exploratory, this one was to establish the JDC program in the Soviet Union. Yet as the Goldmans landed in Moscow, very little of substance had been scheduled, other than a meeting with Kharchev, because anything the JDC might want to do would have to be approved by Kharchev.

One of the most fruitful elements of a future program emerged on a walk from the National Hotel toward the Choral

Synagogue. Goldman walked and talked with Cantor Pliss and Pliss raised with Goldman the idea of establishing a professional-level choir. Goldman liked the idea and agreed to it, but then, drawing on his principle of extending the Jewish content of life through education, raised the ante: What about a cantorial school? Pliss, though a graduate of a conservatory of music, was modest enough to believe he was not qualified to lead a cantorial school so they agreed to go slower on that idea, but the cantor was bold enough to be an entrepreneur in Jewish affairs, with dreams of after-school programs for students and publications of liturgical music.

As they discussed the costs and structure of a professional choir, and possibly arranging a concert in Moscow by renowned New York cantor Joseph Malovany, Goldman sought advice from Pliss on dealing with Kharchev. The cantor suggested the JDC donate $10,000 to a general children's charity fund, a non-sectarian operation, as a gesture of goodwill that the minister would appreciate. There was also a practical side to linking up with the Children's Fund. The arrangement that Pliss and Goldman eventually worked out was for the JDC to buy blank audiotapes and send them to the Children's Fund. The Fund sold the tapes; 30 percent went to them and Pliss got 70 percent of the profit. "This arrangement had the effect of tripling the underwriting that the JDC was providing to the choir," Goldman recalled.

The Goldmans arrived for services an hour early and were heartened to see a crowd of more than two thousand people waiting in Arkhipova Street for the opening of the Simchat Torah services. Since the era when Golda Meir had been Israel's Ambassador to the Soviet Union and had made a point of attending services at this synagogue, it had been important for Soviet Jews to demonstrate their Jewish identity by showing up at the synagogue on this annual holiday; the show of strength in numbers had been an important symbol of the resilience of Jewish life during the latter stages of the Soviet empire. Now that Communism had softened a bit, and open expression of religious affiliation was permitted, the tradition of massing for

Simchat Torah on the hill of the street sloping down to the main synagogue still continued.

The synagogue had been built to house perhaps twelve hundred people. The Goldmans found every seat occupied and the aisles jammed. Before the service, Goldman was approached by various people in the crowd. These sorts of approaches had been made to the JDC group on the earlier trip, who had gently rebuffed them out of the fear that contact might result in actions that might not be approved by the authorities. But now Goldman felt he could listen to private requests. One man asked for religious articles to be sent to Vilnius by the Joint, a request to which Goldman agreed. A second, who had been refused permission to emigrate to Israel, wanted to tell Goldman that his mother had worked for the Agro-Joint and long ago instructed him to thank any representative of the Joint he might encounter. Others asked Goldman to convey greetings to their relatives in the United States or handed him envelopes containing names of relatives in the United States with whom they had lost touch.

The aisles were so full that a procession taking the Torah scrolls around the congregation had difficulty in making its way. Goldman felt overwhelmed by the emotion of finally being able to take part in this service in the heart of Moscow and by the tears visible on members of the congregation as they reached to kiss the Torahs that were being carried around the synagogue. Outside, he was told, thousands more people were standing on the street, straining to hear the service broadcast from loudspeakers.

The service was conducted by Rabbi Shayevich. After the lengthy service, Goldman was asked to address the assembled. He deliberately spoke again in Hebrew, and Shayevich translated. Goldman talked of the opportunity the JDC now had of extending help to Soviet Jews and said that this help would be in the area of Jewish religious and cultural matters. Goldman told the crowd in the Moscow synagogue that the JDC would try to have the Steinsaltz Talmud also translated into Russian and published in the Soviet Union.

Leaving the synagogue, the Goldmans were further surprised to see perhaps as many as eight thousand additional Jews of all ages jamming all the surrounding streets, talking in groups, unwilling to leave each other's company even after more than three hours of standing.

At breakfast two days later, just hours before a scheduled meeting with Kharchev, Goldman asked Shayevich and Pliss for suggestions about the agenda and requests that he could make of the minister. They wanted better housing for themselves—the Chief Rabbi had an apartment so small that his family spent much of the time in Hungary, and the cantor had only a small rented room while his family lived one hundred kilometers outside Moscow.

Minister Kharchev's opening proposal to Goldman was what he and the JDC had feared: to reestablish the Agro-Joint in the form of Jewish farms to produce kosher meat and kosher wine. The government would provide the land, not far from Moscow, and the JDC could bring in the tractors and experts. "I found myself in a dilemma, not wanting to reject immediately a proposal made by the Chairman of the Council for Church Affairs," Goldman recalls. "It was not an economic issue as it was in the early 1920s, when Agro-Joint was established, but our agenda was really to help Jews regain their cultural background and tradition—there was no need to retrain them, as before."

Years later, looking back, Asher Ostrin, the current JDC director of programs in the former Soviet Union, dubbed this moment the critical juncture for the JDC in the USSR. "A lesser man than Ralph would have said 'yes' to reestablishing the Agro-Joint, would have said 'yes' to almost anything that the minister proposed, just so that we could have our foot in the door of the Soviet Union."

What Goldman did say was based on all the years of preparation for this moment that the JDC had put in, especially in its work with Eastern European countries, and on the themes that Goldman had pursued throughout his long career. His goal was, "This time, we come to Judaize the Jews." At the meeting with Kharchev, Goldman responded to the chairman's suggestion by pointing out that sixty-four years earlier, when the Agro-Joint had been set up, the task of the Soviet government had been to turn former Jewish shopkeepers and artisans into productive agriculturalists and to establish collective farms, but that objective no longer existed since Gorbachev's reforms were encouraging free enterprise rather than more collectives. This mild demurral was enough to deflect Kharchev and spur him to ask Goldman what the JDC had in mind; Goldman wisely replied that it was not his agenda he was pursuing but that of Rabbi Shayevich, and he asked the rabbi to present the program that the community wanted.

This led to substantive discussions on the parameters for kosher restaurants, meals-on-wheels programs for the elderly, the importation of books for the teaching of Hebrew and Jewish history, the establishment of a choir, and the Malovany concert. Kharchev agreed to them all with little hesitation and asked whether proceeds from the concert could go to the Children's Fund. "Of course," Goldman said, and added that the donation would be in honor of Kharchev, as would a separate JDC $10,000 donation to the fund. The chairman "smiled and appreciated that," Goldman's later memo recalled.

It appeared that the door of the Soviet Union had been officially opened for the JDC to walk through, bearing to Soviet Jews the sort of gifts the organization had hoped to be allowed to bring.

An inkling of what the JDC commitment to working in the Soviet Union would entail came from a whirlwind tour of far-flung cities that the Goldmans then took, accompanied by Pliss and an interpreter. "I was so touched at the initial opportunities provided in my discussion with Kharchev," Goldman recalls, "that I thought my presence in the Soviet Union must not be interpreted as though I had just come to Moscow to deal with Ashkenazic Jews; so I decided on the spot that Helen and I should travel to Tashkent and Samarkand, to also give a signal to the Sephardic Jews."

The group arrived in Tashkent, Uzbekistan, a semitropical, mostly Moslem city seventeen hundred miles and three time zones distant from Moscow, on the eve of an enormous celebration—the millennium of Christianity in Russia. They were taken to visit a Moslem Institute where 180 students trained to become mullahs because the deputy minister of religion in charge of the region wanted to make certain that Goldman understood that liberalization of attitude toward religion included *all* religions. The intricately carved Sephardic synagogue, hung with woven tapestries, reminded Goldman of those in North African countries. At a Sabbath dinner, because Jews are constrained by Jewish law not to write during the Sabbath, the regional head of the ministry of religion was requested and gallantly performed the task of noting the community's requests. As Goldman later confided in a note to the files, "It was a wonderful opportunity to have him participate in what the synagogue felt they needed, and of course, at the same time get not only his involvement but his approval of what they were asking for." At Samarkand, a four-hour bus trip from Tashkent, they visited an old Jewish cemetery in which some of the gravestones bore portraits etched in stone and covered in glass. In this predominantly Moslem city, a kosher butchery existed, and there were services in the synagogue three times a day. Goldman was thrilled to see these expressions of Judaism in such a remote and isolated place. Rabbi Steinsaltz had compared the Jews of the Soviet Union to a tree that seemed dead above ground but whose roots were alive and could be watered and nurtured back to health. Now Goldman had seen for himself how alive those roots were and could determine their immediate needs for nurture.

The trip was not without its frustrations, though. Someone with a videotape camera was recording the proceedings in Samarkand, and when Goldman asked the regional leader of the ministry of religion (who had accompanied them from Tashkent) to join him in being taped, the representative of the government took the opportunity to ask pointedly difficult questions of Goldman, attempting to embarrass him. Goldman eased himself out of the situation, but not before imagining that this tape might be sent to Kharchev to undo all that had been accomplished so far.

A similar but more disturbing worry perturbed Goldman after returning to Moscow, when a last-minute meeting with

Kharchev failed to produce a written summary of the planned programs that the minister had agreed to. "One must have strong nerves and a great deal of patience to deal with the Soviet bureaucracy," Goldman noted to the files, recalling "humiliations" such as unreturned phone calls and personal slights. Unwilling to leave without written agreement from the government on the details of the program, he persisted until he had reached Kharchev by phone. The minister told him that everything was going to be fine, that whatever Goldman worked out with the community leaders Kharchev would ratify, and that he might soon accept Goldman's invitation to visit the United States. "This telephone conference with him gave me great gratification that my mission to Moscow was successful," Goldman noted with relief.

For more than a decade, Goldman had been carrying around a simple brass key ring—found by his friend, Motke, in a London flea market—decorated with Russian buildings, along with a hammer and sickle, and marked "Kremlin Front Door." Now that front door to the Soviet Union, the door that he had insisted upon going through rather than entering through any other door, was being opened to the JDC.

CHAPTER ELEVEN

Keeping Faith With Israel

The JDC's Work in Israel Into the Present

O NE OF GOLDMAN'S most deeply held organizational beliefs, a derivative of his tenet about the importance of
Israel in world Jewish affairs, was that a candidate for JDC executive director must have served for a while as the chief officer of
the JDC-Israel. He had sent Michael Schneider to do so in the
mid–1980s, with just that objective in mind. Schneider's Israel
experience was one of many things that in 1987 made him the
clear choice of Goldman and the board to become Goldman's
successor as executive vice-president in 1988.

At the time of Goldman's second retirement, the JDC's activities in Israel still amounted to one-third of the organization's annual budget and were organized according to the guidelines
Goldman had elucidated years earlier: sponsor programs that assist
the vulnerable, build communities, and further the long-term interests of the State of Israel; begin such projects with adequate
partners who can later take over their funding; only undertake
projects that permit a phased withdrawal of JDC funding; and
only fund projects whose effects can be studied and measured, so
that future projects will gain from present experience.

Since the mid-1980s, several factors deeply affected and
complicated the JDC's attempts to assist the development of
Israel. One was the huge influx of immigrants from the Soviet

Union in the years 1988–1993, an influx that by its sheer size changed many priorities in Israel. Another factor was what in polite language was called "structural changes" in the American Jewish community—really, a revolution in the ways in which local federations, the UJA, and the JDC went about conducting their business.

In the earlier configuration, local federations forwarded their collected donations to the UJA, which, by contract, funneled a share of them to the autonomous JDC. In the 1980s, that arrangement was in the process of radical change for several reasons. The foremost had to do with the current belief of large numbers of American Jews that the State of Israel was now mature and needed less assistance from American Jews. It was complicated by the belief that Israel was not assiduously enough pursuing opportunities to achieve peace with its neighbors, and that money earmarked for overseas relief ought to be directed to populations other than Israel's. Joined to these new beliefs was a feeling on the part of local American Jewish organizations that they should be more directly involved with the disbursement of their donations.

Part of the reason for their feelings of alienation was the JDC's historic unwillingness to publicize its operations, publicity that might have allowed donors to better understand (and celebrate) where their dollars had been going. The JDC had not been modest or closemouthed in any arrogant way. Rather, its refusal to pat itself on the back or publicly celebrate its achievements derived mainly from the fear that publicity could easily have jeopardized JDC-backed sensitive operations, such as rescue missions, assistance rendered in Eastern Europe, and the support of the Lishka's work in the Soviet Union.

Given the new parameters in the 1980s and 1990s, Schneider and the JDC lay leaders, with Goldman acting as elder statesman-consultant, needed to reshape what the JDC could and should do in Israel. The basic tasks of the JDC-Israel in earlier decades had in large measure been adequately addressed. The outlines and many details of Israel's social services infrastructure were now mostly complete, and institutions to take them further—dealing with research, training, and community development—had been established.

PARTNERSHIPS

Reasoning from the basic Talmudic premise that all Jews were responsible for one another, the JDC decided to redirect its attention and dollars toward a revised and exceedingly difficult-to-accomplish goal: helping Israel become a more inclusive society.

Concentration on vulnerable groups was once again the key, though the target groups were not the same ones that had previously constituted its major concerns. Progressively less JDC attention would be paid to the mentally ill, the retarded, and the disabled, since other organizations and public agencies were now more actively serving those groups; similarly, community centers had reached full maturity, and there was less need for JDC involvement. Relying more heavily on these efficient partners permitted the JDC to increasingly concentrate on assisting other vulnerable populations that a burgeoning post-industrial economy was leaving behind: the elderly; children and youth; and people in transition or in temporary distress, such as new immigrants.

CARING FOR THE "OLD-OLD":
KIRYAT MOSHE TODAY

A Brookdale study in the 1980s revealed that previous estimates of future services needed for the elderly were wrong because they had not adequately forecast the phenomenal growth of the "old-old"—those over the age of seventy-five, a group that was growing faster than that of the population as a whole. New questions followed: Would there be adequate facilities to care for the old-old? Could ways of caring for the elderly be designed that were viable alternatives to institutionalization?

Partly due to the guidance of Goldman, the JDC had become thoroughly convinced that the answer to both questions was "yes," and that an attendant concern was the development of possibilities for what is called "aging in place." Aging-in-place programs would make it more possible for the elderly to remain in their communities at a lower cost to society than that incurred when the elderly are institutionalized. The major programs to encourage aging in place were "supportive communities" and day-care facilities; these communities are still vital and thriving today.

One of the eighteen extant supportive communities is located in the long-settled, Jerusalem residential neighborhood of Kiryat Moshe, a collection of seventeen three-story buildings with 236 small apartments, over half of which are occupied by people who have lived in them since they were built in the 1950s. Transforming such a neighborhood into a supportive community has entailed a host of minor alterations, some modest communal effort, and rethinking of what would help people feel comfortable and confident in their old age. The minor alterations include changes to outdoor lighting, walkways, and stairways; putting in hand-rails; removing obstacles to walking; and painting caution signals at difficult spots so that the elderly can move around within the community more readily and easily. Alterations are also made inside the apartments, principally to bathrooms and kitchens. "These alterations are very inexpensive," says Dr. Zvi Feine, the chairman of ESHEL, "but they do a great deal in helping people exist on their own."

The communal effort includes transportation, meals, communal facilities, and medical assistance. The elderly not only have a reliable support system, but they also feel they are in the company of friends and extended family. With such help, they are more able to maintain their independence. For such supportive communities, ESHEL often makes the initial "capital investment"—the physical improvements, the buying of alarm systems and communal kitchens—then within a few years cedes operational responsibility to a consortium of partners that includes the municipality, the national social security program, insurance institutes, and others.

The other major program is day-care centers for the frail

elderly. There are currently several dozen of these centers in Israel, with another dozen being completed each year. In Azzatta, a rural center near the Negev, an ESHEL day-care center draws participants from fifteen surrounding *moshavim*, communities of private farms that sell their products as a cooperative. The fifteen communities have a population of about fifteen thousand people; the Azzatta center director estimates that no more than 10 to 15 percent of the people who could use the center's services agree to come each day. In the early morning, the day-care center arranges for the frail elderly to be picked up at their homes by a fleet of several vans and then transported to the center, a one-story building mostly given over to a dining hall, kitchen, and meeting-room facilities, with a garden and walkways outside. Many of the clients need walkers or wheelchairs. At the center they receive breakfast and lunch, and in between they are stimulated by exercise, discussions, study programs, and counseling. Because many of the center's clients have no running water at home, some are given baths at the center, and many bring their laundry to be done.

Although the cost of operating a daily center is considerably higher than that of maintaining a supportive neighborhood, it is still lower than the cost of institutionalization, which is one reason why the number of such centers continues to expand yearly. The second reason for these centers' success, and one that's equally important, is that such centers increase the feeling of community in rural areas, and thereby contribute to the stability of the country.

ESHEL has not neglected building institutions, however, and in recent years has led a national consortium to produce three thousand new beds for the elderly, in response to the huge influx of elderly from the Soviet Union; ESHEL also aggressively pursued funding for these new beds from the Conference of Jewish Material Claims Against Germany (Claims Conference) set up to compensate victims of the Holocaust. Additionally, ESHEL has assisted many municipalities in creating their own master plans for services to the elderly, which include buying computer equipment to assist the planning process.

Caring for the Handicapped

The JDC-Israel's long experience with the elderly spills over into its work with another particularly vulnerable population—the mentally and physically disabled. The Sabbah Center in Jerusalem, partially funded by the JDC-Israel, deals with the moderately retarded, and those in wheelchairs or with other physical limitations. The clients of this educational center arrive there daily, some by public transportation and some on special buses, from group homes and family residences. In addition to receiving daily care, the disabled are trained in certain skills that can enable them to lead more productive lives and to stay out of institutions.

The JDC's experience with people who are having difficulty existing comfortably in their own homes has informed its long relationship with the national voluntary association Yad Sarah, which dates back to a start-up grant in 1976, when all Yad Sarah did was loan medical equipment to those who needed it. Today, Yad Sarah is Israel's largest voluntary association, with six thousand volunteers delivering all sorts of medical and maintenance services to 250,000 families each year. A recent survey reported that one of every three families in Israel had been helped by Yad Sarah, and the organization estimates that its services save Israel about $250 million each year in hospital and long-term care costs. Today, most of Yad Sarah's operational funding comes from private donations in Israel, yet recently, when Yad Sarah needed a headquarters and training facility for its varied activities, the JDC agreed to be a major underwriter in recognition that the facility would provide added capacity for helping the vulnerable in a way that few other building projects might do.

New Brookdale programs investigate the areas of vulnerable children, people with disabilities, and the absorption of immigrants. "Ralph was instrumental in this expansion of Brookdale," director Jack Habib recalls. "He helped create a constituency within the JDC board for support for the idea."

Similarly, today, Brookdale's funding comes mostly from the government in specific contracts for research, but the Institute still receives what Habib characterizes as "significant though minor" JDC funding "that assures our independence." Brookdale's steady production of innovative practical ideas, its support for pilot programs that are later replicated in multiples, and its collection and analysis of data make it a key resource in the field of the elderly. The growing need for these elements in other fields of social services encouraged Brookdale in 1987 to do what Israel Katz had foreseen when he insisted on adding "Human Development" to its title: expand beyond the field of aging into that of general health policy.

The thoroughness with which Brookdale covers a subject is revealed in a sampling of its recent projects in the area of youth: the preparation of a "national agenda for Arab children," an evaluation of the effectiveness of police work with youth, a quality assurance system for residential facilities serving more than ten thousand children at risk, a study of the integration of immigrant Ethiopian youth into Israeli society, and studies on youth violence.

ALIENATED YOUTH IN ISRAEL

The alienation of youth from Israeli society became, in the 1990s, a critical problem, one linked to other problems such as the widening disparity of incomes between the rich and the poor, the rising rates of poverty among the Arab minority and other ethnic groups, and what a JDC report called "the declining effectiveness of the public service system to deal with the disadvantaged" in a government climate that was increasingly turning to privatization and decentralization of such services.

Demographic projections show that the composition of Israel's children is changing in the direction of ever-higher percentages of Arab children, of those of Asian-African descent, of those of very recent immigrant families, and of those from ultra-Orthodox families. In trying to cope with these children and their families, the study warned, "we are dealing with an area in which all [other developed] countries are finding themselves inadequate, and the question is whether Israel can succeed where others have not."

In Beer-Sheva and Haifa, comprehensive community planning units—already working with troubled youth, compiled statistics showing that almost 15 percent of children in Israel could be defined as high risk. The category included those suffering from physical, sexual, emotional, or educational neglect; those exhibiting behavioral problems; or those becoming dropouts or in severe danger of dropping out. Extrapolating from these local statistics, the JDC-Israel estimated that about 300,000 children throughout the country were at risk. To reduce that overall number, and to make a difference in the lives of children at risk, the JDC found, would require double and triple the investments in them previously made by the government and private agencies. In 1996, JDC-Israel director Arnon Mantver, a veteran of government ministries and social services, took steps to create a new entity, modeled on ESHEL, but aimed at children.

Called ASHALIM, the new entity officially came into being in January of 1998. Like ESHEL, ASHALIM is made up of partners from the JDC-Israel and the several government agencies whose services were aimed at these youth. ASHALIM extends the Goldman-inspired ESHEL pattern by including new partners on the decision-making level, such as the New York City Federation.

ASHALIM draws on many pilot programs and already existing projects supported by the JDC. One, called MIFNE, deals with high school dropouts. The JDC-Israel sponsors intensive one-year programs that use computerized learning technologies and individual counseling; through these programs, many young lives have been turned around. Of one group of students, 30 percent returned to full-time academic studies, 38 percent began vocational training, and 19 percent found full-time employment. The lead sponsor of the MIFNE program is the Jewish community of Paris, whose programs have proved effective in dozens of schools.

"This is a good example of how outside groups like the Jewish Community of Paris, or the New York Federation, can find a way to directly participate in programs in Israel through working with the JDC," Goldman points out. "It's important because it increases the direct interest of many volunteers. Most donors want direct involvement in activity rather than to just write checks."

Several JDC-sponsored programs are in the process of being absorbed within ASHALIM, including emergency drop-in centers that offer immediate asylum to children from abusing families and counseling for the families. Nineteen community-based Centers for Prevention of Family Violence, based on a JDC-Israel sponsored model, try to prevent casualties from domestic violence; often, abusers and their families are referred to the centers for help by local police forces. Residences for abused children and community group homes are also being tried.

Further work in the area of children-at-risk is undertaken in schools with potential dropouts, in a JDC program called New Educational Environment. Currently, the program is operating in thirty-five schools. Additionally, as the JDC has done with ESHEL in the field of the aging, the JDC is multiplying the effectiveness of its efforts in ASHALIM and the arena of youth by putting its money and resources behind the training of professionals and lay workers in the field, including teachers, nurses, child welfare workers, police, and district attorneys.

"We are proceeding in a classical JDC way with ASHALIM," says Hannah Primack, finance and budget director for ASHALIM, "concentrating on planning and development, not on direct providing of services." Even so, JDC-Israel director Mantver adds, "we are very much in the practical world—our fingers are dirty all the time." Mantver points out that while the problems associated with children at risk are large and immediate, the JDC-Israel must proceed in a deliberate way, starting with pilot projects and then replicating them, "in order to be comprehensive and not go wrong, to use real experience to shape the best way of doing things."

INTEGRATING THE INFLUX

The largest recent challenge for Israel, in terms of numbers of people affected, may be the absorption of the huge influx of Soviet Jews who arrived between 1988–1993. Where to settle the nearly one million new immigrants, how to house them, how to care for them during the transition period, and how to accomplish their integration into Israeli society were the foremost questions to be answered during that period. An indication of the scope of the problem is given by the statistic that the group included 57,000 men and women who in the Soviet Union had held the job title of "engineer" or "technician." While the general educational level of the immigrants was a cause for joy, many of them, especially the engineers and technicians, came with skills that were inappropriate for Israel's more narrowly defined engineering-related jobs, and most had to be retrained for other positions. Another challenge was the large number of elderly among the immigrants.

The major difficulty associated with absorbing the immigrants was profound and basic. As Dr. Seymour Epstein, the JDC's director of Jewish education, noted, more than 500,000 Soviet Jews arrived in Israel in a short period of time having,

> no Jewish past and not a drop of Jewish present. . . . They came without any sense of the Jewish calendar, no genetic knowledge of the life cycle, no identification with the heroes of Jewish history, no love of Zion, and an overwhelming desire to be elsewhere. . . . All the sad rules of dislocation apply, but in this case they are exacerbated by the ignorance of all things Jewish and the indifference to the Zionist dream.

While the basic responsibility for absorbing former Soviet Jews into the mainstream of Israel rested with the government, the Jewish Agency, and other Israeli entities, the JDC assisted in many of the endeavors, especially those with an educational component, for instance, making its already-extant libraries of Russian-language Judaica available in Israel for the benefit of the recent immigrants and giving baskets of books to Soviet Jews as they arrived in Israel.

To work extensively with the new immigrants in fields in which it already had significant strength—manpower training, care of the elderly, children-at-risk, training of professionals— the JDC cut back on the operating funds for its other projects, because, as an internal report put it, "the immediate consequences of absorbing the immigrants were so great that this had to be given more priority." Very rapidly, 40 percent of the JDC-Israel's budget was absorbed in helping the immigrants. Media reporting about the absorption of the immigrants tended to stress the negative: the mismatch in skills, the immigrants' unrealistic expectations of being cared for, and antisocial behavior by immigrant teenagers, such as refusing to serve in the armed forces. However, a 1992 Brookdale study found in a survey of all Russian immigrants in the city of Lod that those who had been in Israel more than two years had the same rate of employment as that of the general population; a nationwide survey later found the same result. Equally as important, 80,000 Soviet-born children were readily absorbed into Israel's public education system.

An innovative way to address the needs of immigrants is being mounted by eighteen small business development centers for which the JDC-Israel has served as partial sponsor. Modeled on the Hebrew Free Loan Society's program of loans given without interest, the Jerusalem Business Development Center (JBDC) began with help from the JDC-Israel, which arranged collateral for the loans that came from banks and from a special government fund. This arrangement was another collaboration between two old friends, Teddy Kollek and Ralph Goldman, with major funding coming from The Jerusalem Foundation—a foundation Kollek established and on which Goldman continues to serve as an executive board member. In keeping with Goldman's tenets, the JDC's input was critical at the outset of the business-center program and receded in importance as the program matured. The JBDC provides special courses in the "rules of business" in

Israel, and mentors and special expertise in areas such as marketing and manufacturing. Other sectors of the population served
by the JBDC include Arab women who want to start home-
based businesses, ultra-Orthodox Jews, and recently discharged
members of the armed forces who can use their discharge grants
for education or to start their own businesses.

THE MOST DIFFICULT GROUP TO ABSORB

While the influx from the Soviet Union was the largest group of
immigrants needing to be absorbed, the group that has proven
to be the most difficult to absorb has been the Ethiopians. The
reasons for the difficulties lie in the backgrounds of the 30,000
Ethiopians brought to Israel in Operation Moses in 1984 and
Operation Solomon in 1991. Unlike many other groups of immigrants, including the Soviet Jews who were in comparison
reasonably well-educated and cognizant of Western ways, the
Ethiopians, who came from rural villages, arrived "lacking not
only basic materials possessions, but also language and basic survival skills," according to a leading group caring for the
Ethiopian immigrants, the Association for the Advancement of
the Ethiopian Family and Child in Israel. Long after the bulk of
recent Soviet Jews had found niches in Israeli society, Ethiopians
had not, with jobless rates among adults nearing 50 percent and
with some children unable to cope in school or stay within the
educational system. Race is a factor in the difficulties of absorption for the dark black Africans, but the more contributory factors are cultural, the Ethiopian Family Association suggests. For
instance, some of the employment possibilities made available to
the Ethiopian immigrants were fruit- and vegetable-picking on
farms; earlier waves of immigrants from Yemen and North
Africa had successfully held such jobs and then moved on to better jobs, but the male Ethiopians, former farmers, have rejected
harvesting jobs as lacking in dignity and inappropriate to their
positions as heads of families. In many ways, Ethiopian cultural
traditions have frequently clashed with the requirements of a
more modern society, as when entire communities of

Ethiopians would stop their work and schooling to attend weddings and funerals, shutting assembly lines and educational programs, resulting in firings and other sanctions.

To counteract such difficulties has required the highest per capita investment for any immigrant group, says Ruth Paz, the director of the Association whose facilities in Beer-Sheva are in a housing project in an outlying neighborhood. While unemployed fathers sit in a hallway and prepare meat for a traditional stew, upstairs in converted apartments their children are learning how to take part in a new society while absorbing enough about the land and culture from which their parents came so that they can respect and appreciate it. There is a small kindergarten, after-school classes, and materials such as black dolls and models of rural Ethiopian villages. "For me," says Ruth Paz, "the most exciting aspect of the program is training young adult Ethiopians to do the teaching and counseling."

In Paz's Beer-Sheva program, as in a half-dozen others in Israel aimed at Ethiopian absorption, the JDC's involvement is relatively small. In cumulative terms, however, the drive to ensure that the Ethiopians succeed in Israeli society is heavily backed by the JDC. A broad-based Coalition for the Advancement of Ethiopian Education was brought into being by the JDC in 1997, and provided intensive Headstart-type summer courses for three thousand Ethiopian children to ready them for the forthcoming school year. Another program fosters volunteerism among the Ethiopian communities.

EDUCATION AND POLICY STUDIES

Perhaps the general thread of Goldman's continuing influence in the work of the JDC in Israel can be best summed up in the label most frequently applied to him by others, but which he himself does not claim: great teacher. Learning exudes from him. He teaches by example and also by sharing his vast knowledge and experience with those he works with, both directly and indirectly, and he enables study and training in many communities.

More than by any other quality, Goldman's influence is

defined by his belief in the appropriateness and effectiveness of education in all endeavors. Communities must and can be educated to accommodate the elderly in their midst, immigrants educated to adapt to Israeli society (and society educated to properly welcome them), families educated to adopt less abusive relationships with their children, and so on. In the JDC's contemporary work in Israel, education is increasingly viewed as the preferred route to moving society in socially-just ways, to enabling poorer citizens to lift themselves out of poverty, and to raising the general populace's level of knowledge about Judaism and Jewish culture. Education accounts for nearly one-third of the JDC budget and an even larger fraction of the JDC-Israel's budget.

For Goldman, though, the ultimate educational aspect of the JDC's work is that expressed in the mission of the Center for Social Policy Study (CSPS). During the interval of Goldman's first retirement, there had been an attempt to spin off the CSPS, on the grounds that it could be better administered and underwritten by a university. One of Goldman's objectives in agreeing to step back in as executive vice-president had been to move the JDC to recommit to the importance of maintaining the CSPS. Goldman still feels that CSPS is an effective fulcrum that the JDC has in Israel, because the Center's studies and recommendations are educational tools that directly affect major government policy deliberations.

The JDC Executive Committee, accustomed to perceiving the Joint as a relief agency, at first found it difficult to justify or explain the merits of a research institute. But Louis Zorensky, chairman of the committee to evaluate the CSPS, asserted after a study that the effectiveness of JDC dollars through a policy organization could often be greater than through direct relief. Other committee members came to agree with him.

That aspect of the CSPS work has been most vividly on display in its approach to a new and alarming trend in Israel, the growing income disparity between the rich and the poor. Reversing the trend has seemed a goal amorphous in character and difficult to achieve.

In the past, through its educational activities, the CSPS has been able to reverse some trends in Israeli society that it deemed alarming, for instance, a decrease in the efficiency of government social-service spending, which it helped turn around in the 1990s. The problem of growing income inequality in Israel is a far wider problem, though. "One way we address this problem is by trying to assist the most vulnerable populations in gaining better jobs," says Dr. Arnon Gafni, the former director of Israel's central bank, now a consultant to the CSPS. The theory is that if people are able to obtain better jobs, they will have more income, and the disparity will not be so large. Dr. Gafni recounts one interesting CSPS path toward achieving the goal. "We looked into lengthening the school day, so that children in poor situations can complete their schooling in less time, and get into the job market more quickly." After investigating this possibility, the CSPS presented the findings to a Public Commission that had been appointed to make a recommendation on the matter; the Commission adopted the CSPS staff report as its own recommendation. Briefings on the report and its findings were given to the education ministry and to the Knesset's education committee; this led, in turn, to a press conference at which Prime Minister Netanyahu announced that the recommendations would be adopted by the government and money allocated in the next budget to implement the changes in the school day.

But the CSPS did not stop there. It also analyzed proposed across-the-board increases in education spending by the government and suggested that such increases would do little good. The center recommended instead that more money be directed to the weakest schools in the system, those in recently developed towns and in poor urban neighborhoods. This recommendation was also accepted and became policy, saving millions of shekels from being wasted.

The center's annual report on Israel's social services, widely distributed, is considered the backbone of its research program because it enables the tracking of changes in social policies, whether these are changing as a result of declared policy shifts, or whether they are brought into being because of economic or social processes. In 1996, as it had done with previous yearly "social scorecard" reports, the CSPS held briefings on the report and its findings with many government ministers, Knesset members from several different parties, people in the media, and others, all before the session of the Knesset that was to consider social expenditures for the next fiscal year.

"This report had a red cover," Center director Dr. Yaakov Kop points out, "and one of our proudest moments came during the subsequent Knesset session, when the televised pictures of the parliamentary debate on social services showed that nearly every member had a 'little red book' on his or her desk, and every speaker carried it to the podium and referred to a fact or an idea on this or that page of the book. That was when we knew CSPS was at the point of maximum effectiveness, providing information that was making a difference in the public debate over important issues."

A Personal Tragedy

In 1971, Goldman's son David, who had just graduated from George Washington University, came to Israel to visit his parents and sisters, Judy and Naomi. He had planned to return to the United States to attend the Washington University Law School in St. Louis, but after his visit, he decided to remain in Israel and study law at the Hebrew University in Jerusalem.

Interested in international relations, especially in working towards peace between Israel and her Arab neighbors, after graduating from law school David interned for two years with Israel's Foreign Ministry and eventually became an advisor in its legal department. To be eligible to accept assignments for diplomatic work abroad, he was required to Hebraicize his name; David Joel Goldman became David Ben-Rafael—David, son of Ralph.

David served in the Israeli Embassy in London as Secretary of Information (1983–86); as Consul at the Israel Consulate in Chicago (1986–1988); and as Minister and Deputy Chief of

Mission in Buenos Aires, Argentina. His assignments included attending several intergovernmental conferences dealing with nuclear subjects, serving as a member of the Israeli delegations dealing with the "normalization" of relations with Egypt, and representing the Legal Department in the discussions of the Kahn Investigation Committee on the subject of Sabra and Shatilla. As the Israeli Legal Department's representative to the United Nations General Assembly, he gave a speech before the Sixth Committee on International Terrorism, on October 18, 1989:

> The problem of international terrorism is an issue of grave concern to my nation, as Israel has been targeted and victimized for years by internationally linked terrorism. Yet Israel is by no means the only victim of international terrorism. It is a phenomenon knowing no geographic bounds and showing no signs of eradication.

He stressed the need for countries worldwide to work together to combat terrorism, little knowing that he would himself become victim to such terrorism.

On March 17, 1992, as Ralph Goldman was returning from lunch with his close associate and friend, Herbert Katzki, he was informed that the Israel Embassy in Buenos Aires, Argentina, had been bombed. A car bomb, launched by terrorists, destroyed the Israel Embassy, killing twenty-nine people and injuring more than 180.

At first, reports came in from friends in many parts of the world suggesting that they had seen David on television, assisting with the rescue of survivors. However, at 6:30 A.M. the next morning, the Goldmans' daughter Judy called from Israel to say that the Israel Foreign Office was going to announce that David was among the missing.

Ralph and Helen immediately flew to Buenos Aires. Soon after their arrival in Argentina, and forty-eight hours after the bombing, their worst fears were confirmed. David's body was found. Another heartbreaking journey was organized as Ralph and Helen, David's wife Elisa, and their two very young children, three-year-old Noa and baby Yonatan, prepared to accompany David's remains to Israel.

Even at this moment of intense personal tragedy, Goldman's sense of the larger issues did not desert him. Before leaving Argentina for Israel, he wrote a letter to President Carlos Menem, enclosing a Spanish translation of Haim Nachman Bialik's poem, "In the City of Slaughter," about the notorious pogroms of Kishinev. "My son was killed because he was a Jew and an Israeli," he wrote and then added, "I hope that Buenos Aires does not also become a 'city of slaughter.'"

At David's graveside in Jerusalem, several eulogies were offered. Elyakim Rubenstein, then Secretary of the Government and former head of the Legal Department of the Foreign Office, spoke of David's dedication, honesty, and hard work. Robbie Sabel, then chief of the Legal Department of the Ministry of Foreign Affairs, spoke about David's skillful legal knowledge, humility, unlimited intellectual honesty, his sense of humor, and his standing as a precious member of the Foreign Service.

Since the day of his son's death, Goldman has waged an intense campaign to learn the truth of what happened in Buenos Aires and to bring the perpetrators to justice. Hardly a week goes by when he does not make an inquiry about the matter; in his office at the JDC, one desktop is covered with files dedicated to the bombing. With the same persistence and diligence that he brought to his professional work throughout his career, Goldman pursues the matter with the United States State Department, the United States and Israel anti-terrorists groups, and Israeli intelligence; he has even testified before a United States Congressional Committee on Foreign Relations headed by Congressman Benjamin Gilman. Sadly, in July 1994, the AMIA building, headquarters of the Jewish community, was also bombed and Buenos Aires did indeed become a "city of slaughter."

The Goldman family and their friends have established the David Ben-Rafael Fellowship at the Truman Center for Peace at the Hebrew University in Jerusalem. And in July 1998, a community center that also houses a synagogue was dedicated at the

JDC-Lauder International Camp at Szarvas, Hungary, and named Beit-David, in David's memory. A fitting memory, it is a summer camp joining together teenagers from across Eastern and Central Europe, the former Soviet Union, Israel, and North America, supported by the JDC and the Ronald S. Lauder Foundation.

For Goldman and Helen, their daughters Judy and Naomi, their daughter-in-law Elisa, and their grandchildren, the pain and sorrow have not eased. Their memories of David's warmth, hospitality, intelligence, sense of humor, and his love for his family remain an integral part of their daily lives.

CHAPTER TWELVE

Realizing the Dream

The JDC and the Former Soviet Union Today

T HE EVENTUAL RETURN to the Soviet Union, the dream of
Goldman and the upper echelons of the JDC for so many
years, was not a moment of triumph like the winning of a race or
striking it rich. Their dream was a dream of service, and the re-
ward for realizing it was to be reaped in the form of hard work in
service to one of the largest and least-well-served Jewish communities in the world. "I seek my brethren," the JDC had said;
now, having found them, the organization faced the formidable
task of helping its brothers spiritually and materially to rebuild
their own communal houses.

To that task, Goldman, appointed after his retirement by
Michael Schneider to assist in the supervision of programs for all
the Soviet states, brought all of his experience of the past fifty
years of his work in Israel and in the Eastern European countries. And for that task, the JDC also brought new generations of
social service workers, trained not only in the skills necessary for
their jobs, but in the commitment that is essential to their work.
What Goldman embodied to the younger Soviet-born, Israel-
born, and American-born people of the JDC who signed on to
work in the Soviet Union was an ideal of dedication to the
cause, a passion that ennobled and transcended the work to be
done. Any good bureaucrat could supervise programs, they

learned, but it took passion to invest those programs with meaning beyond the immediate succor of needy people, to energize recipients and service workers alike to continue on in the face of adversity. And they learned that there were all sorts of ways of saving lives other than overt rescue; in particular they imbibed from Goldman the idea that to reinvigorate a life with passion was to save it for the long term.

The Joint's return to the Soviet Union after fifty years' absence coincided with the beginnings of the tidal wave of Jewish emigration from the USSR. As the number of Jews allowed to emigrate by the Soviet authorities increased from a trickle to seven thousand a month, this "sudden expansion of Soviet transmigration," JDC President Sylvia Hassenfeld wrote to board members in January of 1989, created budget problems for the JDC so severe that there was "a possibility that we might have to stop accepting new arrivals into our system in Vienna"; JDC money that might have been applied to the work inside the Soviet Union was becoming absorbed by the growing need to take care of the transmigrants.

The UJA wanted a coordinated campaign to jointly fund the absorption of Soviet Jews in Israel and in the United States. Goldman was quite upset at this idea, which he felt would put Israel into competition with the United States for immigrants, because in Goldman's view there was no way that Israel could adequately vie for Soviet Jews with the much wealthier United States. As he had in the past, he emphasized that since the Soviet Jews who wanted to emigrate to the West were not technically refugees—they could go to Israel—their migration costs ought to be funded by their relatives, not by philanthropic money. In this instance, Goldman's idea did not prevail. It was overwhelmed by a special UJA joint campaign to raise $75 million for absorption in Israel and the United States.

While the numbers of those coming out of the Soviet Union continued to grow and to create problems of transmigration and absorption, Goldman continued to focus the efforts of the JDC on working with the Jews who remained in the Soviet Union.

In Moscow, the concerts by Cantor Joseph Malovany and the

JDC Moscow Male Choir had a practical function but were also symbolically important, as were the public celebrations held in many cities at Passover and Chanukah from 1988 to 1991, the early period of the JDC's return. The Judaica libraries that were established and the concerts that attracted thousands of people put the JDC on the map for Russians by addressing the yearnings for Jewish spirit and culture. These yearnings were reinforced by the holiday services and meals.

During this early period, the JDC also concentrated on establishing working relationships with local groups (most often centered on synagogues), helped to bring into being programs for Jewish studies on the university level, assisted local organizations to establish themselves and find ways of gathering or making money for programs, and collaborated with Rabbi Adin Steinsaltz. Steinsaltz had been invited to set up a Jewish Studies academy, often referred as "Yeshiva," but actually a place for a Jewish experience in the Soviet Union, the first since the Soviet Union had been founded in 1917. As the package program had done in decades past, the JDC work in the years after the return to the Soviet Union aimed at reaching as many cities as possible throughout the various republics; seventeen cities were reached, including outlying ones such as Tashkent, Vilnius, and Novosibirsk. Operationally, the concentration was on three major subject areas, characterized by Michael Schneider as a "massive flow of Jewish knowledge into the USSR . . . community organizational self-sufficiency . . . and community economic self-sufficiency."

ENABLING A COMMUNITY

In the fall of 1989, Schneider gathered several veteran staff members and one Russian-speaking recruit, Stuart Saffer, who became the first resident country director, as well as Goldman's old friends Shaike Dan and Motke Yanai. The JDC's role in the USSR was growing. Schneider established a Soviet Union Team for which he assumed staff responsibility. Asher Ostrin, a JDC staff member, subsequently assumed responsibility to recruit staff, mostly former Soviets living in Israel, to develop the rapidly growing role in the USSR. Goldman continued as senior consultant with responsibility for programs in Moscow and government relations; he also continued to pursue achieving formal USSR accreditation, a goal finally achieved on June 17, 1992, four years after the first official visit of the JDC leadership to Moscow. By then, the USSR had disintegrated, and the JDC received its accreditation from the Russian government. Since the Russian government had legal precedent only to issue commercial accreditation, the Deputy Minister of Justice, Svetlana Tetuke, upon presenting the certificate, said, "we're giving accreditation 'to restore historic justice.'"

The fall of Communism and the swift dissolution of the USSR during the course of 1991 created more opportunities for the JDC to work with Soviet Jews who did not emigrate to Israel or to the West, and who chose to start new lives in the former "republics." Such states as Russia, Ukraine, and Uzbekistan, as well as former vassal countries like Estonia, Latvia, and Lithuania, all became independent. They all formed their own governments, some more autocratic than others, and all had their contingents of people who could now live openly as Jews—if they wished to do so, and if the support system for their Jewishness was viable and available. In the new Confederation of Independent States (CIS), Judaism continued to be categorized not as a religion but as a national identity; Jews were considered a national ethnic minority group, in a similar category as the Tartars or the Kurds, and were eligible for similar treatment.

For the JDC, in addition to creating opportunities, the fall of Communism also brought added responsibilities. The new state governments wanted to take care of pensioners, for instance, but did not have the resources to do so in the manner that had been possible under the Communist system. Moreover, under the new system, things that were previously provided almost without charge, such as rides on public transport, electricity and phone service for flats, and maintenance help, now cost money, which also placed undue burdens on pensioners and on those who could not find adequately paid jobs in the newly capitalist economy. The JDC was challenged to find ways of assisting those in need and developing local communities' responsibility for their own needs without making the needy into permanent dependents.

The opportunities and responsibilities entailed palpable dangers: for instance, when the UJA announced that the JDC would distribute emergency kosher food to needy Jews in the former Soviet Union, some press organizations in the CIS interpreted this to mean that Jews would only help other Jews and would allow non-Jews to starve.

After the Gulf War, the United States government selected the JDC to distribute food to all the needy, no matter what their background, in Moscow and St. Petersburg. Steve Schwager, associate executive vice president of the JDC, assembled a staff of Americans and Israelis to do the work. Articles appeared accusing the JDC of being no more than a new version of the hated Jewish middleman, taking a cut of the funds. It became necessary for the JDC to tread very carefully, to institute controls so that emergency food deliveries were not diverted to the black market, to stress that all such distribution was done through local organizations and was not in any way anti-Christian, and to ensure that the American government's 600,000 pallets of food, in particular, were given to all who asked for them. Briefings to such influential newspapers as *Izvestia* and to the Moscow mayor's office helped to prevent further anti-Semitic backlash.

In the early 1990s, mostly through the efforts of local Jewish organizations and leaders, aided by the JDC and other organizations—notably the JDC's continuing partner, the Lishka—Jewish life was reemerging throughout the CIS, as evidenced by an average of one new synagogue opening each month. Dozens of rabbis were imported from outside countries, often through the Lubavitch organization.

The scope of the JDC's involvement was already large and continued to broaden monthly. A set of Jewish books in Russian was sent to the each of the 11,000 children attending Jewish religious schools in the former Soviet Union; 750 teachers of Hebrew were sponsored, many traveling there from Israel; two million Jewish study items in Russian were shipped in, including videos, computer programs, study aids, teacher-training kits, and other written materials; and dozens of new Jewish books were translated into Russian for later distribution. In 1992, twenty-seven public Passover Seders were organized, more than half of them in cities that had not held Seders at any time in living memory. Twenty local food and welfare councils were organized, and ten summer camps were supported, some of them so recently converted from Communist Young Pioneer facilities that Communist statues, slogans, and paraphernalia still adorned the walls.

"We are trying to turn book shipments into libraries, and libraries into cultural centers," a 1992 internal JDC memo reported and wondered how best to do so. Subsidize the librarians' salaries? Make libraries into communal cultural centers for holiday celebrations? Train librarians as cultural and communal center directors? Attach libraries to soup kitchen programs? Eventually, all these approaches would be tried. Similar development questions were raised in the fields of welfare, Jewish education, medical assistance, and the like. In the JDC's internal discussions, as a guide to answering these questions and shaping programs, it was often Goldman who stressed that all programs in the former Soviet Union must attempt to follow the paths and patterns the JDC had established in its work in Israel: working with local partners, limited-year involvement of the JDC, emphasis on training professionals, and the use of pilot projects that could later be replicated.

A typical success in terms of evolution was that of Yad Ezra, the Moscow Jewish social service organization. It was originally formed to assist refugees from the Baku region who had come to Moscow, by Rabbi Adolf Shayevich and Mikhail Chlenov— men who had been at cross purposes in the past. While Shayevich was the establishment leader, Chlenov was one of the dynamos of the Jewish underground in the 1970s and 1980s, a demographer by profession, known widely for having taught Hebrew to Sharansky. They determined to work together in 1990, forming a handful of volunteers attached to the Choral

Synagogue who would accept a thousand food packages from the JDC and deliver them to home recipients. According to senior administrators of Yad Ezra, Goldman helped shape its name and purpose, so that in just two years, Yad Ezra grew into an organization well-enough regarded to be able to obtain premises from the Moscow city government, raise some of its own funding locally, and continue welfare work in the areas of food packages and especially in providing medically related services to the homebound elderly.

Goldman's way has always been to help people to ultimately help themselves. His outlook is very much in the tradition of Maimonides' *Mishneh Torah* which explains that the highest level of *tz'dakah*, or Jewish charity, is "to strengthen the hand" of the people being helped. "My job is basically as an enabler," he says.

A FLOURISHING OF JEWISH EDUCATION

One of the people who had most impressed Goldman in his earliest meetings in Moscow was Eugeny Velikhov, a leading academician, and vice-chairman of the Soviet Academy of Sciences. In addition to assisting Rabbi Steinsaltz with a new training school for rabbis, a Russian-language version of the Steinsaltz Talmud, Velikhov, in discussions with Goldman, expressed strong interest in fostering the teaching of Jewish subjects at the college level. That sort of education was a notion close to Goldman's heart, and he made the most of the opportunity of having the blessing of the prestigious Academy of Sciences to pursue it.

Education at the university level proceeded in several directions. Under the aegis of the Academy itself, there evolved an umbrella organization called SEFER, which was created to help energize and coordinate the teaching of Jewish subjects in regular and specialized universities throughout the CIS. SEFER has its headquarters in the architecturally striking modern campus building of the Academy of Sciences in Moscow, and benefits from the association, which gives it important status throughout the academic community of the CIS.

Dr. Victoria Mochalova, SEFER's executive director, recalls the birth of the idea for the organization, at the 1994 International Center for University Teaching of Jewish Civilization (ICUTJC) conference, which Ralph Goldman attended as chair of the Board of Regents.

"At the meeting, Dr. Rashid Kaplanov decided to create a new organization that would unify and coordinate all the academic programs in the Jewish education field of the former Soviet Union," Mochalova recalls, an organization that would be "connected to the ICUTJC and have the Joint's support." By August 1994, SEFER official Kaplanov became the academic chairman and Mochalova the executive director. The JDC's Rabbi Jonathan Porath was appointed to serve as liaison to help Sefer and other academic Jewish Studies Programs.

According to Mochalova, thousands of Jewish-related courses were being taught at more than a hundred institutions in the many new states, courses ranging from Hebrew as a language to Biblical archaeology, the study of the Talmud, Jewish contributions to Russian history, Yiddish literature and theater, socialist influence on Israel, and more. "This is an explosion maybe even Goldman did not expect," Mochalova comments. "To 'Judaize the Jews' cannot be done here only through the synagogue. Jewish education is the key to the future of the Jewish community in the former Soviet Union."

SEFER runs two annual conferences, one for professors, and another for students, from which volumes of studies are published; it also sponsors conferences on individual subjects, such as the history of Polish Jewry or Jewish music, and provides assistance and technical support to universities in establishing new Judaica courses. At its most recent professorial conference, more than a hundred papers were presented by attendees from many CIS states and from a half-dozen foreign countries. "No one should forget," Mochalova recalls, "that this gathering took place not in Ann Arbor, or at Brandeis, or in Jerusalem, but in

Moscow [and] at the Russian Academy of Sciences, which in itself gave off a powerful message: Jewish studies in Russia is officially a part of the Academy."

Mochalova attributes the explosion of interest in Jewish studies to the historical moment. "Being Jewish was shameful for so
many years, a negative identity—a secret illness, we were forbidden to speak about it, were treated like criminals. It was politically incorrect to mention our national niche." Today's study of
Jewish subjects is the beneficiary of having been forbidden for so
long; it has the feeling of "forbidden fruit," but it also "provides
people with a sense of their own heritage. Today, to study
Judaism in the former Soviet Union is 'heroic,'" Mochalova says.
"SEFER's goal is to make it normal and ordinary."

JDC support for SEFER is small but ongoing, including the
underwriting of conferences, publications, teacher training, and
the like. "Actually," Goldman observes, "the support is so small
that I'm amazed they can do so much." On the other hand, the
JDC provides no current, direct support for one of the principal
state academies for Jewish studies, the Maimonides Academy in
Moscow. But in 1992, when that academy began, says director
Chlenov, the JDC was there and essential.

He recalled in a recent interview that before 1971, there had
been no Jewish communal activity in the USSR and no Jewish
studies permitted by the authorities. The instruction in Hebrew
and Judaism organized by the stalwarts of the underground was
"illegal, if not exactly secret" and became closely tied to
Zionism. It was their Zionism and their insistence on teaching
Hebrew while it was legally outlawed which placed the people
of the underground frequently at odds with the "official" Jews
of the Choral Synagogue and their rabbi, Shayevich.

Chlenov recalls that when Goldman first came to the USSR,
in 1988, Goldman had been "reluctant to establish contact with
us," because of the JDC's insistence on dealing first with officially sanctioned organizations, but that the attitude had
changed in 1989 when Goldman went out of his way to attend
an unauthorized conference and to explain to the conferees that
"the goal of the Joint was to help all indigenous organizations

and institutes. For most of us who remain here, staying in Russia was a positive choice," Chlenov explains. For Chlenov and his university colleagues, for example, the founding of a leading academy to teach Jewish subjects was the fulfillment of a lifelong dream.

JDC assistance to the nascent university-level teaching of Judaism was important in what Chlenov calls the "crucial years" of 1991–1992, but more recently he has been able to replace JDC underwriting of Maimonides with funds from private donors, notable among them the recently formed Russian Jewish Congress.

One of the earliest university-level teaching of Jewish studies is at the JUM, the Jewish University in Moscow, which holds evening classes in a part of the journalism building of the state university, located just opposite to the Kremlin in downtown Moscow. Initially, the JUM was an outgrowth of the Steinsaltz academy but now it receives no money from that source. Funding currently comes mostly from tuition, from the Russian Jewish Congress, and, for textbooks and other supplies, from the JDC, which has also stimulated other private foundation grants. A similar Jewish University, also partially supported by the JDC, is in operation in St. Petersburg.

In the early 1990s, the Jewish Theological Seminary and YIVO, with help from the JDC, established a Jewish Studies program called Project Judaica at the Humanitarian State University. In the late 1990s, the Hebrew University of Jerusalem established at the Moscow State University the Stanley Chais Center for Jewish Studies, which is also providing great impetus to the development of Jewish studies. In many other universities, SEFER has developed mentoring programs on Jewish Studies for faculty who are accomplished scholars in history and philosophy to receive mentoring programs in Jewish studies.

THE RUSSIAN JEWISH CONGRESS

The revolution that toppled Communism in the Soviet Union in 1991 drastically changed the republics' economic system as well as their political governance. In the outburst of capitalism that followed, a new class of wealthy people were quickly produced. As it happened, a sizable proportion of these people were Jewish, and their wealth and prominence resulted in the creation in 1996 of the Russian Jewish Congress (RJC), with an annual budget of $15 million and a headquarters in a skyscraper in Moscow. (In contrast, the JDC's 1996 budget for the CIS, exclusive of money from the Conference on Jewish Material Claims Against Germany, also known as the Claims Conference, was $11 million.) According to the RJC's chief staff executive, Alexander Osovtsov, "People come to us with projects, and we decide about the funding and supervise the projects." They prefer projects that have the objective of community building, and the RJC's goal is "to establish a normal Jewish community" similar to those in New York, Paris, and London. Forty-seven local RJC branches undertake projects throughout the CIS, including the operation of the university programs discussed above, religious schools, soup kitchens, newspapers and other communications, the restoring of synagogues, and the furnishing of religious materials and kosher food.

The RJC's most ambitious single project, funded separately from its welfare, education, and cultural activities, has been the completion of the newest synagogue in Moscow, on the outskirts of town, in a park dedicated to war heroes and located on the grounds where Napoleon halted in front of the city. Opened officially in September of 1998, the starkly modern synagogue in memory of Jewish war dead, designed by an Israeli architect, is at once a memorial, a museum, and a religious building that recalls the Holocaust in the Soviet Union, as well as the contributions of Jews in the Soviet armed forces and to the cultural life of Russia.

Rabbi Shayevich, a member of the RJC executive board, notes that longer-established projects such as the welfare programs and other projects of the Choral Synagogue still require substantial financial assistance from the JDC, "because the local organizations do not yet have enough stability and money to support them."

One way in which local communities try to raise that money is through property reclamation. Since 1985, the property reclamation institute set up by Goldman personally had helped Jewish communities in European and Moslem countries investigate and try to recover community buildings that had once been owned by Jewish communities and which had been seized by the state, or had simply been taken over when the Jewish populations were killed or had emigrated. In 1998 in the former Soviet Union, more than a hundred such properties had been reclaimed, mostly former synagogues, and some were sold or rented to raise money to operate current welfare and educational programs. JDC-supported annual conferences, archival research, and a national steering committee for local property reclamation efforts assist the efforts.

Although the JDC's programs and support for the Jewish communities in the former Soviet Union is the largest of all externally funded efforts, sixteen other foreign-based organizations and eight foundations are all at work there. They range from those led by former Soviet Jews, now residents of Israel, to large American organizations—religious, such as Reform, Conservative, and Orthodox, and other philanthropic groups. Cooperation among them, and with local wealthy Jews such as those who compose the leadership of the RJC, have resulted in significant programs.

WELFARE OF ALL TYPES

Currently, in the former Soviet Union states, the JDC administers not only its own budget but also about $24 million a year that comes from the Claims Conference. The largest portion of this money is allocated to direct welfare programs.

Much of the welfare work is aimed at assisting the elderly, the majority of whom are survivors of Nazi persecution. The situation of the elderly in the former Soviet Union since the fall of Communism has become critical. Pensions average around $15 a month, a very modest amount—not enough to cover daily meals, much less pay for electricity, phone, apartment upkeep, transportation, and medicines for the large population fifty-five years of age and older. Health care is practically unattainable for those without money, despite the socialized nature of medicine.

The JDC's response to this situation has been to develop and foster an innovative welfare facility known as the Hesed model. So profound has its effectiveness been that in March 2000 the Russian Academy of Languages added the word *Hesed* to the Russian language, meaning "programs of social services with special compassion." Dr. Amos Avgar, a JDC veteran staff member, developed the Hesed programs, which provide a structure through which communities can galvanize the resources that exist within them to provide for the needs of their most destitute and vulnerable members. For example, volunteer Jewish physicians act as medical consultations and volunteer engineers make repairs in people's homes. There are now Hesed welfare centers in 145 cities, serving 250,000 Jewish elderly in 2,100 locales. Assistance includes food packages, meals-on-wheels, soup kitchens, medicines, medical equipment, winter relief, home-care, day centers, and more. The Hesed centers are run by an army of more than 14,000 volunteers and thousands of additional paid personnel, all trained by the JDC at the Rosenwald Institute for Communal and Welfare Workers in St. Petersburg.

At one soup kitchen in Moscow, in a crumbling building at the confluence of several streetcar lines, more than a hundred lunches a day are distributed to Jewish pensioners. Volunteer waiters and waitresses serve the meals, and the pensioners frequently take home extra bread and fruit to tide them over until their next visit.

A kitchen in a Moscow residential neighborhood is operated by Chamah, an international organization derived from the Lubavitch, which also operates a kindergarten, several grade schools, and a religious high school at other locations around the city, all of which are partially supported by the JDC and by the Russian Jewish Congress. The evolving character of the Chamah facility is that it now includes a Jewish activities center and JDC-stocked library on the second floor, as well as a medical office with a doctor who is "vastly underpaid," according to the center's director. The clients are mostly retired professional people, many of them former academics; their pensions are increasingly unable to pay for medical treatment, especially for medications. The center's cultural and spiritual activities bring the otherwise isolated clients together, and, no less important, provide them with a sense of Jewish community, an anchor in the fast-changing world of post-Communist Russia.

Community centers have long been one of Goldman's favorite bases for various program operations, and in the former Soviet Union he has nudged JDC-supported projects in the direction of establishing and continually enlarging the purview of such centers. Typically, the JDC helps renovate a donated space, contributes a library and office equipment, and lets the community do the rest, providing occasional suggestions based on what is known to work elsewhere. The Meod Center in Moscow, for instance, began in a building that already housed a well-attended Yiddish theater and started serving elderly walk-ins. The clientele is an odd but interesting mix of generations; parents seem less interested in things Judaic, but the children who are taking Hebrew lessons attend, and so do their aged grandparents, many of them survivors of ghettoes and concentration camps, who remember something of Judaism from their distant childhoods.

The National Institute for Communal and Welfare Workers, brought into existence in St. Petersburg, conducts seminars and training courses using experts from Israel and the United States in addition to those already at work in the CIS; its purpose is to develop a cadre of professional and volunteer community workers for the entire CIS. Located on an inner courtyard in one of the city's historic nineteenth century buildings, the Institute shares premises with an extensive library stocked by the JDC and with a small kindergarten. Some programs last for weekends; others last for two hundred hours over the course of many months and include on-the-job supervision. Branches of the Institute have been established in Dnepropetrovsk, Minsk, Kishinev, and Kiev. As the guiding thought has been in the JDC's sponsorship of training programs in Israel, in the St. Petersburg Institute the idea is to develop Jewish community workers who can initiate and manage their own projects and have some knowledge of how to raise funds to underwrite them.

A large community center was recently dedicated in Moscow by the Lubavitch as part of a new synagogue erected mostly with funds from that organization and from wealthy local businessmen. A previous wooden synagogue on the site was destroyed by fire, and there have been two bomb blasts at the site of the temporary structure there—incidents that have been decried by the Russian Orthodox patriarch and other religious leaders. The building is so large that in addition to the synagogue, it contains sports facilities, classrooms, computer rooms, ritual baths, and other amenities; there are also plans for an entire kosher hotel complex adjoining the synagogue. Some of the Chabad center's current programs for youth are cosponsored by the JDC. The Chabad community center claims to be in touch by telephone or mail with 15,000 Jewish families in Moscow, or approximately 50,000 people, a large fraction of the city's Jewish population, which is estimated at 250,000 people.

On May 16, 2001, there was a groundbreaking for a new JCC opposite the landmark Choral Synagogue on Arkhipova Street. The campus will include an administrative center for the Moscow Jewish Community Council, a welfare Hesed to serve the Jewish elderly, and a children's home. According to Joel Golovensky, director of the JDC Russian Department in Moscow, "This campus will be the realization of a dream of Ralph Goldman, who brought the Joint back to Russia after its fifty year banishment by Stalin."

Reaching a New Generation

The Moscow Jewish population is the largest concentration in the CIS, but the Jewish population in the CIS is estimated at 1,350,000 people, 450,000 of whom are elderly. Clusters of Jews are found in virtually all of the larger towns and even in rural enclaves throughout the huge land area of the former Soviet Union; for instance, in Cherven, fifty kilometers south-east of Minsk, there are twenty Jewish families, eighteen of them elderly. The JDC maintains regional offices in sixteen cities and employs hundreds of people to serve as liaisons to Jewish communities; most of them are local Jews, but about twenty-five are Israelis. The depth of their dedication is reflected by such stalwarts as Yitzhak Averbuch, the Israeli logistics expert who had initially returned to Moscow in 1991.

The JDC representatives visit sponsored projects and community organizations in many towns in the CIS on a regular basis. JDC food packages—still an integral part of the program—are sent to 235,000 people throughout the CIS, many located in communities that have less than fifty Jews in residence.

Increasingly, and much to the gratification of Goldman, the JDC is turning over the raising of funds for welfare work and the administration of welfare programs to local organizations, and concentrating on education and community building activities in the CIS. Annual book festivals, for example, are now being held by local Jewish organizations, with the help of the JDC, in 99 towns from Siberia to the Ukraine. There are 148 Jewish community centers and 179 Jewish libraries in more than a hundred towns. The specifically Jewish libraries are mostly single rooms, but their existence has spurred already-established depots to examine their own holdings of Jewish materials; one of the largest collections of these, in Minsk, was brought out and put on display as a group in 1997 for the first time in fifty years. The JDC helps to support 34 Jewish kindergartens, 54 day schools, and 225 Sunday schools to prepare new generations of Jewish-born children to take part as Jews in communities where little or no Jewish activity has taken place since the time of their great-grandparents.

The main educational task is to bring knowledge of all things Jewish to families who had all but entirely lost their base of information about Judaism—to introduce them to such fundamental matters as the schedule and meaning of annual holidays, and the contents of the five books of Moses. But such education must also counteract the mountain of misinformation about Jews that had been amassed and disseminated during the seventy years of the Soviet Union—anti-Semitic outpourings that even after the fall of Communism still resonate with many among the non-Jewish sectors of the population. In 2001, youth gangs with fascist armbands and attitudes are active in dozens of cities, numerous newspapers carry articles with anti-Semitic messages, and members of the Duma, the Russian parliament, openly blame the country's recent economic ills on the Jewish politicians, bankers, and media titans who were in Boris Yeltsin's inner circle.

Despite such vitriol, the appeal of Judaism is spreading among young Jews. When the Moscow Hillel began in 1994 it consisted of only a handful of students, says director Yevgenia Mikhailyeva. Today, in the former Soviet Union, there are twenty-six Hillels in twenty-six cities, enough to be organized into three regional clusters centered in Moscow, St. Petersburg, and Kiev, and all with professional staff directors. The JDC supports much of the Hillel activity in the former Soviet Union in association with several private foundations, the foremost being the Charles and Lynn Schusterman Family Foundation, which had the initial idea to bring Hillel to the Soviet Union.

Young people often show up at the former Soviet Union Hillels initially "looking for companionship," as one member put it, but many stay to take part in projects with serious religious content. "At our first shabbats," Mikhailyeva recalls, "people were afraid to speak Hebrew, and they said 'Oh, it's too religious for us,' but they kept coming back." Among the more successful projects are the weekly Shabbat services, Torah study, which grew out of those services, and Passover seders that Hillel students have been trained to conduct in towns where rabbis or cantors are not available. In 2001, some 900 Hillel members led Seders in 350 communities that were attended by more than 37,000 people. One young Moscow woman who speaks Yiddish traveled several thousand miles to lead a seder for Yiddish speakers in Siberia. "The parents were asking questions like children," she recalled, "and for the first time, I felt that I was doing something important."

Since 1994, the Moscow Hillel has been sponsoring a special Rosh Hashanah service for young people; the first year's celebration drew seventy people and was largely given over to Russian intellectual games, a meal, and a minimum of prayer. These services have been replicated all over the former Soviet Union. In September 2000, more than 12,000 people gathered in a stadium in St. Petersburg for services.

In 1996, Eugene Wiener, representing the JDC, arrived in Moscow. An American-born sociologist, rabbi, and author who had been a professor at the Haifa University, Wiener wanted to expand and upgrade the Rosh Hashanah service. "It had been thought that Soviet Jews in general, and the young people in particular, were not interested in Judaism as a religion but only as a cultural heritage." However, Wiener found that young people were interested in the great moral questions, and he believed that these could be addressed at Rosh Hashanah and Yom Kippur services. "'We don't like prayer,' the Moscow Hillel told me," Wiener recalled, "and they said we could have only fifteen minutes of it, and then they would get on to the intellectual games." Some 250 young people showed up at the 1996 Rosh Hashanah celebration for youth, and many not only endured the prayer portions of the service but thereafter began to attend weekly Shabbat services. In 1997, with JDC assistance, Hillel students telephoned friends and lists of potential attendees, inviting them for "prayer and religious questions" at Rosh Hashanah, and 550 showed up. Wiener and the Moscow Hillel determined to hold the 1998 Rosh Hashanah celebration in a larger hall and chose an auditorium that seats a thousand people, located in the luxurious new Radisson Hotel.

As dusk approached in the late afternoon of September 19, 1998, many hundreds of young Jewish people arrived at the Radisson-Slavjanskaya, gathering in groups in the lower and upper lobbies, some dressed in good clothes, others in denim; they wandered among the fashionable shops whose prices were well beyond their means. Some knew that many floors above, in the same complex, was the headquarters of the Russian Jewish Congress; others knew that the Joint was cosponsoring the event. Kits of *kippahs, tallit,* and prayer materials were handed out. Around the upstairs lobby that serves as ante-chamber to the theater, Hillel and other organizations had set up information tables, covered with information touting social outings, genealogical searches, and reading materials, as well as soft drinks and snacks.

In a short while, the entire auditorium was packed, every seat taken, and every aisle jammed with people ranging in age from teenagers to men and women in their early thirties. Some 1,400 people sat or stood in the auditorium, while several hundred more participated from the lobby, unable to find seats inside.

A service lasting more than two hours was conducted by a rabbi from New York City, whose occasional remarks in English were translated into Russian by the Hillel director. As in a synagogue, prayers were dutifully recited, but as in a theater, excited applause greeted the offerings of an all-girl choir led by Hillel instructor Masha Samolyova. One reason for the length of the service was the detailed explanations given for the various parts of the ritual. In between listening to the hymns and songs, everyone pored over the seventy-four-page booklet put together for the event. Printed in Russian, Hebrew, English, and in a Russian transliteration of the Hebrew, the booklets featured a compilation of prayers, outlines of Jewish history, readings, Judaic artwork, and even photographs of events important to the recent history of Israel. The booklet reminded some observers of the JDC-funded prayer books that Shaike Dan and Motke Yanai had clandestinely brought into Romania by boxcar in the 1960s, books containing Jewish calendars and Hebrew alphabets as well as prayers, all designed to keep alive a religious tradition in danger of dying out. Now, similar booklets were to be taken home by Russian youth to serve the same purpose.

The ram's horn, or *shofar,* was sounded—to applause—the final prayers were intoned, and the huge crowd filed out into the lobby, where many stayed for additional hours, playing games, making acquaintances, comparing notes. To see the celebrants looking at one another, to see the sheer number of young people willing to publicly express and embrace their Jewishness, was to catch a glimpse of the true importance and excitement of the celebration, as well as of the work of Goldman and the American Jewish Joint Distribution Committee. Their hard work had gone into making this moment possible, sending the message that even after nearly a million Soviet Jews had emigrated to Israel, Judaism was reviving in the heart of the former Soviet Union, and that the presence and commitment of its young Jews would ensure that revival into the new century.

EPILOGUE

Over the course of the 20th century, almost one out of every three Jews changed countries. Some were forced to leave homes, others chose to move. In many of those transitions, the JDC played a role, whether in the foreground or quietly in the background. This new century begins with less movement among Jews, and the JDC's work is focused on helping Jewish communities and the disadvantaged worldwide. Many of the organization's current efforts—rebuilding Jewish life in the former Soviet Union, bolstering Jewish communal structures in Eastern Europe, fostering vitality among communities around the world—can be traced back to the philosophy and the work Goldman began in the 1970s.

During the 1970s and 1980s, Ralph Goldman never gave up his hope—not even for a moment—that the JDC would be able to reconnect with Jews behind the Iron Curtain. Goldman inspired his colleagues, staff, and board members with the mantra, "Be ready for the day." On an ongoing basis, they prepared for the time when the JDC would be back in Budapest, in Bratislava. Under Goldman's leadership, those dreams became reality. Now, in the former Soviet Union, the JDC is involved in hundreds of cities, where Jews are again able to express their Jewish identity; in Eastern Europe, where communities were thought to be extinct, there is a new vitality and new leadership.

Ralph's office at JDC headquarters in New York, overlooking Third Avenue, is filled with the tools and memorabilia of a lifetime of service to the Jewish community. On the walls are several plaques presented to him, a wall hanging from Ethiopia representing the creation of the world, photographs of Ralph with David Ben-Gurion and with the grandnephew of Leo Nikolaevich Tolstoi, and a watercolor painting of Jerusalem with a note from Teddy Kollek marking their fifty years of friendship. His bookshelves are lined with volumes of the Talmud, the *Encyclopedia Judaica*, Salo Baron's *History of the Jews,* and other works in Hebrew, Russian, and English, and a countertop next to his computer is crowded with items of Judaica and folk art—and every object has a story.

And he has a shelf of open, active files dedicated to unresolved issues: the 1992 terrorist bombing in Argentina that took the life of his son David, and the 1967 murder of one of his JDC predecessors, Charles Jordan, in Czechoslovakia. He won't let these matters rest.

Sitting at his desk during the summer of 2001, Ralph speaks with enthusiasm about his continuing work. He won't dwell on his achievements—and there are many—rather, he looks ahead to a time when Jewish communities around the world are economically self-sufficient and interconnected because of their shared tradition, history, culture, and religion. He sees the Joint's present work as "enabling" communities, leading them toward a position of equal footing with other Jewish communities, whether in Israel or anywhere in the Diaspora.

"When I began here, the Joint was Big Brother, or 'Uncle Joint.' Now we are in the position of equals," he says. The relationship between the JDC and the communities it serves is one of partnership and mutuality. To Ralph, the JDC remains a "humble servant of the community." He is quick to give credit to other organizations. "A sign of our success is that we're now not the only player," he says, adding, "I welcome that."

When Ralph discusses his long and distinguished service, even his characteristic modesty can't obscure his many successes and the high regard in which he is held internationally. In 1985, he was awarded the French Legion of Honor. He has also been awarded the Amit Yerushalayim (Guardian of Jerusalem) and was granted honorary doctorates from Baltimore Hebrew College, Hebrew Union College-Jewish Institute of Religion, and the Jewish Theological Seminary of America.

Ralph has a rich memory and an intense power of recall; he'll often mention an event and tie it to a date as specific as "Erev

Rosh Hashanah, 1962," or he might make a passing reference to Shakespeare, Cicero, or Bialik. As he talks of his adventures, it's easy to picture the idealism of his days at Hebrew College and as a young social worker, the passion and excitement of his work with the Haganah, qualities which he has retained over decades. Some of his JDC experiences in Europe sound like the stuff of best-selling thrillers, with Ralph lifting an ashtray on the coffee shop table while having a conversation with a colleague to find a hidden microphone, being followed repeatedly, and once having to tear up and swallow his notes so that airport officials wouldn't seize them. But they're all true, and there are still some stories he won't tell.

When asked about Biblical quotes that are most meaningful to him, one of his choices may at first seem surprising. "Don't depend on philanthropy," he says, paraphrasing Proverbs. "What I've tried to do," he says, "is to make people independent of support." Through education, professional input, and the development of local resources, the JDC fosters among its clients—whether individuals, communities or institutions—the ability to survive and flourish on their own. Ralph is a great believer in people: He sees qualities of resiliency and great potential in all.

Throughout his tenure, Goldman felt that the work of JDC had to go far beyond the delivery of supplies, and must also provide Jewish content, "to Judaize the Jews," in his words. The goal is nothing short of ensuring Jewish survival. He's proud that his JDC predecessors made volumes of the Talmud available in D.P. camps after the war. (He recently came across one such copy when he paid a shiva visit to the home of the late Knesset member, Dr. Yosef Burg, the long-time leader of Israel's National Religious Party.) Ralph likes to point out that the Talmud proves Jews can have differing opinions on all sorts of things. Respecting those differences, he gets along well with Jews of all backgrounds, and has friends across the spectrum. He thinks of himself as a traditional Jew, although in his own way, and he eschews denominational labels. With his natural dignity and ease among people, he often serves to bridge others' differences.

Being an executive is about two things—ideas and people. Ralph generates ideas about everything—Jewish, political, historical, philosophical, artistic…

And he truly loves people. He draws close to him the old, the young, the experienced, and those just starting out in their careers.

To honor his career, the JDC established the Ralph Goldman Fellowship in 1985. Every year, one or two young people are selected to work abroad for the JDC as Fellows, with training in the New York office as well as hands-on fieldwork in foreign countries.

"Mentor" is a word that is widely used, but a relationship that is rare in practice. But with Ralph, it is a reality. There are countless people of different ages across the Jewish world and beyond who can truly call Ralph their mentor. He has the time and patience for everyone. I was fortunate to be one of the first Ralph Goldman Fellows and, as he did for so many others, he shaped my career and professional life.

In every generation of the Jewish people, there are a few who walk a little bit taller than the rest of us. They see things, understand things, and do things in a way that is different from the rest of us. They are larger than life. Ralph is one of these people.

He looks at every problem and sees beyond it. He sees its background, its context, and its place in Jewish history.

In a world that is all too often devoid of those who understand where we have come from and where we are going, Ralph has that indefinable quality that makes him one of the great Jewish leaders of our times—the gift of "vision."

—Gideon Taylor
Former Ralph Goldman Fellow,
Executive Vice President
Conference on Jewish Material Claims Against Germany

BIBLIOGRAPHY

Avriel, Ehud. *Open the Gates! A Personal Story of Illegal Immigration to Israel.* New York: Atheneum, 1975.

Bauer, Yehuda. *Out of the Ashes.* Oxford: Pergamon Press, 1989.

"Compassion in Action: A Continuing Task." New York: The American Jewish Joint Distribution Committee, Inc., 1976.

Eliav, Arie Lova. *Land of the Hart: Israelis, Arabs, The Territories, and a Vision of the Future.* Philadelphia: The Jewish Publication Society of America, 1974.

Ettinger, Amos. *Blind Jump: The Story of Shaike Dan.* New York, Herzl Press, 1992.

Gilboa, Yehoshua A. *The Black Years of Soviet Jewry, 1939–1953.* Boston: Little, Brown & Co., 1971.

Goldman, Ralph I. "The Role of the Professional in Developing and Shaping Jewish Communal Policies and Strategies." New York: American Jewish Joint Distribution Committee, 1981.

Grobman, Alex. *Rekindling the Flame: American Jewish Chaplains and the Survivors of European Jewry, 1944–1948.* Detroit: Wayne State University Press, 1993.

Gruber, Ruth. *Destination Palestine: The Story of the Haganah Ship Exodus 1947.* New York: Current Books, 1948.

Handlin, Oscar. *A Continuing Task, The American Jewish Joint Distribution Committee, 1914–1964.* New York: Random House, 1964.

Hurwich, Louis. *Memoirs of a Jewish Educator.* 1960.

Kollek, Teddy, and Amos Kolek. *For Jerusalem*. New York: Random House, 1978.

Morrissey, Evelyn. *Jewish Workers and Farmers in the Crimea and Ukraine*. New York: privately printed pamphlet, 1937.

Pacepa, Mihai. *Red Horizons: The True Story of Nicolae and Elena Ceaucescus—Crimes, Lifestyle, and Corruption*. Washington: Regnery Gateway, 1987.

Potok, Chaim. *Gates of Numbers*, p. 121.

Rosen, Moses, and Joseph Finkelstein. *Dangers, Tests and Miracles: The Remarkable Life Story of Chief Rabbi Rosen of Romania*. London: Weidenfeld and Nicolson, 1990.

Sachar, Abram L. *The Redemption of the Unwanted: From the Liberation of the Death Camps to the Founding of Israel*. New York: St. Martin's Press, 1983.

———. *Diaspora: An Inquiry into the Contemporary Jewish World*. New York: Harper & Row, 1985.

Slater, Leonard. *The Pledge*. New York: Simon & Schuster, 1970.

Szulc, Tad. *The Secret Alliance: The Extraordinary Story of the Rescue of the Jews Since World War II*. New York: Farrar, Straus & Giroux, 1991.

Waldman, Menachem. *The Jews of Ethiopia: The Beta Israel Community*. Jerusalem: Ami-Shav, 1985.

White, Theodore H. *In Search of History*. New York: Warner Books, 1978.

Zertal, Idith. *To Save a World: American Jewish Joint Distribution (AJJDC) 1914–1984*. New York, 1985.

ACKNOWLEDGMENTS

It is commonplace in acknowledgments to avow that *This book could not have been written but for the help of.* . . . Surely, that sentiment has never been truer than in this instance. Heinz and Ruthie Eppler and Louis and Mary Zorensky helped envision this book and kept it on course. Its most enduring champion was Margy-Ruth Davis, and its next was my agent, Mel Berger. Ralph Goldman, his wife Helen, and their children and grandchildren, both in the United States and in Israel, were unfailingly helpful to me.

At JDC headquarters in New York, Ralph's long-time assistant Sherry Meltzer Hyman and his secretary Freyda Reiss Weiss dug into files, searched their memories, and in a thousand other ways aided the writer's task. This work is the beneficiary of files and interviews that had been accumulated for years, and which provide its wide perspective on the organization's disparate and far-flung activities. Among the others at headquarters whose assistance was essential were Jonathan Kolker, Gene Ribacoff, Executive Vice President Michael Schneider, Steve Schwager, and Amir Shaviv. At JDC-Israel, I was greatly helped by Arnon Mantver, Zvi Feine, and Vicky Mevorach. I was also given warm welcomes and assistance by JDC personnel in Moscow, St. Petersburg, and Bucharest. Aiding the book's progress to its final form were Sandee Brawarsky, Michelle Howry, and publisher Esther Margolis. I thank you all; had it not been for your efforts, this book would still be a dream.

—Tom Shachtman
August, 2001

INDEX

ABOUT THE AUTHOR

Tom Shachtman is the author and co-author of two dozen non-fiction books for adults and children, as well as being an award-winning documentarian whose work has appeared on ABC, CBS, NBC, PBS, in syndication and on local stations. His most recent book, *Absolute Zero and the Conquest of Cold* (1999) was characterized by *The New York Times Book Review* as written "with passion and clarity," by *Library Journal* as "a truly wonderful book," and by the *Atlanta Journal-Constitution* as "an absolute delight."

Around The Block: The Business of a Neighborhood (1997), was labeled by *The Economist* "a 'near-classic' .... [It] tells you more about social conflicts, immigration, education and, indeed, America itself than countless loftier works." *The New Yorker* dubbed it "A grand idea, splendidly executed," and the *Washington Post Book World*, "A thoughtful, interesting book ... a good and useful book thatæunlike so much else these daysægives cause to look to the future with hope."

His earlier histories include *Skyscraper Dreams: The Great Real Estate Dynasties of New York* (1991), *Decade of Shocks*: 1963-1974 (1983), *The Phony War*: 1939-1940 (1982), and *Edith and Woodrow* (1981). His collaborative works include *Torpedoed* (2001, with Edmond D. Pope); *Whoever Fights Monsters* (1992, with Robert K. Ressler); and *The Gilded Leaf* (1989, with Patrick Reynolds). He holds a B.S. in psychology, an M.F.A. in playwriting, and taught writing for many years at New York University and at Harvard's Extension School.